UNDERSTANDING CHILDREN

UNDERSTANDING CHILDREN

Volume 2:
Changing Experiences and Family Forms

Edited by Anne Cleary,
Máire Nic Ghiolla Phádraig and Suzanne Quin

Oak Tree Press
19 Rutland Street,
Cork, Ireland
www.oaktreepress.com

Volume 1: State, Education and Economy
ISBN 1 86076 228-X

Volume 2: Changing Experiences and Family Forms
ISBN 1 86076 229-8

A catalogue record of this book is
available from the British Library.

Printed in Ireland by ColourBooks Ltd.

Contents

UNDERSTANDING CHILDREN

Volume 1:
State, Education and Economy
(ISBN 1-86076-228-X)

PART 3: CHILDREN AND THE ECONOMY

About the Contributors

Nollaig Byrne is a clinical director, consultant child psychiatrist and family therapist. She is based in the Department of Child and Family Psychiatry, Mater Misericordiae Hospital, Dublin. She has written and presented widely both nationally and internationally on the topics of child sexualised abuse and families in poverty.

Anne Cleary is a lecturer in Sociology in University College Dublin. Her research and lecturing interests include health, particularly child and mental health, and gender. She has produced a number of publications in the health area and has co-edited a textbook *The Sociology of Health and Illness in Ireland*. She is a member of the editorial board of the *Irish Journal of Sociology* and a board member of the Health Research Board. Her recent research activities include a longitudinal study of Irish children.

Niamh Flanagan is a Research Officer with the North Western Health Board having previously held research positions in UCD, the Combat Poverty Agency and the St. John of God order. She holds undergraduate and masters level degrees in social policy from UCD and a post graduate diploma from the National College of Industrial Relations. Her research interests include family structure and labour market access with specific reference to women's employment, lone parent's employment and supported employment for people with a disability.

Eilis Hennessy is a lecturer in developmental psychology in the Psychology Department in University College Dublin. Her research interests include child care quality, after-school care and parents' views on child care. She has been involved in many research projects on these topics and has co-authored a book on the impact of child care on children's development.

Louise Higgins is currently training as a clinical psychologist at Stewart's Hospital in Dublin. She is a former researcher at The Children's Research Centre, Trinity College where she conducted research on the needs of children of drug users, and on crime prevention programmes for young people.

Diane Hogan is a lecturer in Developmental Psychology in the Department of Psychology, Trinity College Dublin. She is also a Senior Research Fellow with the Children's Research Centre, TCD. Her research interests include the social and cultural contexts of parenting and parent-child relationships, children's social-emotional development, and children's experiences of family life. She is also interested in the methodological and conceptual issues associated with conducting research with children.

Máirín Kenny, former Principal of St Kieran's NS for Traveller Children, Bray, is a research consultant. She recently collaborated in a research project on the experience of young people with disabilities in second level schools (commissioned by the South West Regional Authority; publication pending). Her other projects include a study of travellers' experiences of assimilation policies for Pavee Point. She is currently researching racism in Irish schools for the Department of Health and Science as well as child protection and welfare procedures in relation to travellers for the ERHA.

Gabriel Kiely holds the Jean Monnet Chair in European Family Policies at University College Dublin where he is also the Director of the Family Studies Centre. He has published extensively on family policy issues and is currently carrying out research on fathers in families, children and divorce and fertility patterns. He is the Irish member of the European Observatory on Family Matters.

Imelda McCarthy is the Director of a PhD programme in families and systemic therapies, college lecturer and family therapist. She is based in the Department of Social Policy and Social Work, University College Dublin. Her work has been translated into eight languages and she is the editor of *Irish Family Studies: Selected Papers* (1995) and *Poverty and Social Exclusion* (1994).

Máire Nic Ghiolla Phádraig is a Statutory Lecturer in Sociology at University College Dublin and is also Director of the Social Science Research Centre there. She was a member of the "Childhood as a Social Phenomenon" project co-ordinated by the UN Centre in Vienna and is a member of the COST Action 19 Children's Welfare management committee. Her research publications have included work on religion, family, childhood and Irish language.

Valerie O'Brien lectures in the Department of Social Policy and Social Work at UCD. She was employed for many years in the child welfare field as a social worker. Her current research and practice interests are in the areas of alternative care for children, family and professional decision making and developing systems of intervention and service delivery that are based on best practices.

Pat O'Connor is Dean of the College of Humanities and Professor of Sociology and Social Policy at the University of Limerick. Her fourth book, *Emerging Voices: Women in Contemporary Irish Society*, was published by the Institute of Public Administration in 1998. She has recently been involved in a cross-national study of young people's ideas about work and family and is also currently analysing the material written by young people in the *Write Now, Write Now* Millennium Book Project.

Gemma O'Donoghue completed her MsocSc (Sociology) in University College Dublin in 1997. Her thesis explored the situation of marital situation from the viewpoint of children. Since then she has worked in administration with local authorities.

Brendan O'Keefe is Local Development Co-ordinator with IRD Duhallow, a rural development organisation based in East Kerry and North West Cork. A graduate of University of Limerick (Social Research Option), with a Masters from UCG, he has considerable experience of working on community development and social inclusion projects and has undertaken extensive socio-economic auditing.

Suzanne Quin is a Senior Lecturer and the Director of the Masters of Social Science (Social Work) Course in the Department of Social Policy and Social Work in University College Dublin. She has undertaken a number of research studies and published articles in the area of health care. She is the author of *Untimely Lives, Uncertain Deaths* (1996) and is the co-editor of *Contemporary Irish Social Policy* (1999) and *Irish Social Policy in Context* (1999).

Preface

We have many nostalgic accounts of childhood in Ireland in the first six decades of the twentieth century, notably Alice Taylor's *To School through the Fields*. Books such as these give a somewhat rosy picture of childhood given what we now know of child sexual abuse and bullying. More recent publications have emphasised the darker side of Irish childhood, Frank McCourt's *Angela's Ashes* being the most successful of the genre. Corporal punishment was legal in schools and a daily experience for many children at the hands of parents, teachers and older siblings. Relative poverty was not as marked as in recent times, but absolute poverty was probably more acute and there were fewer social welfare safety-nets. In the 1960s, emigration was still rife (many fathers went to England to support their families), Dublin tenements still housed up to six per room and over half of rural dwellings still lacked indoor sanitation and running water. If the "normal" family circumstances were not in place, through birth out of wedlock, marital separation/desertion or the illness or death of a parent, a child could well end up in an orphanage. Many of the legislative and regulatory changes introduced since the 1970s have removed or reduced some of the graver sources of suffering for children and improved their rights and quality of life. The main thrust of such changes has been to support the upbringing of children with their biological parent(s).

While acknowledging what is good about these changes for the quality of life for children, we need to look also at the negative aspects of the changes and to see if there are ways of improving matters for children today. Within living memory, the context of childhood in Ireland has been transformed from a matrifocal neighbourhood within which to range freely, to a looser network of carers and activities, often scattered over several localities, to which the children are driven or bussed. It is important to examine the implications of such changes for the experience of childhood today.

In setting out to produce this book we set a goal of focusing on children in the context of a changing Ireland. Despite the changing nature of childhood and children's lives over the past 30 years, no book has charted these changes specifically for children. Existing work on Irish children tends to focus specifically on child welfare and child abuse and therefore on negative aspects of childhood. Insofar as such matters will be dealt with in these volumes, the emphasis is not on "social problems affecting children" but on how do children cope with, resist, or accommodate to adversity of various kinds.

Scholarly interest in children in Ireland initially surfaced in the context of social problems. Concerns around children and childhood began to be voiced in the 1980s in relation to revelations about child sexual abuse. This gave rise to a series of commissions, fora etc. The discourse of these reports and the terms of reference of the bodies producing them both illustrate what the norms of childhood in Ireland are and how these are perceived to be threatened or inadequately served. Children were also constituted as a "residual" problem in the process of a more comprehensive incorporation of women within the labour force. This is very much the emphasis within the Expert Working Group on Child Care Report. Children are identified as a barrier to women's continued participation and promotion in the labour force. Children emerged as a "muted group" in marital separation cases and very little evidence pertaining to them was uncovered in analysis of legal documents (Fahey and Lyons, 1995). Ireland ratified the UN Convention on the Rights of the Child in 1989 and this has acted to set standards and provide greater moral weight to the work of child advocacy groups such as Barnardos and the Children's Rights Alliance. It has also helped to heighten awareness of children as persons with rights and to stimulate research questions around the situation of children generally.

The aim of this book is to present a more comprehensive and positive profile of childhood and children in Ireland by bringing together recent research and analysis of the lives of Irish children. The focus would be on contemporary aspects of children's lives and on the challenges facing children in adjusting to the changing context of childhood. The contributors are drawn from a range of disciplinary backgrounds in the social sciences, but share a similar approach to the study of childhood in their questioning of common assumptions of childhood as a passive, residual category of "becoming adults" who may be simply described as being in the process of being socialised. In this the book is allied with the contemporary approach to the study of childhood and its concerns:

> Most of the new sociological thinking about childhood is *structural* rather than individual; it is *relational*, first of all with respect to an intergenerational perspective; and it seems to be far more interested in typical, normal and common conditions for the majority of children, i.e. the focus is no longer merely on children in particular critical situations (Qvortrup, 1995, p. 10).

Childhood cannot be taken as a biological given but is socially constructed, deconstructed and reconstructed in changing times. The social construction of Irish childhood is contributed to by the State, families, the churches, the legal and administrative system and the media among others, but also, to some extent, by children themselves. While children are among the least powerful categories of people in society, they are more than objects of socialisation, concern, abuse, neglect, parental ambition etc. Children may also be viewed as social actors in their own right who contribute to the culture and social groups in which they participate. The degree of social competency and agency of children is likely to vary not only by age but also by context. While it is important to examine the contexts and social forces influencing childhood and children's lives, a more important focus is that of the experience of childhood in different contexts. How do children react to and engage in different situations, changing conditions, new cultural trends, etc.? In accordance with international convention, the upper age-limit of childhood is taken to be the minimum school-leaving age (i.e. 15 years).

Accordingly, contributors were requested to draw on primary research with children themselves, where possible. Many were able to do so, using a variety of techniques — questionnaires, interviews, focus groups, ethnography, observation — with sometimes unpredictable findings. The range of research methods employed in the study of children and childhood is as extensive as that used in the study of adults. While there are limits of lack of literacy and articulation in the methods used with younger children, the choice of method is fully comprehensive from the age of about 8 or 9 years (Hill, 1998, p. 15). Very young children can only be studied by observational methods or indirectly by interviews with carers, whereas older children can co-operate with written questionnaires, interviews, focus groups, etc. "Visual sociology" methods utilising photography or video are highly suited to recording children's group interactions (see *Visual Sociology*, 1999, Vol. 14). Particular ethical issues arise in relation to research on children. It is usually necessary to negotiate access and consent from parents and guardians. To the extent that the child population of study is constituted through institutional arrangements such as schools or day care facilities, such access and consent must first be negotiated with the management; the consent of children themselves is less frequently prioritised. This may not be very realistic if children are very young, but the option to refuse should be available as soon as children are capable of understanding they are being sought to co-operate in research (Hill, 1998, p. 15).

The project of producing this book was originally inspired by our former colleague and mentor, Emeritus Professor Helen Burke. It was conceived as offering a vehicle for co-operation between members of the Department of Social Policy and Social Work and the Department of Sociology. We are pleased that papers were produced by contributors from a broad range of social science disciplines.

In inviting contributions, we sought to provide an analysis of as broad as possible a cross-section of children in Ireland (a term not co-terminus with "Irish children"). Another goal was to examine the impact of social and cultural processes in varied institutional settings. Sadly, there are gaps which we did not succeed in filling. In particular, the impact of the media on the lives of children in Ireland is not represented here. Neither is that most negative element of peer culture, namely bullying. And try as we might we were unable to discover a researcher who had studied the situation of being children of a religious minority in Ireland.

Despite these gaps, we are confident that *Understanding Children* will introduce readers to many facets of the lives of children in Ireland not previously published. It is our hope that the gaps in our knowledge and understanding of childhood in Ireland that remain will soon begin to be filled by further re-search — indeed, the National Children's Strategy planned Longitudinal Study of Children promises to do so.

The quantity of papers resulting from our invitations was so large that, at our publishers' recommendation, we have divided it into two volumes. *Volume 1: State, Education and Economy* deals with the macro-structures which define children's lives and the way in which children themselves respond to them. *Volume 2: Changing Experiences and Family Forms* looks at mi-cro-level aspects and cultural variations in the experience of childhood in contemporary Ireland. The Table of Contents of the companion volume is listed after the Table of Contents for this volume.

References

Expert Working Group on Childcare (1999), *National Childcare Strategy*, Dublin: Stationery Office.

Fahey, Tony and Lyons, Maureen (1995), Marital *Breakdown and Family Law in Ireland: A Sociological Study*, Dublin: Oak Tree Press and ESRI.

Hill, Malcolm (1998), "Ethical Issues in Qualitative Methodology with Children", in Hogan, Diane and Gilligan, Robbie (eds.) *Researching*

Children's Experiences: Qualitative Approaches, Proceedings of conference, The Children's Research Centre, Trinity College Dublin.

National Children's Strategy (2000), *Our Children — Their Lives*, Dublin: Stationery Office.

Qvortrup, Jens (1995), "Childhood in Europe: a New Field of Social Research" in Chisholm, L. et al. (eds) *Growing Up in Europe: Contemporary Horizons in Childhood and Youth Studies*, Berlin: Walter de Gruyter and Co.

Introduction

PART 1: NEW FAMILY FORMS

For most children the family is the social context within which initial relationships are built and an understanding of the world absorbed. Traditionally, children were viewed as dependent within this structure and, according to Lynch (1998), this subordinate status of children is reflected in constitutional references to the family in Ireland. However, recent analysis of the family has incorporated a more active role for children, in line with new perspectives on children and childhood. As Hill and Tisdall (1997) have said, children are not just dependent on adults and contribute in significant ways to family life. At the same time, the status of parents as well as parenting approaches is changing. LeVine and White (1992) suggest that the new parenting goal is to optimise the life chances of children and that this task is being undertaken in the context of more equitable parent-child relationships. Parenting is coming under increasing scrutiny from outside the family for reasons such as neglect and abuse, although, as Lynch (1998) notes, State intervention in the family in this country is confined to exceptional circumstances. However, parenting is now subject to some degree of external evaluation and many parents must try to achieve this in less than optimal circumstances such as poverty, poor health and lack of support in relation to childcare (Report of the Commission on the Family, 1998). That most parents try hard to achieve this is illustrated by Hogan's account, later in this volume, of the attempts of drug using parents to protect their children. Good parenting does appear to be one indicator of present and future well-being for a child. According to Fahlberg (1994), children at a young age need to develop both satisfactory relationships and independence. Parents need to be available and capable of supporting children in these endeavours. Fitzgerald and Jeffers' (1994) study attests to the importance of parenting, yet it is clear that there is a good deal of flexibility both in the type and form of parenting (Hill and Tisdall, 1997). Furthermore, it is becoming increasingly apparent that children are resilient and capable of negotiating quite difficult home environments (Gilligan, 1993).

The structure and dynamics of Irish families have altered considerably over the last 30 years and there is now a diversity of family types. Children are increasingly reared in lone parent family units or in reconstituted families, although the majority of children still grow up in two-parent households (McKeown et al., 1998). Family size has also changed. As recently as 1981, the vast majority of children had an average of three siblings (Clancy and Nic Ghiolla Phadraig, 1995) and were in two-parent households with a father in full-time employment and a mother who was a full-time homemaker. It is the increased levels of participation in employment by mothers of young children which probably marks the most important change in the lives of children, particularly of the pre-school age group. The home situation of the under five-year-olds has changed significantly in Ireland, even in the last 20 years. Barely half of these children now have a mother full-time in the home, as compared with three-quarters as recently as the beginning of the 1980s, and children increasingly experience out-of-home care facilities (Hennessy and Hayes, 1997).

Children are also affected by marital breakdown and the implications of family recomposition to a greater degree. According to Nic Ghiolla Phadraig (1991), increasing levels of parental separation have two main implications for young children: first by increasing the numbers of children in poverty and welfare dependence, and secondly, by reducing the level of contact with the non-custodial parent.

Increased levels of mothers' participation in the labour force may also have affected the balance of power within families

(Cleary et al., 2001). This, in turn, has influenced child rearing practices. Fatherhood and related roles are changing and fathers, as Kiely's paper shows, are becoming more involved in child-rearing and are less likely to adopt a patriarchal authoritarian role.

These changes in family patterns have prompted debates on the effects this may have on children. Existing evidence in relation to the effect of differing family type on children suggests that the nature of the household is not the most significant factor, but rather the quality of the relationships and this applies to lone parent families also. The fact that studies have shown that a higher proportion of children in lone-parent households have scholastic or emotional problems, compared to those living with both parents, is more likely to be due to poverty than to parenting factors (Cleary et al., 2001).

The issues raised here demonstrate the changing nature of Irish families and the possible challenges for children involved in these changes. In this first section, "New Family Forms", the contributors examine the types of family that have emerged in Ireland and the experiences of children within these families.

The changing role of fathers within the family is the theme of the first paper in this section. Kiely argues that fatherhood is a social construct defined by the prevailing culture. However, he says, this construct is ill-defined and variable and is dependent not only on the constructs of children and their fathers, but on society in general. This lack of an agreed definition, according to Kiely, reflects not just our different experiences of fathers, but the changing nature of the social role of fatherhood in Western society. Existing constructions of fatherhood range from the detached provider of material goods to the caring, emotionally involved parent. These various conceptualisations, as Kiely points out, are all relevant to our understanding of fatherhood but, he contends, they are uni-dimensional. Fathers are still the main providers for their children. They are also, he states, significant role models for their children and their involvement in quality parenting is important for the development and well-being of their children. Fathers, according to Kiely, are seeking a new identity and a redefined position in their children's lives. Yet this process is hampered by the fact that neither work nor legal institutions are facilitating fathers, in giving time to their children, nor in assuring access to them should families break up.

Fathers and fatherhood is an important theme also in Flanagan's paper that picks up on contemporary debates about the absence of fathers in families. Her paper is written against the backdrop of a significant rise in single-parent female families in Ireland and her focus is on the children of such units. The findings dispel some notions about children in single-parent families and confirm others. According to Flanagan, the social implications of being born outside marriage are determined by the subsequent parenting and living arrangements of the family. Children living in unmarried two-parent families are largely undifferentiated from their counterparts born to married parents across a range of factors including behavioural difficulties. Although, as Flanagan shows, the changes experienced by children born outside marriage but living in a two-parent family by age four years are more likely to have a positive rather than a negative effect. Children who are reared in an extended family household with grandparents are also in comparatively good circumstances. The social implications of being born outside marriage for most pre-school children, therefore, appear to be transient. However, for the identifiable grouping of those who live in lone (female) parent households the disadvantages are ongoing. Flanagan's research reveals a strong association between lone-parent families and disadvantage, both social and economic. The level of paternal involvement in these families was often very low and sometimes non-existent. Perhaps most worryingly, Flanagan identified a trajectory to this disadvantage. The mothers of these children were economically and socially disadvantaged prior to giving birth, suggesting, she contends, a grouping of children and mothers trapped in a disadvantaged lifestyle.

O'Donoghue's paper picks up on a similar theme of disengaged families and examines how children cope with, and accommodate to, parental separation. Most studies of parental separation, as O'Donoghue notes, concentrate on the negative outcomes for the child but she attempts a revision of this approach. Her analysis is based on a small sample of young people who, as children, experienced parental separation. This research indicates that, while children are affected in a negative way by this experience there are crucial intervening factors that modify this effect. The important mediating element is the child's exposure to inter-parental conflict, either in the pre- or post-separation period. Where there was little conflict and the separated parents were co-operative and supportive of each other, the child transcended this short-term adversity and appeared even to gain from the process, in terms of long-term emotional and behavioural skills.

O'Brien's contribution removes the child conceptually from parental to "relative care", an increasingly important child care option. Her paper presents children's views of the different stages of this care option, from the decision-making procedure and assessment practices to arranging contact and future planning. Relative care, as O'Brien suggests, meets the needs of many children who cannot live with their own parents although, as her research shows, children would prefer to live at home. However these children also demonstrated that they had come to terms with the fact of living away from the family home. They indicated a preference for being fostered by relatives rather than by strangers. Their stories reinforce the need for frequent contact with families, both parents and siblings. The children considered that initiating this was the responsibility of their parent(s) and that their relatives should initiate this contact. Overall, they wanted adults to take more control and allow them to get on with "an ordinary life". According to O'Brien, the study demonstrates the resiliency of children in coping with significant challenges to themselves and their family attachments.

Hennessy's paper examines the experiences of children in day care, a form of care with much greater applicability in Ireland today. As Hennessy says, the topic of day care has moved from being of specialist concern for a minority of parents and experts in child development to a subject of national debate, legislation and controversy. This increased interest reflects the growing usage of non-parental day care for children of all ages. Here Hennessy quotes an ESRI study (Williams and Collins, 1998) which estimates that almost 10 per cent of Irish children

(46,000) between the ages of six and twelve are cared for by someone other than their parents after school each day. The number of younger children in day care is even greater. Hennessy's research shows differences in the experiences of children in the different types of care. Her study showed that children cared for by a relative, usually a grandparent, were the least likely to have someone to play with. Children cared for by a childminder were the least likely to have access to books and children attending crèches were less likely than other children to be able to play outside. Yet despite these differences, the findings suggest that the majority of children view after-school care as a positive and enjoyable experience, whatever the type of care setting.

PART 2: CHALLENGES FOR CHILDREN AND FAMILIES

"The unique and essential family function is that of caring and nurturing for all its members" (Report of the Commission on the Family, 1998, p. 56). The problem of raising children in less than optimal conditions and the question of what constitutes "good enough parenting" are important ones for contemporary society. Parents vary in their capacity to parent effectively. Sometimes factors within the family result in it becoming, for the child, a far from the safe place to be and issues of power and control predominate in place of love and nurture.

Changing social attitudes have allowed the devastating experiences of some Irish children to be acknowledged more openly, rather than remaining hidden within the institution of the family. One of the key objectives of the National Children's Strategy (2000, p. 61) is to ensure that children "will be safeguarded to enjoy their childhood free from all forms of abuse and exploitation". Unhappily, this is not the current reality for some children within their own families. The existence of child sexual abuse, by no means a new phenomenon, has only relatively recently entered the public arena.

McCarthy and Byrne discuss the changing societal and familial contexts that have supported children making disclosures about sexual abuse when it occurs. Their chapter illustrates the resources and strengths demonstrated by such children in their attempts to find solutions to a problem they should never have had to encounter. The experiences of children in such circumstances have been graphically conveyed in McColgan's book based on personal history and, in broader terms, in the report of the Kilkenny inquiry into child sexual abuse, both referred to in the chapter. What is remarkable is the extent of resilience that the children interviewed demonstrated and articulated so vividly in the interviews recorded in McCarthy and Byrne's chapter. Further, the range of coping mechanisms used to distance themselves from their immediate experiences is notable and shows the sophistication of thought processes that even very young children can be capable of in difficult circumstances. Butler and Roberts (1997) refer to perceptions of the "relative powerlessness of children to be significant authors of their own biographies, both literally and figuratively". McCarthy and Byrne's chapter draws attention to the importance of professionals reinforcing the child's sense of autonomy and self-worth in the aftermath of experiencing powerlessness and victimisation.

In other situations, caring families may be faced with particular challenges arising from children's serious illness or disability. In such circumstances, children and their families may need additional supports from the wider society in helping them to accomplish their task successfully. Increased medical knowledge and technology has resulted in a higher proportion of low weight babies now surviving infancy, a factor which has implications for future health problems, including disability (Nolan, 1992).

Children with cancer illustrate a group of children in particular circumstances of adversity. It is shocking to contemplate that even very young children can be faced with a life-threatening illness. Furthermore, often this illness requires painful and debilitating treatment to promote survival. It is the fact that the illness is so untimely within the expected lifecycle that makes the diagnosis, treatment and, for those who survive, post-treatment stages so challenging in emotional, physical and social terms. The question arises of how the initial and subsequent stages are experienced from the viewpoint of the child affected. Perhaps one of the most surprising of the research findings in Quin's chapter is that the children's memories and views about their experiences are by no means solely negative. The positive attention they receive and the sense of support they feel are compensatory factors that help them to cope. It is the perceived lack or withdrawal of such factors by parents that account for the negative effects of the illness on their siblings. This points to the importance of the child's immediate environment of family and social supports in determining the effects of extra-familial adversity on their coping responses.

For children with cancer and their families, the aspiration and, for the majority, the reality is long-term survival and a return to "normality" in spite of what has occurred. This is not an option for children whose physical disability poses ongoing challenges that continue and change through childhood and into adolescence. Such children and their families, as Cleary's chapter demonstrates, face issues that, in part, are determined by the child's dependency needs arising directly from the physical effects of their condition and, more importantly, by a social and physical environment that takes little account of their situation.

Families in the research undertaken by Cleary did not see themselves in a negative light, but rather as an ordinary family having a child with specific needs. Most of the children in her study had the potential to participate fully in society, given appropriate and sufficient equipment and support services. That these were not available was evident from the research findings. It is of particular concern that very basic equipment (such as wheelchairs) was not readily available and that one-half of parents whose children had support needs regarded their attempts to access suitable and sufficient services as a constant struggle with officialdom. The Report of the Review Group on Health and Personal Social Services for People with Physical and Sensory Disabilities (1996) specifically acknowledged "present deficiencies in the supply and repair of technical aids" in the overall context of "significant shortfalls in the provision of community services" (p. 72-3). This is further recognised in the National Children's Strategy 2000 that refers to the "challenge to ensure that these children have a range of supports they and their families need and the opportunity to participate equally and effectively in education, employment and social life" (p. 68).

The research population in Cleary's chapter discussed above represented a broad range of socio-economic groups within the population. This is in sharp contrast to the children in research undertaken by Hogan and Higgins concerning children growing up in a context of drug abuse. In keeping with the statistics that identifies drug abuse as essentially a feature of economically deprived urban areas, their study focused on two groups of children growing up in such an environment, the difference between them being based on whether or not their parent(s) were themselves drug abusers. In the case of the latter group, it might be supposed that they were potentially the most neglectful of parents arising from their addiction. The research findings show this not to be the case, in that protecting their children from witnessing the effects of drug use was regarded as being of major importance and was evident in their parenting practices. All were aware and concerned about the potentially negative effects on children of such exposure. This was so even for those who, in practice, were less successful in this respect on account of their level and type of addiction. For parents who were not drug users themselves, there was concern to protect their children from direct knowledge and sight of drug taking in the immediate surrounding of their home environment. This was a particular issue for children in the inner city context where the living environment of a flat complex meant that drug dealing, drug use and discarded equipment were readily evident. Growing-up in conditions of adversity, in this instance, arose not from experiences within the home, but in the geographical, economic and social environment within which the home is situated.

PART 3: CHILDREN AND CULTURAL MINORITIES

This section addresses the issues of diversity in Irish childhood. In keeping with the overall theme of the book, the focus is on children as active participants within their social contexts. Hutchby (1998) emphasised the social competence of children in a variety of settings. The children referred to in the chapters in this section have to cope with significant differences in their family and social experiences to those of their peers. Some of the key themes that emerge in the different chapters arise from the changes that are taking place within society, while others are rooted in traditional values, prejudices and socio-economic divisions. A factor in common, however, is that all of the children will have experienced a childhood that differs in some, or many, respects to the majority of children in this country on account of race, ethnicity and/or language.

Many, but not all, of the chapters refer to situations in which material disadvantage coincide with difference. This is not necessarily so in relation to the children who are the subject of Nic Ghiolla Phádraig's chapter. It is concerned with children who have been raised as Irish-speaking in a cultural context which pays lip service to the importance of the Irish language, but in which the vast majority live in households that are English-speaking only. The fact that most Irish children are, in effect, monolingual is unusual in that, as Nic Ghiolla Phádraig points out, globally, bilingualism is the more common pattern. Moreover, in most countries, children speak their native language from the outset. It is of particular interest, therefore, to know how children raised through the medium of Irish regard their linguistic inheritance.

Further, what is the difference, if any, between those growing up in a Gaeltacht area and those whose parents make the conscious choice to counteract the prevailing norm of English-speaking areas. The results show varying experiences and viewpoints of children raised in similar circumstances. It highlights the importance of taking account of children's individuality and their ability to take cognisance of the many variables that inform their views.

What of those children who, at the outset, may be unable to communicate in either of the two officially recognised languages in Ireland? This deficit may be only one of the many limitations experienced by the children of refugees or asylum seekers. The number of those seeking asylum in Ireland has grown substantially, even though the total number still represents a small minority of the population. Nolan's chapter draws the distinction between programme refugees who have formal status and specific services, though limited, directed towards their particular needs. Asylum seekers, on the other hand, enjoy neither of these rights and live in a state of uncertainty and marginalisation. Little is known about the lives of the children of asylum seekers in Ireland. Unsuitable accommodation, poverty, and unemployment are all evident in the limited documented evidence about the lives of their parents. Bleak as this may be, it may be as nothing in comparison to the past experiences of both parents and children. The question arises of the effects of such circumstances on these children and the material, social and emotional supports needed to enable them to thrive in their new environment. The Combat Poverty Agency has recently commissioned a study on child poverty among refugee and asylum seekers in Ireland. This will go some way to developing greater awareness of the current life experiences of this visible, but unknown, group of children in Ireland.

While much more is known about Traveller children, their deprived and marginal position in Irish society remains. That a group of children experiences such levels of poverty, poor health and reduced life expectancy (Task Force Report on the Travelling Community, 1995) in a prosperous Ireland is hard to explain, other than in terms of prejudice and indifference. The recent update on the Report (2001) indicates that, in the past five years since the publication of the Task Force Report, little has changed in their economic and social conditions, in spite of the continuing growth in the Irish economy. Kenny, in her chapter, describes Travellers as a reviled ethnic minority in Irish society which, in the past, was dealt with by policies designed to eliminate their difference by the process of assimilation. However, in spite of the change in policies towards the recognition of difference, the educational system has failed to take cognisance of Traveller children's socialisation, of their different definition of what constitutes appropriate childhood experiences and even when childhood comes to an end.

Where childhood ends is another theme of import in relation to refugee and asylum seekers. Nolan refers to the foreshortened childhood of such children, who are forced into adult roles by expedience. They may become the interpreters and mediators between their parents and the wider social systems on account of their greater exposure and ability to understand and speak the English language. Also, they may comprise the little emotional and social support available to their parents, many of whom will be traumatised by past experiences. Further, refugee and asylum-seeking children may be required to adopt a parenting role in relation to younger siblings, a role common among female Traveller children. How, then, will they find the space, energy and opportunity to become part of their new society?

In part this will depend upon the attitudes of other children towards them. In their chapter, O'Keefe and O'Connor examine attitudes towards Travellers as an existing minority within the largely ethnically homogeneous population in Ireland. Their chapter focuses on the attitudes of peers to Traveller children, by exploring the views of school-going children, male and female, coming from both working class and middle class backgrounds. Using a standardised scale measuring social distance, they found that racist attitudes were prevalent amongst each group at cognitive, affective and behavioural levels. The greatest level of prejudice was found among working class boys. However, in exploring this further by means of focus groups, negative attitudes were modified, in part, by direct experience. The further away in terms of social distance, the greater likelihood that less strong, but prevalent, stereotypes existed. Girls, they found, displayed a different form of prejudice, couching differences in terms of patronising pity. O'Keefe and O'Connor consider that the educational system has a key part to play in changing attitudes towards ethnic minorities towards a greater recognition of the value of difference. This view is reinforced by the National Children's Strategy which states that "learning to appreciate and recognise positively each others' differences and similarities in childhood, should be seen as a critical investment towards Ireland's new multiculturalism" (2000, p. 70).

It is the primacy of a child-centred focus that enriches these chapters on children dealing with wide-ranging situations of challenge and difference. Overall, the research contained in the chapters has produced findings, some to be expected and others less easily anticipated. What is evident is the importance of incorporating the child's viewpoint in order to facilitate greater understanding of children's experiences in different situations of adversity. Without such understanding, there is the danger that negative experiences of difference and/or adversity may be compounded for children by the interventions and institutions that are intended to ameliorate them.

References:

Butler, I. & Roberts, G. (1997), *Social Work with Children and Families: Getting into Practice*, London: Jessica Kingsley.

Clancy, P and Nic Ghiolla Phádraig, M. (1995) "Marital Fertility and Family Planning" in McCarthy, I. (ed) *Irish Family Studies: Selected Papers*, UCD: Family Studies Centre.

Cleary, A., Corbett, M., Galvin, M. and Wall, J. (2001) "The Context and Experience of Marginalisation amongst Young Men in Ireland". A Report Commissioned by the Katherine Howard Foundation, Dublin: Social Science Research Centre, UCD/Katherine Howard Foundation.

Commission on the Family (1998), *Strengthening Families for Life, Final Report to the Minister for Social Community and Family Affairs*, Dublin: Stationery Office.

Department of Health (1995), "Report of the Review Group on Health and Personal Social Services for People with Physical and Sensory Disabilities", *Towards an Independent Future*, Dublin: Stationery Office.

Department of Health and Children (2000), The National Children's Strategy: *Our Children — Their Lives*, Dublin: Government Publications.

Department of Justice, Equality and Law Reform (1995), *Task Force on the Travelling Community*, Dublin: Stationery Office.

Department of Justice, Equality and Law Reform (2001), *First Progress Report of the Committee to Monitor and Co-ordinate the implementation of the Task Force on the Travelling Community*, Dublin: Stationery Office.

Department of Social, Community and Family Affairs (1998), Report of the Commission on the Family, *Strengthening Families for Life*, Dublin: Stationery Office.

Falhberg, V. (1994), *A Child's Journey Through Placement*, London: BAAF.

Fitzgerald, M. and Jeffers, A. (1994), "Psychological factors associated with psychological problems in Irish children and their mothers", *The Economic and Social Review,* 25, 4, pp. 285-301.

Gilligan, R. (1993), "Adversity in the child's home: The protective role of the teacher and the school", *Studies in Education*, 9, pp. 53-66.

Hennessy, E. and Hayes, N. (1997), "Early childhood services in Ireland", *International Journal of Early Years' Education*, 5, 211-224.

Hill, M. and Tisdall, K. (1997), *Children and Society*, Harlow, Essex: Addison Wesley Longman.

Hutchby, I. (ed) (1998), *Children and Social Competence: Arenas for Action*, London: Falmer.

LeVine, R.A. & White, M. (1992), "The Social Transformation of Childhood" in Skolnick, A.S. & Skolnick, J.H. (eds), *Family in Transition*, New York: HarperCollins

Lynch, K. (1989), *The Hidden Curriculum*, London: Falmer Press.

Lynch, K. (1998), "The Status of Children and Young Persons: Educational and Related issues" in S. Healy and B. Reynolds (eds), *Social Policy in Ireland: Principles, Practice and Problems*, Dublin: Oak Tree Press.

McKeown, K., Ferguson, H. and Rooney, D. (1998), "Fathers: Irish experience in an international context". Abstract of a report to the Commission on the Family.

Nic Ghiolla Phadraig, M. (1991*), Childhood as a Social Phenomenon: National Report — Ireland*, Vienna: European Centre for Social Research.

Nolan, B. (1992), *Perinatal Mortality and Low Birth Weight by Age, Parity and Socio-Economic Basis*, ESRI Working Paper No 37, Dublin: Economic and Social Research Institute.

Williams, J. and Collins, C. (1998), "Child-care arrangements in Ireland — A report to the Commission on the Family June 1997", in *Strengthening Families for Life, Final Report of the Commission on the Family to the Minister for Social, Community and Family Affairs*, Dublin: Stationery Office.

Part 1:
New Family Forms

Chapter 1

The Changing Role of Fathers

Gabriel Kiely

There has been a growing interest in recent years in the significance of fathers for the well-being of their children. Increasingly, the interest has moved from focusing on fathers as primarily providers for their children to fathers as parents. This chapter will examine the changing role of fathers in Irish society. This will include a discussion of the social and symbolic significance of fathers for their children and will draw on what research findings are available. While the chapter will include a discussion on the changing legal position of fathers in relation to their children, the focus will be less on rights and more on the social construction of fatherhood and the reciprocal needs of children and their fathers.

DEFINING FATHERHOOD

Father is the term used to distinguish the male parent from the female parent, the mother. Fatherhood, therefore, refers specifically to the relationship between children and their male parent. There are two components to this relationship, i.e. biological and social. The biological father is the person who conceives the child with the child's mother. The social father is the person who may or may not be the biological father, but who carries the role of father in relation to the child. In this sense, fatherhood is a social construct which is defined by the culture.

However, there is no clear understanding of what this definition constitutes. It can include all aspects of parenting, or only some. How fatherhood is perceived in society depends on the ideas and beliefs of not only children and their fathers, but of all society. A further complication in defining fatherhood is that it is difficult to distinguish what is distinctly fathering from parenting, i.e. what tasks are uniquely performed by fathers which are not also performed by mothers.

Blackenhorn (1995, p. 25), in an attempt to overcome the difficulties in defining fatherhood, describes fatherhood rather negatively as a social role that obligates men to their biological offspring. While this description is largely correct, it fails to take account of the great variation in the ways in which fathers carry out their role and that many fathers are not the biological fathers of their children. Most commentators avoid giving such definitions. For example, not one of the papers read at the highly significant conference on fathers held in Denmark in 1993 (Fathers in Families of Tomorrow, 1993) put forward a definition of fatherhood. Thus, while each of us might have an image of what we mean by the term "father", when it comes to some common shared image, we seem unable to go beyond the simple description of a father as the male parent. This lack of an agreed definition reflects not just our different experiences of fathers, but the changing nature of the social role of fatherhood in western society.

THE CONSTRUCTION OF FATHERHOOD

Theories of fatherhood in the social sciences have shifted their focus over the past few decades. This is because ideas about fatherhood are the product of different cultures and changes over time. The classic structural-functional approach of Parsons and Bales (1955) in the 1950s, for example, emphasised the instrumental, as distinct from the expressive, role of fathers. This conceptualisation was based on notions of the nuclear family in which tasks were divided between family members based on a complementary gender role differentiation which assigned the provider role to fathers and the homemaker role to mothers.

In the 1960s, research attention began to focus more on the importance of the father as a role model for his children, especially for boys. In addition, the negative effects of absent fathers on children's behaviour, including school performance and crime, received particular attention. This was due largely to the rise in divorce and the subsequent increase in the number of households headed by lone mothers (see Lamb, 1986). Psychoanalytic theory, in a similar vein, emphasised the importance of fathers for the psychological development of children. Much of this focused on what is termed the "symbolic father", i.e. a real or imagined person whom the child perceives as significant during the early years of childhood. In the 1980s, attention shifted to a discussion of fatherhood in the context of the equality debate (see Carlsen and Larsen, undated). Increased emphasis was placed on the need for fathers to share household and childcare tasks with mothers. Now the focus is more on the issue of identity. As de Singly (1993, p. 4) describes it, "men are having trouble forging an identity for themselves as fathers". They are confronted with a blurring between the gender-neutral role of parent and the gender-specific role of father.

All of these conceptualisations continue to be relevant to our understanding of fatherhood. However, each only describes an aspect of fatherhood. Fathers in most families are still the main providers for their children and act as significant role models. Their involvement in quality parenting is important for the development and wellbeing of their children and their participation in this parenting can contribute to increased parental equality, both within and outside the home. The difficulty in conceptualising fatherhood is in how to integrate all of these aspects into a coherent identity when there is no clear cultural prescription for doing so. Fatherhood, in so far as it is a social construction, changes as people's ideas and beliefs about it change. We have, therefore, many and sometimes conflicting conceptualisations of fatherhood, all existing simultaneously. These range from the detached provider of material goods to the caring, emotionally involved parent. Fatherhood, therefore, is not simply one social construction but several, with each reflecting different beliefs about the nature of what it means to be a father. As McKeown et al. (1998, p. 18) put it, "fatherhood is a social practice which is shaped by its social context".

THE CHANGING ROLE OF FATHERS

In traditional families, fathers had a clear role as the family patriarch. He was the head of the family, its protector and the person who provided for the family's material needs. Aldous (1998), in tracing the changing concept of fatherhood over time, shows how this traditional model of fatherhood evolved to meet the needs of a changing society and, in particular, the needs of pre-industrial and industrial societies. Fathers were heads of the households and they controlled procreation and the social validation of their children. They were the primary and usually the sole breadwinner. This patriarchal position was upheld not only by custom and tradition, but also by law.

Fathers no longer hold this position within families (see Kiely, 1995, p. 155). Headship is no longer vested in the father. Procreation, as a result of contraception, abortion and artificial insemination, can now be controlled by women. With the advent of the welfare state and the increased participation of mothers in the paid labour force, fathers are no longer the exclusive providers. Social validation of children comes through employment and education, and not through one's father. In addition, children's rights are protected by law, thus removing this element of control by fathers over their children. These changes have confronted fathers with the need to redefine their role and function within the family and, in particular, their role as parents.

With the loss of many of these traditional aspects of their role, fathers are searching, as noted above, for a new identity. The search is reflected in the increased public attention given to fatherhood in the media (see European Commission Childcare Network, 1994) and as a subject of international conferences (see, for example, Fathers in Services for Young Children (1996), Rome; Fathers in Families of Tomorrow (1993), Copenhagen; Men as Carers (1993), Ravenna, Italy; and Men as Carers for Children (1990b), Glasgow). Fathers have also been the subject of political debate. However, much of this debate has focused rather negatively on the need to make fathers take more responsibility for their children which generally means financial responsibility. Much less attention has been paid to the caring and parenting function of fathers. This is in spite of the fact that caring is the one area in which fathers can enhance and expand their involvement with their children more than any other. This lack of attention in public policy to the role of fathers as carers is reflected in Ireland and in many other European Union member states by the absence of provisions like paid parental leave. If fathers are to be encouraged to develop their caring role, then both public attitudes and official policy concerning fathers will need to change.

FATHERS AS PROVIDERS

Sociological studies of the family have been criticised for identifying fathers with the instrumental function of breadwinner, claiming that such a description no longer fits families in modern society. However, any analysis of the labour force participation of fathers and mothers shows that fathers continue to be the family's primary breadwinner. This is shown by McKeown et al. (1998) in their analysis of the Irish Labour Force Survey data of 1996. Fathers are the exclusive breadwinners in half of all families, with only three out of ten families consisting of dual-earners (p. 123). In addition, they show that fathers work longer hours outside the home than male non-fathers, with 33 per cent of fathers working 50 hours per week or more, compared to 27 per cent of non-fathers (p. 132). In contrast, mothers work 15 hours less per week outside the home than fathers (p. 132). Similar patterns of employment are found across the European Union. An analysis of employment patterns by the European Commission Childcare Network (1990a, p. 2) shows that, in the EU, less than 44 per cent of mothers with a child aged 0-9 were employed, compared to 92 per cent of fathers. The same study shows that 17 per cent of the mothers were employed in part-time work, compared to only 2 per cent of fathers, and that 67 per cent of fathers usually work over 40 hours a week, compared to 29 per cent of mothers (pp. 6-7). This difference in working hours is partly accounted for by the higher percentage of mothers in part-time employment. However, when parents in full-time jobs only are compared, the study shows that fathers work an average of 40-49 hours per week, while mothers work 30-39 hours. Another study (European Commission Childcare Network, 1990b, appendix) shows that married and cohabiting men with children work on average from 42 to 44 hours per week, depending on the age of the youngest child, compared to 39 hours by single men.

The continued dominance of the breadwinner role of the father has significant consequences for other aspects of his relationship with his children. Work outside the home, as McKeown et al. (1998, p. 124) observe, is one of the greatest determinants of a father's involvement with his children since it determines the amount of time he can spend with them. The more time he spends in his role as provider at work outside the home, the less time he has to spend on the physical and emotional care of his children.

FATHERS' INVOLVEMENT IN THE HOME

In spite of the emphasis in recent decades on the role of fathers as carers within the home, their participation continues to be significantly less than mothers'. While this can be explained in part by the long hours they spend in paid employment outside the home, the reality continues to be that mothers are the primary carers, even in dual-earner families (see Kiely, 1998). For example, a Eurobarometer (1991, p. 122) study found that 61.6 per cent of men surveyed across the European Union said that they did not do as much as one of a range of household tasks presented to them by the survey. In Ireland, 84 per cent of the men "claimed to do nothing" (p. 124). This is consistent with the findings of the Family Studies Centre study in Ireland in which mothers reported that very few of their husbands took responsibility for household tasks apart from household repairs or for a range of child care tasks (Kiely, 1995, p. 149). The Irish study showed that even where mothers were employed outside the home the rates of participation by fathers remained low.

When fathers do participate in child care tasks it tends to be with the more pleasurable aspects of child care. For example, the study by Kiely (1995, p. 149) showed that fathers participated more than mothers in such activities as going on outings and playing with the children. Mothers were more involved with such tasks as putting the children to bed, helping them with homework and attending school meetings. The European Child Care Network (1990b, pp. 1-2) also reported that fathers' involvement in child care is concentrated "on the more enjoyable, cleaner and less demanding aspects, such as play". Turner (1993, p. 153), in her review of studies on the sharing of child care between parents, concluded that "fathers' participation is most likely in the more pleasurable child care activities with mothers taking far more responsibility for day-to-day routines and chores".

Time-budget studies on the amount of time spent on childcare and housework by fathers and mothers also show the low level of participation in these tasks by fathers. Künzler (1994), in an analysis of 65 studies covering the period 1970 to 1992 including time-budget studies, found that all studies showed that the lion's share of housework chores is done by women. In addition, the analysis concluded by stating "in a way, time has stood still; the distribution of housework tasks has not changed its sex-stereotyped bias from the 1960s" (p. 8).

These behaviours within the home do not, however, reflect attitudes of men and women to the involvement of fathers in bringing up their children. For example, another Eurobarometer (1993, p. 92) study found that 96.3 per cent of men and 87.4 per cent of women surveyed in the European Union agreed that men should be involved in bringing up their children. In the Irish study (Kiely, 1995, p. 148), 80.7 per cent of the mothers thought that husbands and wives should share housework equally. This discrepancy between actual behaviour and attitudes is most likely accounted for by changing cultural expectations about fathers, compared to descriptions of what the so-called "new age" father actually does.

In addition, fathers are more likely to share tasks with mothers than to undertake them on their own. The Irish study (Kiely, 1995, p. 149) clearly shows this. However, while fathers' participation increases somewhat when sharing the household tasks on child care duties with mothers, the rate is still low relative to the participation in carrying out these tasks by mothers on their own. It is interesting to note that, while the 1993 Euro-barometer study found that men and women thought that most child care tasks were part of the maternal role, and that women considered that these tasks should be shared by both parents, men had a "greater tendency than women to emphasise the separate roles of the father and mother" (p. 95). This would seem to challenge the argument sometimes put forward that the low level of fathers' participation is related to a resistance on the part of mothers to share their traditional child-caring role with fathers.

From an equality perspective, fathers are far from sharing child care tasks equally with mothers. From a children's per-spective, however, a somewhat different picture can be dis-cerned. The old authoritarian, emotionally detached father is being gradually replaced by a more caring, involved father. Even though fathers are slow to share in the routine tasks nec-essary in caring for children, there is a movement, however slight it may be, towards some sharing with mothers. More sig-nificantly, attitudes are changing about the role of fathers in the home which, in turn, permit the creation of an environment conducive to greater contact by fathers with their children. On the basis of a child's need for intimate relationships with the significant adult in the child's life, this move, from the child's perspective, is certainly welcome.

FATHERS AND THE LAW

In Ireland, the child's legal relationship to their father varies depending on the father's marital status, i.e. whether he is mar-ried and not legally separated from the child's mother, legally separated/divorced from the child's mother, or not married to the child's mother. Thus, the distinguishing variable determin-ing the legal relationship between children and their fathers is not the nature of the relationship between both of them, i.e. the child and the father, but the relationship between the father and the child's mother.

In the case of fathers who are married and not legally sepa-rated/divorced from the child's mother, paternity is presumed to exist by virtue of the father's marriage to the mother, unless both parents agree that he is not the father. With the presumption of paternity, the father's name appears on the child's birth certificate. Consequent on his paternity, the married father has guardianship rights to his child and rights to custody of and access to his child. However, these rights are not absolute and can be restricted by the courts under the Guardianship of Infants Act (1964) if the court deems it to be in the child's best interest.

In the case of legally separated or divorced fathers, guardianship, custody and access are generally determined either by joint agreement between the parents or by the courts. The courts have the right under the Judicial Separation and Family Law Reform Act, 1989 or the Family Law (Divorce) Act, 1997 to remove or restrict the guardianship, custody and access rights of either parent. The guiding principle, as laid down by this legislation, is what constitutes the best interest of the child and the court will not grant a judicial separation order unless it is satisfied that provision has been made for the welfare of any dependent children, including matters of custody and access. Similar provisions apply in the case of divorce. Although the courts under the Children Act, 1997 have the power to grant joint custody to both father and mother, the practice has been to generally award custody to the mother. Fahey and Lyons (1995, p. 28), for example, in their analyses of family law cases, found that married fathers were the most likely applicants to the District Court for guardianship, which were also most often applications for custody and access. McKeown et al. (1998, p. 181) argue that joint custody should be the norm with both parents having equal rights of custody and access and that the "onus should be on the courts to prove why joint custody would not be in the best interest of the child".

In the situation where the father is not married to the child's mother, the father has no automatic rights in relation to the child. He does, however, have the right to apply to the court under the Guardianship of Infants Act, 1964 as amended by the Status of Children Act, 1987 to establish paternity and/or guardianship and, if the mother agrees, his name can appear on the birth certificate, thus establishing paternity. In the event of establishing guardianship, custody and access, the court — as in other situations — can restrict these rights if it is deemed to be in the best interest of the child.

Irish law and legal practice reinforces the position of mother as the primary parent. Some of this gender bias can be attributed to the Constitution, which prescribes the woman's role as within the family, while also basing family life on married life. This gives rise to an ideology of motherhood which, by implication, weakens fatherhood. To overcome this difficulty, the Constitution Review Group (1996, p. 325) recommends that the Constitution be amended to give constitutional rights to natural fathers, provided those fathers had a stable relationship with the child's mother. While such a change would help to equalise the rights of both parents to their children, the key concern from the child's point of view is not the rights of parents but the rights of the child to both parents.

Children's rights and parents' rights are not always compatible. The guiding principle of what is in the best interest of the child is paramount. The problem, however, is in how this principle is interpreted and applied. Undoubtedly, children need to be protected from abusive parents, but this hardly explains why so many fathers lose custody of their children in family law cases (see Fahey and Lyons, 1995). The explanation is more likely due to a combination of factors which includes the use of an adversarial approach in family law cases. McGrath (1998) argues that the use of the adversarial approach in cases of child protection does not serve the best interest of the child. He advocates the use of an inquisitorial system in which the judge gathers information and then comes to a decision, unlike the adversarial system which is a competitive argument between two sides (McGrath, 1998, p. 44). The parties, he says, are "engaged in a struggle with each other, not in a mutual search for the truth" (p. 44) and "the emphasis is on winning" (p. 58). When this adversarial approach is combined with the gender bias in the law and the prevailing ideology of motherhood, it is easy to see why fathers do not fare so well. It is difficult to see how this can then be in the best interest of the child.

Fahey and Lyons (1995, p. 135) found that in family law cases solicitors represent their clients, i.e. the parents, and that children are secondary figures. They go on further to state that, while the law requires the Circuit Court to ensure that adequate provision is made for children before a judicial separation is granted, "it institutes no mechanism through which the child's requirements or the child's preference can be directly expressed to the court". Unfortunately, as Fahey and Lyons observe, "it seems that the child's voice is heard only through the parents, sometimes in the context of a bitter conflict between the father and the mother as to what is best for the child" (1995, p. 136). The legal position of fathers in relation to their children is, therefore, not only weakened by defining this relationship on the basis of his relationship with the child's mother, but also by the manner in which the law itself is practised.

NON-RESIDENT FATHERS AND THEIR CHILDREN

Non-resident fathers are fathers whose primary residence is not with their children. There are three broad categories of non-resident fathers: non-residence as a result of marital separation; non-residence following the termination of a cohabitation relationship; and non-residence by fathers who never married or resided with the child's mother. A distinction can also be made between non-resident fathers who are biological fathers only and non-resident fathers who are the social fathers. The discussion in this section is primarily concerned with non-resident social fathers.

It is difficult to calculate the extent of non-resident fathers. Official statistics do not seem to include this as an important or relevant piece of information. According to figures from Eurostat (2000), 7 per cent of the population in the EU live in lone-parent households. This represents 11.4 per cent of all family types (i.e. couples without children, couples with children, and lone parents with children). Lone-parent families in Ireland amount to 10 per cent of all private households (Central Statistics Office, 1997), with 8 per cent of families consisting of lone mothers and their children, and 2 per cent of lone fathers and their children. While those lone-parent families headed by mothers consist of widows, non-married parents and lone-parents as a result of divorce/separation, the figures give some indication of the prevalence of families with non-resident fathers.

While there are conflicting views about the extent of non-resident fathers' contact with their children following separation, the evidence seems to show that, for many, the frequency of contact diminishes and, for some, ceases. Bradshaw and Miller's (1991) study, for example, found that five years after separation 40 per cent of non-resident fathers had lost contact with their children. Seltzer (1991) found that 37 per cent of the children in her study had no contact, including letter or telephone contact, with their separated, non-resident father.

There are many obstacles to fathers' contact with their children following separation. These obstacles can be attitudinal, behavioural and structural (see Kiely, 2000). Attitudinal obstacles primarily consist of attitudes about fatherhood and the role of men as carers of children. This also relates to men's own identity as fathers, as discussed earlier. Behavioural obstacles primarily arise from the nature of the relationship between the child's parents after separation. Several studies show that there is a relationship between the level of contact and the level of partner conflict and/or resistance by the resident mother to contact by the non-resident father (Arditti and Keith, 1993; Ahrons and Miller, 1993; Arendel, 1995). There are two types of structural obstacles. The first are those that arise from legal and social provisions such as custody and access agreements and social welfare provisions. The second are those that arise primarily from the father's living circumstances, such as inadequate accommodation, distance from the child's residence and demands of work.

In recent years, as already noted, public attention given to the need to have "absent" fathers take more responsibility for their families has meant financial responsibility and, to some extent, reflects welfare reforms. Very little attention has been given to the need to assist fathers in maintaining their parenting contacts with their children. This is in spite of the existence of research findings which consistently show that the maintenance of a relationship with both parents in a spirit of co-operation mitigates the stresses of divorce for children (Kroll, 1994).

The UN Convention on the Rights of the Child states that children have the right to maintain contact with both parents if separated from one or both (Art. 9). It would appear, however, that this is a much overlooked right when it comes to the child's right of contact with their non-resident father.

CONCLUSION

One of the striking features in reviewing the literature on fatherhood is the dearth of research on children's perceptions and experiences of their fathers. The same applies to fathers' own perceptions of their role and their contribution as parents to their children. In spite of the increased attention paid to fathers, especially over the past decade, the rise in awareness of their importance to their children and the UN Convention on the Rights of the Child which guarantees the child's right to both parents, fathers are still the invisible parent. His relationship with his children is unique to the role of fatherhood, but how that relationship is experienced is waiting to be told and its value to the child waiting to be fully recognised.

References

Ahrons, C.R. and Miller, R.B. (1993) "The Effect of the Post-Divorce Relationship on Parental Involvement: A Longitudinal Analysis", *American Journal of Orthopsychiatry*, Vol. 13, pp 441-450.

Aldous, J. (1998) "The Changing Concept of Fatherhood" in K. Matthijs (ed). *The Family*, Leuven: Leuven University Press.

Arditti, J.A. and Keith, T.Z. (1993) "Visitation Frequency, Child Support Payment and Father-Child Relationships Post Divorce", *Journal of Marriage and the Family*, Vol. 55, pp 699-712.

Arendel, T. (1995) *Fathers and Divorce*. London: Sage Publications.

Blackenhorn, D. (1995) *Fatherless America*. New York: Basic Books.

Bradshaw, J. and Miller, J. (1991) *Lone Parents in the U.K.* London: HMSO.

Cacace, M. and d'Andrea, L. (1996) *Fathers in Services for Young Children*. Rome: Centro di Cooperazione Familiare.

Carlsen, S. and Larsen, J. (undated) *The Equality Dilemma*. Copenhagen: The Danish Equal Status Council.

Central Statistics Office (1997) *Census 1996, Volume 3, Household Composition and Family Units*. Dublin: Stationery Office.

Constitution Review Group (1996) *Report of the Constitution Review Group*. Dublin: Stationery Office.

de Singly, F. (1993) "The Social Construction of a New Paternal Identity", in *Fathers in Families of Tomorrow*, Copenhagen: The Ministry of Social Affairs.

European Commission Childcare Network (1990a) *Mothers, Fathers and Employment*. Brussels: Commission of the European Communities.

European Commission Childcare Network (1990b) *Men As Carers for Children*, Report of an EC Childcare Network Technical Seminar, Glasgow. Brussels: Commission of the European Communities.

European Commission Childcare Network (1993) *Men As Carers*. Brussels: Commission of the European Communities.

European Commission Childcare Network (1994) *Men, Media and Childcare*. Brussels: Commission of the European Communities.

Eurostat (2000) *The Social Situation in the European Union*. Luxembourg: Commission of the European Communities.

Fahey, T. and Lyons, M. (1995) *Marital Breakdown and Family Law in Ireland*. Dublin: Oak Tree Press.

Fathers in Families of Tomorrow (1993) Report of the Conference. Copenhagen: The Ministry of Social Affairs.

Kempeneers, M. and Lelievre, E. (1991) *Family and Employment within the Twelve* (Eurobarometer 34) Brussels: Commission of the European Communities.

Kiely, G. (2000) Fathers as Parents after Marital Separation, in B. Jans, A. Habisch, E. Stutzer (eds.) *Familienwissenschaftliche und Familien Politische Signale*, Bonn: Vektor-Verlag.

Kiely, G. (1998) "Caregiving within Families", in K. Matthijs (ed). *The Family*. Leuven: Leuven University Press.

Kiely, G. (1995) "Fathers in Families", in I. Colgan McCarthy (ed.) *Irish Family Studies: Selected Papers*. Dublin: Family Studies Centre.

Kroll, B. (1994) *Chasing Rainbows: Children, Divorce and Loss*. Cambridge: Russell House.

Künzler, J. (1994) "Measuring and Explaining Male Participation in Domestic Labour", Paper presented at the *World Congress of Sociology*, Summer, Bielefeld, Germany.

Lamb, M. (1986) *The Father's Role*. New York: John Wiley and Sons.

McGrath, K. (1998) "The Dutch Inquisitorial Legal System: What Lessons Has It for Child Protection Services within an Adversarial System", *Irish Journal of Social Work Research*, Vol. 1, No. 2, pp 43-65.

McKeown, K., Ferguson H., Rooney, D. (1998) *Changing Fathers?* Cork: The Collins Press.

Malpas, N. and Lambert, P. (1993) *Europeans and the Family* (Eurobarometer 39). Brussels: Commission of the European Communities.

Parsons, T. and Bales, R. (1955) *Family Socialization and Interaction Process*. New York: Free Press.

Seltzer, J. (1991) "Relationships between Fathers and Children Who Live Apart: The Father's Role after Separation", *Journal of Marriage and the Family*, Vol. 53, pp 79-101.

Turner, J. (1993) "Childcare", in J. Kremer and P. Montgomery (eds.) *Women's Working Lives*, Belfast: HMSO.

Wood, K. and O'Shea, P. (1997) *Divorce in Ireland*. Dublin: The O'Brien Press.

Chapter 2

Born Outside Marriage:
The Social Implications for
Irish Pre-school Children

Niamh Flanagan

INTRODUCTION

The latter half of the 20th century has been characterised by an unprecedented rise in the proportion of births in Ireland which are outside marriage (Figure 2.1). In 1998, births outside marriage accounted for almost 28 per cent of all births.

Figure 2.1: Births Outside Marriage as a Percentage of All Births in Ireland, 1950-1999

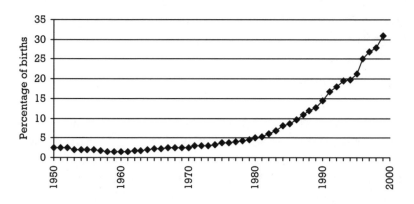

Note: Figures for 1999 are based on the first three-quarters of the year.
Source: CSO, *Statistical Abstract*, 1950-1966 & C.S.O., *Vital Statistics*, 1966-1999

Irish research on the subject of births outside marriage has, for the most part, concentrated on the social characteristics of women who conceive out of wedlock. For example, the backgrounds of the women delivering outside marriage, the circumstances surrounding their pregnancy and their ultimate parenting decision have been examined in a number of studies (Vincent, 1961; Viney, 1964; Kirke, 1974; Powell, Swain and Dockeray, 1982; Rynne and Lacey, 1983; Darling, 1984; Dockeray and Powell, 1984; Richardson, Keenan and Kernan, 1987; Richardson and Winston, 1989; Donohue et al., 1990; and O'Grady, 1992). With two exceptions (O'Hare et al., 1987; Flanagan and Richardson, 1992), these static, point-in-time studies of unmarried parenting "tend to be small scale and [or] limited" (O'Grady, 1992, p. 1). Thus, there is a distinct lack of information on the post-natal lives of unmarried mothers and their children in Ireland. National statistical reports[1] document rates of unmarried maternity, placement for adoption, lone-parenting and welfare dependent maternity. However, each source enumerates a different sub-group and the entries, exits and overlaps between the groups are masked. It is unclear, therefore, if such roles as unmarried mother, common-law spouse and lone parent are transient or permanent roles. Moreover, there is virtually no research on the long-term fate of children born to these women. This study examines the social implications of being born outside marriage for Irish pre-school children, in terms of family structure, living arrangements, risk of poverty and behavioural difficulties.

THE STUDY SAMPLE

The paper draws on data from a longitudinal study of 86 unmarried women, and a control group of 52 married women, who delivered in the National Maternity Hospital, Dublin in 1987 or 1988. The longitudinal study involved interviewing the women twice antenatally, in the neonatal period, one year after delivery and finally, four years after delivery. This sample represents the respondents who completed all stages of the longitudinal study.

An initial sample of 200 unmarried pregnant women was randomly sampled at their first antenatal clinic. A control group of 99 married women was added to the initial sample during their postnatal stay in hospital. An attempt was made to match the control group of married women with the unmarried sample for parity and age. A total of 161 respondents from the initial sample were not included in the final phase of the study because they were untraceable (54 per cent), did not wish to continue (32 per cent), had miscarried (4 per cent) or placed the child for adoption (10 per cent). Review of the demographic profiles of completed (n=86) and incomplete cases (n=161) showed no significant difference in terms of age, education, employment, social class or parity.

The married sample was matched with the unmarried sample for age and parity. The married sample, however, did have significantly higher levels of education and were significantly more likely to originate from higher social classes than the unmarried sample. Moreover, the age profile of the unmarried sample was comparable with national profiles.

A Note on Terminology

Some of the unmarried sample changed their marital status in the course of the study, however this group are referred to throughout as the "unmarried sample two-parent families" in order to distinguish them from two-parent families from the control group of married women. Unmarried mothers who live alone with their child are referred to as lone parents to distinguish them from unmarried mothers living in the maternal family home (without a partner).

THE FAMILY STRUCTURE

While children born to married parents are, by and large, reared in a stereotypical two-parent family with siblings, children born outside marriage experience a somewhat more irregular family structure. The family structures of four-year-olds in the current study are examined in terms of: (a) the mother's decision to parent or place the child elsewhere; (b) The presence of siblings in the home; (c) the status of the parents' relationship; (d) non-resident paternal involvement in the life of the child.

The Decision to Parent

National figures have shown a general decline in the number of children being placed for adoption since the late 1960s. Indeed, by 1997, the number of children placed for adoption with non-relatives was equivalent to 1 per cent (n=127) of births outside marriage. Statistics also show an increase in adoption orders granted to the natural family (n=12) and the child's stepfather (n=238), further reinforcing the trend away from placing a child with non-relatives .

Flanagan and Richardson (1992) documented the significant trend for unmarried mothers to choose to parent their own child, with 93 per cent choosing this option in 1990. Moreover, some of those recorded as placing the child for adoption did not complete the adoption process, opting to keep their child.

By definition, none of the children in the current sample were placed for adoption, although 8 per cent (n=16) of the unmarried mothers in the initial sample left the study having placed their children for adoption. At the age of four, most children (n=82, 95 per cent) in the current sample were living with their mother. However, two children had been placed in care and one was living with maternal grandparents.

Siblings

Most of the children (n=132, 96 per cent) in the study were the first-born of the women. At the age of four, two-thirds of the children born outside marriage (n=54, 63 per cent) remained an only-child. In contrast, only 21 per cent (n=11) of children born to married parents had no siblings at this stage (χ^2=22.5, P≤.001).

At this point in their child's life, women who gave birth outside marriage had an average of 1.4 children, significantly fewer than their married counterparts at 1.9 (t=4.12, P≤.001). Most of the children born outside marriage who had siblings were living in two-parent families (n=22, 71 per cent), and most (n=22, 73 per cent) shared a father with their siblings.

Parents' Relationship

Over the five years of the study, the relationships between the 86 women who delivered outside marriage and the father of their child changed substantially (Figure 2.2). At the mother's first antenatal visit to the hospital a majority (n=58, 67 per cent) were involved in a boyfriend-girlfriend relationship. Five years later, only a minority (n=6, 7 per cent) remained in a boyfriend-girlfriend relationship, although four of these six couples had made plans to marry. Nearly a quarter (n=21, 24 per cent) of the unmarried women had married the father of their child and the proportion of parents who were cohabiting nearly doubled from 8 per cent (n=7) to 15 per cent (n=13), with most of these couples planning to marry (n=8), or prevented from doing so by the father's previous marriage (n=2).[2] The percentage of parents who had ended their relationship rose from 24 per cent (n=21) at the first antenatal visit to 53 per cent (n=46) by the child's fourth birthday.

Figure 2: Status of Relationships of the Unmarried Parents at First Antenatal Visit and at the Child's Fourth Birthday

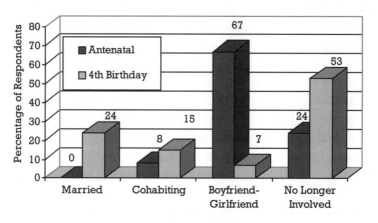

During the pre-school years, a distinct trend was identified toward termination or consolidation of the parents' relationships. By the time they reached school-going age, one in four children born outside marriage had seen their parents marry. However, nearly two in three were not living with both parents. Indeed the parents of half of the children were no longer involved with each other. While these findings imply a high level of lone-parenthood, many unmarried mothers (n=21) in the study had become involved in a further relationship, although few of these had married (n=3) or were cohabiting (n=1). In contrast to these patterns, over 90 per cent (n=50) of parents married at the time of the child's birth, were still married on the child's fourth birthday. Four sets of married parents had separated, although two continued to live in the same house.

The five years between conception and the child's fourth birthday represent a period of change for the majority of unmarried parents' relationships. Nearly two-thirds of children (n=53, 62 per cent) witnessed a change in the status of their parents' relationship before reaching school-going age, and a further ten sets of parents (12 per cent) had changed the status of their relationship during pregnancy. Moreover, the high rate of change in relationships' status stands in sharp contrast to the stability of relationships among parents who were married at delivery, where only 8 per cent (n=4) of couples changed their relationship.

The bulk of relationship changes that occurred over the whole five years of the study occurred in the child's first year. The majority of these changes were progressive (n=42, 54 per cent) but a large proportion were regressive. Analysis of the changes showed that early pregnancy and the first year of childrearing were the key periods when relationships were likely to end. These periods represent crisis points of discovery/ acceptance of the pregnancy and the reality of childrearing, each of which place strain on a relationship, causing it to regress at a faster rate than in the later stages of pregnancy and infancy. The greatest increases in cohabitation occurred during late pregnancy, suggesting that cohabitation more often than not follows the conception or birth, rather than the birth arising out of a cohabitational relationship. Overall, cohabitational relationships proved to be stable and lasting, declines in the pre-school years being largely due to marriage. Parents that married were more likely to do so in the later pre-school years.

A number of antenatal characteristics differentiate parents whose relationships ended from other unmarried parents. Parents who ended their relationship tended to originate from lower social classes and from families where both parents were unemployed. Moreover, the mother's family was more likely to be a one-parent family. The parents' relationship prior to pregnancy was likely to be shorter and less likely to involve a suggestion of marriage during pregnancy. Furthermore, the fathers were less happy about the pregnancy than other fathers. Perhaps most importantly, the support systems afforded to these mothers, both by the father of the child, their own family and other supports, were weakest. Mothers who ultimately terminated their relationship were clearly more vulnerable during pregnancy, given their lack of adequate support structures.

Mothers who subsequently married the father of their child had higher education levels than other mothers. These mothers reported stronger support networks, specifically from their own parents, the father of the child and his family. Their partners were most likely to feel happy about the pregnancy and most likely to suggest marriage.

These clearly divergent antenatal characteristics paint a disturbing picture of social and economic vulnerability among parents who subsequently end their relationships. Moreover, if the lack of antenatal support continues after pregnancy, the cessation of the relationship with the father of the child places the mother and her child in an extremely isolated and vulnerable position. Alternatively, it is not unthinkable that familial and social supports may be re-established at the price of the relationship with the father of the child. While it is not certain if the antenatal vulnerability is the cause or simply a correlate of the relationship break-up, there can be little doubt that antenatal support for these couples is crucial and may provide sufficient support to facilitate the progression of the relationship and ensure that more children born outside marriage have the opportunity of living in a two-parent family.

Paternal Involvement

For the two-thirds of four-year-olds (n=52, 60 per cent) whose parents are not living together, it is crucial to assess the level of involvement of the non-resident father. Less than a third of non-resident fathers (n=16, 31 per cent) were involved in the care of their child, although this was substantially higher among fathers who were still in a boyfriend-girlfriend relationship with the mother (n=5, 83 per cent). Interestingly, the involvement of the mother in a subsequent relationship did not affect the levels of paternal involvement in caring for his child (n=6, 29 per cent).

Paternal involvement in decision making about the child's life represented a distinguishing factor between children who lived with their father and children who did not: 94 per cent (n=32) of the former and only 17 per cent (n=9) of the latter played a role in decision making.

Only a minority of non-resident fathers may be said to play any role in their child's life. Furthermore, nearly half of non-resident fathers (n=25, 48 per cent), the equivalent of 29 per cent of all fathers whose child was born outside marriage, had no contact with their child.

ACCOMMODATION

Accommodation has traditionally represented one of the paramount areas of concern with regard to non-marital family units. This area of concern encompasses the issues of tenure, overcrowding, quality of accommodation and ghettoization as a reflection of economic well-being. Equally important and deserving of attention is the household composition.

Living Arrangements

An examination of household composition (hereafter referred to as living arrangements) identifies the social structure within which the child lives. Such social structures, in turn, may determine the levels of social, emotional, parenting and, indeed, financial supports available to mother and child. These supports cannot be underestimated in the long-term success of non-marital family units.

While a substantial proportion of the literature suggests that lone mothers and never-married mothers are more likely to encounter housing problems, recent literature suggests a dichotomy in the accommodation and living conditions of non-marital family units (Farley, 1986; McDonnell et al, 1988; Kernan, 1990). These studies conclude that the living conditions of two-parent families and the living conditions of one-parent families living in the maternal family home, are comparable. In contrast, it is suggested that mothers who live alone with their children have a much more difficult time creating adequate homes for themselves and their children.

Flanagan & Richardson (1992) identified an increasing tendency for unmarried women to reside in their family home during pregnancy and plan to return there after the baby is born. This tendency, while not exclusive to Ireland, appears to be less prevalent and declining elsewhere. Indeed, Kernan (1990) points out that this pattern of family living differentiates Irish from British non-marital family units, the latter tending to establish separate family units.

Patterns of residency among unmarried mothers in the current study showed distinct trends. While the majority (n=66, 77 per cent) were living with their family of origin during pregnancy, there was a shift in the pre-school years toward independent living such as marriage, cohabitation and lone parenting. By the time the children had reached the age of four, only 29 per cent (n=25) were living in their maternal-grandparents' home. Mothers of these children were younger, more likely to be employed and more likely to be involved with an employed man, than other mothers (see Figure 2.3).

The largest group of children (n=38, 44 per cent) were living in two-parent families (based on marriage or cohabitation). Most of these (n=34) were living with their father and a small number (n=4) were living with a man other than their father. Nearly a quarter of the four-year-olds (n=20, 24 per cent) were living in a lone parent household headed by their mother. The mothers of these children were less educated and less likely to be in paid employment. In addition, these women had weaker support systems, placing them in a vulnerable position both socially and economically. However, local authority housing did afford this group more social status and independence. In contrast, 96 per cent (n=50) of the children born to married parents were living in a two-parent family at the age of four.

Figure 2.3: Living Arrangements of Children of Unmarried Parents on the Child's Fourth Birthday

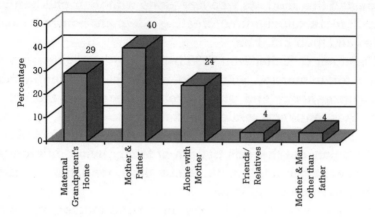

Tenure and Stability

Owner-occupation has been identified as a distinguishing factor between lon e an d two-paren t families, such that lon e-parent households are far less likely to be own er-occupiers (Ferri, 1976; Murphy, 1989;   Haskey, 1991; Crow an d   Hardey, 1991; McCashin ,1995; McRae, 1993). Moreover, lone-paren t hous e-holds are overrepresen ted in ren ted accommodation , particu-larly in local authority housing (Department of Health and Social Security, 1972; Marsden , 1973; Ferri, 1976; Crow an d Hardey, 1991; McCashin, 1995).

The curren t study iden tified n o sign ifican t differen ce in owner-occupation between the married an d un married sa m-ples. However, this was a direct result of the high levels of owner-occupation amon g families livin g in the matern al family home. Among the unmarried sample of two-parent families, the proportion of own er-occupied homes was half that of married sample two-paren t families. As suggested by the literature, mothers who chose to live alone with their child were sign if   i-cantly overrepresented in local authority housing.

It has been suggested that non-marital family units may face difficulties in fin din g an d keepin g suitable accommodation (Ferri, 1976; Darlin g, 1984;   Pascall, 1986; Crow an d   Hardey, 1991) an d thus experien ce numerous accommodation chan ges.

There appears to be no evidence to suggest that this has an adverse effect on a child's development. However, it would seem reasonable to assume that, while one change in accommodation would, to some extent, disrupt and alter a family's pattern of daily life, under normal circumstances the effects would be temporary and satisfactory adjustment soon achieved. Moreover, the option of remaining in the same accommodation and living arrangement, while perhaps valuable to married women who have already formed their family unit, may not hold the same appeal for unmarried women living in essentially "single" living arrangements, such as with the family of origin or with friends. The effect of numerous and repeated changes in accommodation, however, may, particularly if due to adverse circumstances, accentuate the difficulties associated with changing accommodation. Indeed, as Ferri (1976) pointed out, "the risk [is] increased that the sense of security and stability so essential to the young child might be seriously undermined".

Table 2.1: Tenure of Accommodation of Family Units

	Living Arrangements			
	Maternal Family % (n)	Unmarried Sample Two-Parent Family % (n)	Lone Parent Family % (n)	Married Sample Family % (n)
Owned-occupied	60% (15)	26% (10)	10% (2)	54% (28)
Private rented	4% (1)	24% (9)	16% (3)	6% (3)
Local authority	36% (9)	50% (19)	74% (14)	40% (21)
Total	25	38	19	52

In the current study, children living in their grandparents' home had moved house significantly fewer times than other children born outside marriage (F=15.16, P≤.001). Indeed, most of them had lived in the same house since birth. Moreover, this group of children made fewer moves than did the children of married parents. On average, children living in a lone parent household had experienced between one and two moves, although for a few there were as many as six. Almost all children living in the unmarried sample two-parent families had moved house during their pre-school years, while nearly half did so twice or more. Unlike children living in their grandparents' home, moving home at least once was the norm for this group. Indeed, these children were likely to move house more often than any other group.

Overcrowding

Overcrowding has been cited as a characteristic of the living conditions of non-marital families (Ministry of Social Security, 1967; Marsden, 1973) and there can be little doubt that an overcrowded home with inadequate space and privacy is a poor environment in which to grow up. Although children of lone parents in the current study had significantly more room and children living in their grandparents' home significantly less room than other children, no child in the current study was considered to be living in overcrowded conditions.[3]

Quality of Housing

Concerns regarding the quality of housing of unmarried or lone parents are unsubstantiated by this study. With the exception of having a garden, only minimal differences between the homes of the married and unmarried sample were observed. Given the low percentage lacking facilities among the unmarried sample, it was not possible to identify any significant differences among the different types of living arrangements. Notwithstanding this, in all cases the deprivation of facilities was least among those living in the maternal family home. Differences were most significant with regard to use of a telephone and access to a garden. Also, marked differences were observed with regard to structural faults. Women living alone with their child had increased levels of structural faults in their accommodation but were not substantially deprived with regard to other basic facilities.

Overall, a substantial majority of all families were satisfied with their accommodation. Mothers living in their family home reported the highest rates of satisfaction. This is interesting given the suggestion by Fahey and Watson (1995) that families within the maternal family home may suffer from social deficiencies such as lack of independence and privacy. The high level of satisfaction among this group may, however, reflect the fact that those who were not satisfied residing in the family home had moved out by the child's fourth birthday.

Table 2.2: Accommodation Facilities by Living Arrangements

	Living Arrangements			
	Maternal Family %	Unmarried Sample Two-Parent Family %	Lone Parent Family %	Married Sample Family %
Kitchen with cooker and sink	100%	100%	100%	98%
Properly equipped bathroom	100%	94%	95%	100%
Use of a garden	92%	79%	76%	98%
Telephone	76%	38%	29%	60%
Heating	100%	94%	100%	98%
Regular hot water	92%	91%	81%	98%
Structural faults	4%	27%	48%	13%

Ghettoization

Some Irish studies (Kelleher, 1988; Eastern Health Board, 1991; Richardson, 1991) have noted that lone mothers on local authority waiting lists tended to be offered accommodation in the less sought after housing areas, leading to ghettoization of lone-parents. In the current study, all respondents were asked if there were lone-parent families among their neighbours. In contrast to expectation, women parenting alone were less likely to report lone-parent families among their neighbours than the unmarried sample two-parent families or the married sample two-parent families. Thus, while unmarried mothers may be placed in the less sought after housing areas, suggestions that they are being ghettoized are not substantiated by this study.

WELFARE DEPENDENCY OR EMPLOYMENT?

The welfare dependency of unmarried mothers and their children is the cause of most concern for this group and the basis of most criticism. Indeed, the association between unmarried mothers, and high levels of social welfare dependency has long been an issue (Marsden, 1973; Townsend, 1979; Hardey and Glover, 1991; Millar, 1992; Millar et al, 1992; McCashin, 1993).

While welfare dependency among unmarried mothers is undoubtedly high and rising, it is by no means high enough to suggest that it is commonplace among all unmarried mothers, at all stages of family formation. In fact, in the 1970s and 1980s, an average of 62 per cent of children born outside marriage *per annum* did not benefit from the Unmarried Mothers Allowance (UMA) or its successor the Lone-Parents Allowance (LPA) (Flanagan, 1996). This contradicts the perception that unmarried mothers are welfare dependent. Moreover, studies by Miller et al. (1992) and O'Grady (1991) clearly show that, while there is a high level of claims among women immediately after the birth of their child, for the majority of recipients, welfare dependency appeared to be a short to medium term measure.

The risk of poverty declines as labour force participation increases. Moreover, it is likely that entry into paid employment is not only the best exit from poverty but, for women parenting alone, it is also a means of establishing financial independence from family and the state. The employment levels of mothers are influenced by a series of factors that limit their opportunities for employment. The generic factor of high unemployment is compounded by gender specific factors such as low pay and job segregation (Durkan et al., 1995; Conroy and Flanagan, 1994; Nolan, 1993; Daly, 1989). For mothers, these barriers are added to by limited and costly childcare provision as well as by the traditional expectation that mothers remain on home duties. When the fieldwork for the current study was undertaken, the further barrier of an earnings disregard on the LPA[4] added to this list of disincentives, placing many families in a "poverty trap".

Welfare Dependency

Findings in the current study showed that the proportion of un-married mothers who were welfare dependent rose during pregnancy, peaking at delivery and declining thereafter. Not-withstanding this trend, only 17 per cent (n=15) of the mothers reported continuous dependence on social welfare. However, a further 19 per cent (n=16) reported moving into welfare from employment or family support. In contrast, 19 per cent (n=16) reported continuous income from employment,[5] while the larg-est group (n=29, 34 per cent) reported moving from welfare to-ward an income from employment over the years of the study.

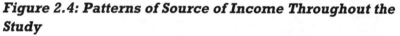

Figure 2.4: Patterns of Source of Income Throughout the Study

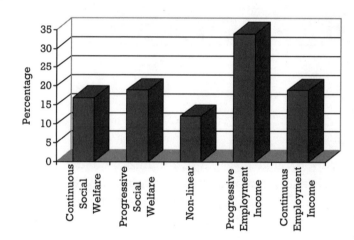

By the child's fourth birthday, social welfare payments consti-tuted a main source of income for 37 per cent (n=31) of the un-married sample and only 22 per cent (n=11) of the married sam-ple. However, the three sub-groups of the unmarried sample were found to be significantly different from each other with re-gard to welfare dependency ($\chi2$=15.92, P$\leq$.001). Lone-mothers emerged as most likely to be welfare dependent. Women living in the maternal family home, while less likely to be welfare de-pendant than those living alone, were nonetheless significantly more likely to be welfare dependant than the unmarried sample respondents who were cohabiting or married. It would appear, therefore, that welfare dependence is not a function of the marital status at delivery. Rather, the choice of living arrangement is a significant factor in determining welfare dependence.

Figure 2.5: Main Source of Income of Married Sample Respondents, Unmarried Sample Respondents and Sub-groups of the Unmarried Sample at the Child's Fourth Birthday

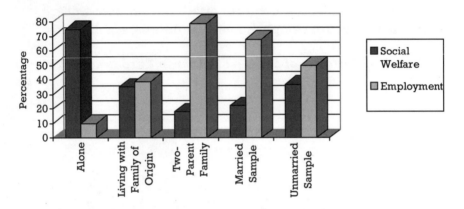

Employment

The perception that unmarried mothers spend all or even the majority of their early mothering years out of work is a fallacy according to the study results. Over the five years of the study, only 33 per cent (n=28) of the unmarried mothers reported that they had no employment throughout this time.

The rate of employment among the married sample (n=23, 47 per cent), at the child's fourth birthday, was similar to that of the unmarried sample in general (n=38, 44 per cent). Interestingly the difference in employment rates between the two groups was substantially smaller than at the time of their initial antenatal visit to the hospital, as many of the married sample respondents gave up work and unmarried sample respondents were more likely to be in employment. However differing trends in employment were evident among the three sub-groups of the unmarried sample (χ^2=9.05, P≤.01). Unmarried sample respondents, who were living in a two-parent family, reported a rate of employment (n=15, 40 per cent) similar to that of the married sample, while those living alone had the lowest rate of employment (n=5, 25 per cent). Those living within the maternal family home enjoyed the strongest employment position, being more likely to be employed (n=17, 68 per cent) than all other married or unmarried mothers. These women were also more likely to be working full-time. Contrary to expectation, women living in the maternal family home were not significantly more likely to get childcare support from their parents, although small numbers make such generalisations unreliable. With regard to the security of employment, as reflected in length in employment and temporary employment, this group living in the maternal family home were less established than the married sample, possibly due to their slightly younger age profile.

Figure 2.6: Source of Income of Unmarried Sample Respondents Throughout the Study

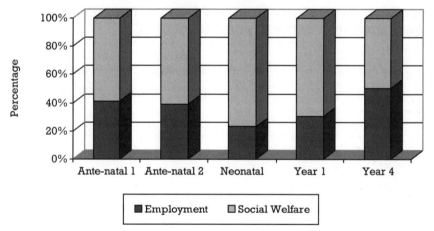

INCOME, POVERTY AND RELATIVE DEPRIVATION

Many studies have documented the risk of poverty and deprivation for lone-parent family units, but the economic prospects for other children born outside marriage are unclear. Income, in its own right, provides little indication of the wealth of families. Any assessment of poverty must, therefore, consider a range of poverty measures such as income, relative income poverty, household deprivation and subjective poverty. Each offers a different perspective on poverty and combines to present a comprehensive picture of economic circumstances.

Income

The average disposable incomes of the married sample and the unmarried sample living in two-parent families were higher than those of lone-parent families and families living in the maternal family home (F=20.36, P≤000). However, this raw data does not take into account the significantly different family sizes (or indeed the possibility that grandparents may bear the cost of overheads). There was little difference in the average disposable income per adult equivalent (p.a.e.)[6] of two-parent families and families within the maternal family. However, lone-parent families reported significantly lower income p.a.e. than any other group (F=4.22, P≤01).

Table 2.3: Average Weekly Disposable Income and Income per Adult Equivalent of Married Sample, Unmarried Sample and Sub-groups of the Unmarried Sample

	Average Disposable Income	Average Income per Adult Equivalent
Married sample two-parent families	£218	£109
Unmarried sample two-parent families	£205	£104
Families within the maternal family home	£128	£106
Lone-parent families	£92	£72
All unmarried sample	£155	£97

Poverty

No family unit from either the married or unmarried sample fell below 40 per cent of average income per adult equivalent of the study population. Fifteen per cent (n=7) of the married sample fell below 60 per cent of average income p.a.e. This compares to 16 per cent (n=2) of the lone-parent families, 8 per cent (n=3) of the unmarried sample two-parent families and none of those living in the maternal family home. Those living alone and the married sample are at most risk of poverty, while women choosing to rear their child within the maternal family home are at least risk.

Comparisons of poverty risk suggest that the unmarried sample as a whole are, in fact, at lower risk of poverty than the married sample, although this was not statistically significant. This finding may be explained by the significantly larger families of the married sample (see Siblings above) as there would appear to be a higher risk of poverty among larger families (χ^2=4.2, P$\leq$.05).

Household Deprivation

Using an adaptation of Callan & Nolan's (1994) household deprivation index, respondents were asked if they possessed seven basic household durables. Married sample families and families living in the maternal family home were significantly less likely to report household deprivation (F=5.0, P$\leq$.01). In comparison, fewer of the unmarried sample two-parent families and the lone-parent families possessed all items on the index.

Table 2.4: Percentage of Family Units from the Married Sample, the Unmarried Sample and the Sub-groups of the Unmarried Sample Experiencing Household Deprivation

	Married Sample Two-parent Families	Unmarried Sample Two-parent Families	Families Within the Maternal Family Home	Lone-Parent Families	All Unmarried Sample
	% (n)	% (n)	% (n)	% (n)	% (n)
Lacking no items	87% (45)	68% (26)	88% (22)	50% (10)	71% (61)
Lacking one item or more	13% (7)	32% (12)	12% (3)	50% (10)	29 (25)

Subjective Poverty

Lone-parent families and the unmarried sample two-parent families were significantly more likely to report economic difficulties than the married sample two-parent families or the families living in the maternal family home (F=3.97, P$\leq$.01). Small proportionate differences emerged with regard to financial debt. However, the differences were not significant and showed similar trends to those observed with the other indicators.

Income and poverty analysis suggests a hierarchy of "wealth". The married sample two-parent families, although at the top of the income scale, are at marginally higher risk of poverty, probably because of their larger families. The unmarried sample families living in the maternal family home and the unmarried sample two-parent families follow close behind the married sample on the income ladder, but appear to have a lower risk of poverty. In general, it can be concluded that these three groups are of similar standing. In contrast, lone-parent families remain firmly at the bottom of the income and poverty ladders.

Analysis of household deprivation makes only minor changes to this hierarchy. Those living in the maternal family home are least deprived in this respect and lone-parent families remain at the foot of the ladder. Subjective measures of poverty support these objective measures with lone-parent families reporting highest levels of economic difficulty and debt. Families in the maternal family home reported the lowest levels of economic difficulty.

This analysis clearly identifies the higher risk of poverty among unmarried lone-parents. The married sample families and the remaining sub-groups of the unmarried sample are not substantially different in terms of income, although it would appear that families living in the maternal family home are cushioned from poverty, household deprivation and subjective deprivation. The most important finding, therefore, is the vulnerability of unmarried lone-parent families. From a social policy perspective, it is crucial that this group are targeted at an early stage and aided so that their children will not fall into a cycle of poverty and deprivation. Indeed, social policy experts have repeatedly called for such early intervention for "at-risk" groups.

BEHAVIOURAL DIFFICULTIES

Limitations of the current study did not permit clinical assessment of emotional or behavioural difficulties among the 138 children surveyed. An adaptation of the Pre-school Behaviour Checklist (PBCL),[7] completed by 131 mothers,[8] yielded a measure of the mother's perceptions of the child's behaviour.

The prevalence rate of perceived behaviour difficulties among all the children in the study was 24 per cent. Reported behaviours of children living in a married sample two-parent family (n=7, 15 per cent), in an unmarried sample two-parent family (n=9, 25 per cent), with the maternal family (n=8, 33 per cent) or alone with their mother (n=6, 32 per cent) were not significantly different. However, there was a trend toward the reporting of fewer behavioural problems among the married sample two-parent families.

Comparison of average PBCL scores showed that mothers of children born outside marriage reported significantly higher scores (*t=-2.81, P<.01*) than mothers in the married sample. However, mothers of children at age four, living in the unmarried sample two-parent families did not report significantly higher scores than their married sample counterparts, although children in one-parent families did (*F=3.76, P<.01*). This suggests that status at birth is less important than parenting arrangements.

The PBCL measures types of behavioural problems: conduct problems, attention difficulties, emotional or nervous behaviour, attention-seeking, poor social skills, overactive and sphincter problems. The two-parent families, regardless of their marital status at birth, did not report significantly different levels of behaviour problems on any of the behavioural subscales. Similarly, perceived behavioural problems among the children of lone-mothers or mothers living in the maternal family home were not significantly different. Significant differences were limited to three specific areas. Lone-mothers reported significantly more attention difficulties than two-parent families (*F=3.79, P<.01*) and significantly more conduct problems than the married sample two-parent families (*F=3.75, P<.01*). Mothers rearing their child alone, or in the maternal family, reported more difficulties with attention seeking behaviour than the two-parent families (F=3.2, P<.05). This latter finding, and possibly the former findings, underline a limitation of the study – significant differences in perceived attention seeking behaviour may be a result of being the sole parent, rather than necessarily indicative of behavioural difficulties. However, these findings may also be a result of poverty and its associated living conditions.

While this analysis shows the possible existence of some behavioural difficulties among children in lone-parent families, it also shows that the four groups of children did not differ in terms of perceived emotional or nervous behaviours, poor social skills, overactivity or sphincter problems.

CONCLUSIONS

For Irish four-year-olds, the social implications of being born outside marriage are, by and large, determined by the subsequent parenting and living arrangements of the family.

Children who are living in a two-parent family at four years of age do not differ substantially from children born to married parents in terms of welfare dependency, maternal employment, poverty or behavioural difficulties. While, by definition, their parent's relationship will have changed and, correspondingly, they are likely to move house, these differences are more likely to be positive than negative in effect. Thus, with the exception of levels of owner-occupation and possession of household durables, children living in two-parent families are largely undifferentiated from their counterparts born to married parents.

Children living with their mother and maternal grandparents live a significantly different life to other children. In essence, their mothers follow the living patterns of young, non-parenting women. These children, although living in a large household, are unlikely to have siblings and only half will have contact with their father. Their accommodation, although not their own, is more stable and established than any other child's. Although there is still a one in three risk of welfare dependency among this group, their mothers are likely to be employed and dating an employed man. Moreover, this group is at lower risk of poverty than most other children.

The most striking feature of this paper is the repeated identification of children in lone-parent families as disadvantaged. In terms of paternal involvement, accommodation stability and quality, welfare dependency and poverty these children are relatively, if not significantly, more disadvantaged. It is not surprising therefore, that their mothers reported more behavioural difficulties. Moreover, the fact that the mothers of these children were economically and socially disadvantaged before giving birth, suggests that these children and their families represent a core group trapped in a disadvantaged life-style. Overall, the social implications of being born outside marriage for most pre-school children appear to be transient. However, for the quarter living in a lone-parent household the disadvantages are on-going and long-term.

References

An Bord Uchtala (1953-1994) *Report of An Bord Uchtala (Adoption Board)*, Dublin.

Callan, T. and Nolan, B. (1994) "Income Poverty in Ireland" in Nolan, B. and Callan, T., *Poverty & Policy in Ireland*, Dublin: Gill & McMillan.

Central Statistics Office (1966-1995) *Department of Health Vital Statistics*, Dublin: Stationary Office.

Central Statistics Office (1989) *Census of Population 1986*, Dublin: Stationary Office.

Central Statistics Office (1994) *Census of Population 1991*, Dublin: Stationary Office.

Conroy, P. and Flanagan, N. (1994) *Women and Poverty in the European Community: Issues in the Current Debate*, Paper prepared for the Equal Opportunities Unit of the European Commission on Employment, Industrial Relations and Social Affairs, DG V/A/3.

Crow, G. and Hardey, M. (1991) "The housing strategies of lone parents" in Hardey, M. and Crow, G. *Lone Parenthood: Coping with Constraints and Making Opportunities*, Hertfordshire: Harvester Wheatsheaf.

Daly, M. (1989) *Women in Poverty*, Dublin: Attic Press.

Darling, V. (1984) *And Baby Makes Two*, Dublin: Federation of Services for Unmarried Parents and their Children.

Department of Health and Social Security (1972) *Families Receiving Supplementary Benefit*, London: HMSO.

Department of Social Welfare (1970-1995) *Statistical Information on Social Welfare Services*, Dublin: Stationary Office.

Dockeray, C.J. and Powell, B.F.M. (1984) "Psychological Aspects of Adolescent Pregnancies in Ireland" (Unpublished Paper), Dublin: St James Hospital.

Donohue, J., Fitzpatrick, A., Flanagan, N. & Scanlon, S. (1990) *Unmarried Mothers Delivered in the National Maternity Hospital 1988*, Dublin: University College Dublin/National Maternity Hospital.

Durkan, J., O'Donohue, A. and Donnelly, M. (1995) *Women in the Labour Force*, Dublin: The Employment Equality Agency.

Eastern Health Board (1991) *Interim Report of the Committee on Single Parent Births and Families*, Dublin.

Fahey, T. and Watson, D. (1995) *An Analysis of Social Housing Need*, General Research Series 168, Dublin: Economic and Social Research Institute.

Farley, F. (1986) "A comparative Study of Living Conditions of Married Mothers and Single Mothers in Cork City", Unpublished M.Soc.Sc. Dissertation, University College, Cork.

Ferri, E. (1976) *Growing Up in a One-Parent Family: A Long-term Study of Child Development*, Berks: NFER Publishing Company Ltd.

Flanagan, N. and Richardson, V. (1992) *Unmarried Mothers: A Social Profile*, Holles Street Hospital/University College Dublin, Dublin.

Flanagan, N (1996) "What the Future Holds: A longitudinal study of family structure and deprivation indices among unmarried mothers in Ireland", unpublished Masters Thesis, UCD.

Hardey, M. and Glover, J. (1991) "Income, employment, day-care and lone parenthood" in Hardey, M. and Crow, G. *Lone Parenthood: Coping with Constraints and Making Opportunities*, Hertfordshire: Harvester Wheatsheaf.

Haskey, J. (1991) "Lone parenthood and demographic change" in Hardey, M. and Crow, G. *Lone Parenthood: Coping with Constraints and Making Opportunities*, Hertfordshire: Harvester Wheatsheaf.

Kelleher, P. (1988) *Settling in the City*, Dublin: Focus Point.

Kernan, E. (1990) "New Families: A Study of Changing Family Patterns in Single Parent Families", Unpublished Thesis, University College, Dublin.

Kirke, D.M. (1974) "A Sociological Study of Unmarried Mothers", Unpublished Thesis, University College, Dublin.

Marsden, D. (1973) *Mothers Alone: Poverty and the Fatherless Family*, Harmondsworth: Penguin.

McCashin, A. (1993) *Lone Parents in the Republic of Ireland: Enumeration, Description and Implications for Social Security*, Dublin: Economic and Social Research Institute.

McCashin, A. (1996) *Lone Mothers in Ireland: A Local Study*, Dublin: Oak Tree Press/Combat Poverty Agency.

McDonnell, K., Fitzgerald, K. and Kinsella, T. (1988) "A Community Based Study of Unmarried and Married Mothers", *Irish Journal of Medical Science* (March) 79-82.

McGuire, J. and Richman, N. (1988) *Pre-School Behaviour Checklist*, Berkshire: Nfer Nelson.

McRae, S. (1993) *Cohabiting Mothers: Changing Marriage and Motherhood?*, London: Policy Studies Institute.

Millar, J. (1992b) *Poverty and the Lone-Parent: The Challenge to Social Policy*, Aldershot: Avebury.

Millar, J. Leeper, S. and Davies, C. (1992a) *Lone Parents: Poverty and Public Policy in Ireland*, Dublin: Combat Poverty Agency.

Ministry of Social Security (1967) *Circumstance of Families*, London: HMSO.

Murphy, M. (1989) "Housing the people: From shortage to surplus?", in Joshi, H., *The Changing Population of Britain*, Oxford: Basil Blackwell Ltd.

Nolan, B. (1993) *Low Pay in Ireland*, General Research Series Paper 159, Dublin: Economic and Social Research Institute.

O'Grady, T. (1992) Abstract of "Married to the State: A Study of Unmarried Mother's Allowance Applicants", Unpublished Thesis, University of Dublin, Dublin.

O'Hare, A., Dromey, M., O'Connor, A., Clarke, M. and Kirwan, G. (1987) *Mothers Alone?: A Study of Women who gave birth outside Marriage*, Dublin: Federation of Services for Unmarried Parents and Their Children.

Pascall, G. (1986) *Social Policy: A feminist analysis*, London: Tavistock.

Powell, B., Swain, E. and Dockeray, J. (1982) "Unmarried Mothers: A Survey of 200 presenting for Antenatal care", *Irish Medical Journal*, 75, 7, pp. 248-249.

Richardson, V. (1991) *Lone Parent Families in Ireland,* Paper presented at the Family Studies Centre Conference, June, Dublin.

Richardson, V. and Winston, N. (1989) *Unmarried Mothers delivered in the National Maternity Hospital 1987*, Dublin: National Maternity Hospital/University College Dublin.

Richardson, V., Keenan, J. and Kernan, E. (1987) *Unmarried Mothers delivered in the National Maternity Hospital 1986*, Dublin: National Maternity Hospital/University College Dublin.

Rynne, A. & Lacey, L. (1983) "A Survey of 249 Irish Women Interviewed while Pregnant and out of Wedlock Between September 1982 and July 1983" (Unpublished Report).

Townsend, P. (1979) *Poverty in the United Kingdom: A Survey of Household Resources and Standards of Living,* Harmondsworth: Penguin Press.

Vincent, C. (1961) *Unmarried Mothers*, London: Collier McMillan.

Viney, M. (1964) "No Birthright: A Study of the Irish Unmarried Mother and Her Child", Dublin: The *Irish Times*.

---

[1] Department of Vital Statistics (CSO), National Census of Population (CSO), Statistics on Social Welfare (Department of Social Welfare), the Annual Report of An Board Uchtala (The Adoption Board).

[2] Divorce was not available in Ireland at the time of the survey

[3] Difficulties arise in comparing levels of overcrowding as a number of statistical formulas have been utilised (see Ferri, 1976:77 and Fahey and Watson, 1995, p. 72 for further discussion of overcrowding formula); Ferri (1976, p. 77) adopted (with some reservations) the standard that a house was overcrowded if there were more than 1.5 persons to a room. This formula was used in the current study.

[4] At the time when the fieldwork for this study was carried out, the earnings disregard for claimants of the LPA was £12. Earnings above this amount made little contribution to the family income, not only because of the £1 for £1 reduction in payment, but because of the concomitant loss of additional benefits such as the medical card.

[5] Income from employment includes respondent's income or resident-partner's income

[6] Equivalence values are calculated based on the number of adult and child dependants in a family unit. Each family unit is assigned 1 for the head of household, 0.66 for each additional adult and 0.2 for each child under 10

years of age. The income reported is then divided by the number of "adult equivalents" to arrive at the disposable income per adult equivalent (see Callan & Nolan, 1994).

[7] The PBCL (McGuire and Richman, 1988) is a 22-item checklist designed for use in group settings to identify children aged 2-5 years who have behavioural or emotional difficulties through use of a systematic and objective description of behaviour, which measures incidence and severity of behaviours. Normative data provides a cut-off point above which further attention to behavioural difficulties may be required.

[8] Five children were excluded from the analysis due to incomplete information and two were excluded due to disabilities, one a learning disability with challenging behaviours and the second with Cerebral Palsy.

Chapter 3

Parental Separation — Children's Responses

Gemma O'Donohoe

INTRODUCTION

This chapter examines how children cope with, resist, accommodate, survive and indeed sometimes transcend adversity in the context of parental separation in Ireland today. While there are a number of theoretical approaches to the study of parental separation, this work adopts a family conflict perspective (Amato & Keith, 1991). This perspective perceives inter-parental conflict as the main characteristic of parental separation affecting the child, while parental absence and economic disadvantage, among other issues, are also considered of some importance in explaining effects on the child. It assumes that marital breakdown is a process which extends over several events (Kiely, 1986) involving inter-parental conflict before, during and after the parental marital breakdown. This process frequently continues for many years. It is this extended series of conflictual events that affects the child's well being, rather than the actual event of parental separation (Needle, Su and Doherty, 1990).

Most studies of parental separation concentrate on negative outcomes for the child. In contrast, this paper focuses largely on positive effects which the child may experience. It is important to take this approach, firstly because the identification of the child's positive emotions and behaviours in response to parental separation is an area which has been under-researched. Secondly, some children may acquire certain positive traits and skills in dealing with issues surrounding parental separation. Furthermore, most previous research has failed to emphasise that it is the child's exposure to inter-parental conflict surrounding the marital breakdown rather than the actual separation of the parents that negatively affects the child. Among the exceptions is the study by Amato et al. (1995) which looked at the long-term effects of marital conflict on later well being in young adulthood.

This paper examines the sources and characteristics of inter-parental conflict in addition to other issues surrounding the separation process, but the main focus concerns children's behavioural and emotional reactions to this conflict. Evidence from these responses portrays the challenges which many children must face in western contemporary society. Before analysing this material, the methodology and limitations of the study are examined.

METHODOLOGY AND LIMITATIONS OF THE STUDY

Methodology

A qualitative method was deemed appropriate, as the issues pursued were sensitive, complex and relatively unexplored. A sample of nine was gained by placing short advertisements on society, club, academic department, and student union notice boards, in University College Dublin's Arts and Commerce buildings. An advertisement also appeared in two monthly editions of the University College Dublin Newsletter. The advertisement sought students, whose parents had separated when they were children, to volunteer to take part in the research. Data for the study were gathered from seven students out of a sample of nine, by semi-structured in-depth face-to-face interviews, lasting on average for two hours. Four students were studying Arts and three were studying Social Science. Of these students, three were male and four were female, while six were undergraduates and one was a postgraduate. The age range of these students was from 18 to 23 years.

Limitations

While this study is very valuable in providing insight into the experience of parental separation, it has a number of limitations. To begin, all interviewees were either Arts or Social Science students from University College Dublin, and all were from predominantly middle and upper class families. There were no controls for socio-economic class differences. Secondly, the study was limited to young adult memories of childhood experiences, some of which, it could be suggested, may have been inaccurate. Time constraints prevented more extensive fieldwork being undertaken. Finally, as most respondents were from Dublin, there is the possibility that the study was limited by regional bias. Despite these limitations, the method chosen elicited a large quantity of good quality data and justified itself in the breadth and depth of information collected. It is to the analysis of this data that I now turn.

THE CHILD'S EXPERIENCE OF INTER-PARENTAL CONFLICT

The data suggest that children frequently have to cope with inter-parental conflict to varying degrees, in the parental separation process. Where inter-parental conflict occurs, parents frequently contrive, often unconsciously, as powerful social actors to deconstruct their children's childhood and to reconstruct a more adult form of childhood than is usual for children of this age in western contemporary society.[1] This occurs because children become involved in adult issues surrounding their parents' separation. Thus, the sources and particularly the characteristics of inter-parental conflict which are outlined below, are of central importance in examining the child's experience of parental separation.

Sources of Conflict

The most predominant source of inter-parental conflict was concerned with financial matters, which is consistent with Masheter's (1991) and Emery's (1982) findings. Also of significance was conflict relating to pre- and post-separation extramarital relationships. The primary source of conflict in this situation occurred in response to one parent's dislike of the other having a new relationship and breaking marriage vows. For example, one respondent notes:

> Mum would bad mouth dad, mainly about him seeing the other woman.

It was common for one of the respondents' parents to have had at least one extramarital relationship before the separation. This has also been identified as a source of conflict in a study of couples who were clients of the Family Mediation Service (Nic Ghiolla Phádraig, 1992, p. 13). Interestingly, there was evidence to suggest that, where both parents had a new relationship after their separation, the child was exposed to less post-separation inter-parental conflict than where only one or neither parent had a new relationship. Respondents attributed this decrease in inter-parental conflict to their parents becoming more detached from their previous marital relationship, where they were more able to "let go" and lead separate lives. One respondent, whose parents both had new relationships, explains that:

> Mum never said anything negative about dad; she was always very supportive and good . . . mum doesn't care about dad's remarriage; mum said she wanted her own life . . . she wanted to live her own life and get on with it, trying to look for someone else.

Other significant sources of inter-parental conflict in the marital breakdown process, as experienced by these respondents, included issues relating to unemployment, alcohol abuse and conflicting relationships with in-laws. Further conflict relating to visitation and parenting of the children also existed, which is consistent with Emery's (1982) and Masheter's (1991) findings. Finally, there was some evidence to suggest that, while parents' decisions to legally separate were mutual, the decision to divorce was not, which led to additional conflict. Similarly, Wallerstein and Blakeslee (cited in McCarroll, 1995) note that the decision to divorce is rarely mutual.

Type of Inter-parental Conflict

The type of inter-parental conflict was found to vary from case to case and it also varied in the pre- and post-separation periods. The inter-parental conflict that the child experienced ranged from verbal and physical abuse to little communication or to being ignored. Similarly, Demo and Acock (1988) distinguish between calm and hostile conflict while Rutter et al. (1979) suggest that conflict may be characterised by apathy or quarrelsomeness.

The predominant type of inter-parental conflict experienced in the pre-separation period was direct verbal abuse. For example, one respondent comments that his mother:

> would swear and scream at his father and call him all the names under the sun . . . very crude language especially with me so young . . . she could be very cruel and insulting and say horrible things.

An indirect form of verbal abuse also occurred in one or both parents' communication with the child which involved the frequent criticising and "bad mouthing" of the other parent in their absence. This was described by a number of respondents as occurring at all stages in the parental separation process, but mainly in the post-separation period, where parents had little or no contact with each other. However, in the post-separation period, conflict between parents was predominantly found to be due to an unwillingness to communicate or compromise on any issue.

All types of conflict were found to have negative affects. However, exposure to both physical and verbal abuse was associated with more negative effects on the child, according to their reflections on the situation as young adults. Interestingly, all of the male respondents and none of the females reported witnessing some degree of aggressive physical abuse between parents in the pre-separation period. It could be suggested that this selective exposure to aggressive inter-parental conflict explains why some research studies suggest that males are more negatively affected by parental separation than females, often becoming more aggressive, with little evidence of any positive effects occurring (for example, Kalter, 1990).

Frequency of Inter-parental Conflict and the Length of Time It Existed

This research suggests that the greater the frequency and duration of interparental conflict, the greater the reported negative outcome. While this is consistent with the findings of Cherlin (1992) and Kroll (1994) who suggest that it is the degree of inter-parental conflict which negatively affects the child, they fail to consider the time period before the separation over which children are exposed to this conflict. Evidence from this study suggests that the child is exposed to inter-parental conflict for a reasonably long period. Most respondents reported being exposed to conflict for at least two years before the actual separation, while others were exposed to between nine and ten years overall.

Direct conflict was at its worst in the year prior to the separation and declined after a time in the post-separation period, findings which support those of Emery (1982) and Masheter (1991). However, this is not always the case. In one case parental conflict was at its worst in the fourth and fifth year prior to the separation, while in another, it was at its most intense in the second to fifth year after the separation. The findings in this study suggest that where children are of primary school age or younger, inter-parental conflict is more likely to occur in the post-separation period. This occurs as parents are likely to have more contact with each other arranging visitation for young children, than where there are older children who were able to arrange their own contact with the non-resident parent.

Extent of Exposure to Inter-parental Conflict

The extent of the child's exposure to inter-parental conflict is another characteristic in the marital breakdown process which has not been examined. Evidence suggests that children are generally exposed to some degree of inter-parental conflict in the pre-separation period, despite the attempts of some parents to hide it. While not all children in the study were direct witnesses to this conflict, they would at least hear their parents' conflict and shouting, sometimes making a conscious effort to listen to it. Commonly, parents would argue in front of the child while the child was present. For example, one respondent explains:

> They'd just fight in front of me, they'd no inhibitions, but not all the time, but all the time towards the end, the year or two before the break up.

In the post-separation period the child was generally exposed to less direct inter-parental conflict.

Interestingly, this study found some inconsistency with the family stress studies (Rutter, 1987; Johnson, 1986 cited in Barber 1992, pp. 73-75) which suggest that the more stresses that a child experiences (including death or serious illness in a close friend or relative and inter-parental conflict), the more negatively affected the child. In this study, however, it was found that in cases where the child was exposed to inter-parental conflict which was continuous and severe, events such as a death in the extended family that would usually be considered extremely stressful actually decreased the amount of stress that the child was experiencing. This occurred because the extent of inter-parental conflict usually decreased temporarily. For example, one respondent reported feeling relieved when his aunt died because the intense pre-separation inter-parental conflict ceased for a period.

In addition to the direct effects of inter-parental conflict on the child, the relationship between the child and their parents was also frequently disrupted, often occurring as the child was forced to "side" with one parent. Where inter-parental conflict was more severe, the child was more likely to side with one parent or other. In this "blaming" environment, the child was often forced to blame one of the parents because this was required to maintain good relations with the other parent.

Positive Emotional Dimensions of the Child's Experience

"Relief"

Relief was a common emotion cited to describe their response to parental separation. This relief was mainly a response to a decline in inter-parental conflict and, in some cases, a response to the child's hope that conflict would decline after the separation. As one respondent explains:

> It was a relief 'cause it hopefully wouldn't be as bad any-more; that mum would stop going on and on and behaving as she did.

This is similar to Mitchell's (1985) and Arendell's (1986) find-ings, that children who witness inter-parental conflict show signs of relief when their parents separate. In one case, relief occurred years after the separation because it was only at this point that inter-parental conflict first declined. The respondent notes that relief occurred:

> When my parents could talk to each other, at least they weren't fighting.

Children also felt relief as the actual separation of the parents became more comprehensible to them. As one respondent ex-plains, for example:

> When the court case was over I felt relieved; there was a conclusion; it was a step forward; it progressed from there.

Children were better able to cope with their parents' separa-tion at a point when they could "normalise" their situation and lose the alienation which they had previously felt. For example, one respondent remarks that:

> The divorce kind of finalised the split . . . I could see what was happening . . . it didn't bother me . . . but I was relieved 'cause it made it legal; it seemed normal 'cause other peo-ple's parents were divorced; so it made it more relateable to other people.

"More Considerate"

Further evidence which suggests that children often transcend the adversity accompanying parental separation was apparent in some respondents' accounts of becoming more considerate and understanding than was usual for their age. This occurred in response to inter-parental conflict but also, to some extent, in response to parental absence and economic disadvantage. Another possible reason for the development of greater consideration and understanding was due to the effect on the child of being "let down" or disappointed by an unreliable and inconsiderate non-resident parent. As the child experienced these negative events, they made a conscious effort to be more mature and understanding in an effort to avoid upsetting others. For example, one respondent explains:

> I'd always make sure to ring mum when I was away camping; I'd always make sure she knew what I was doing, especially when dad went away, 'cause I knew she relied on me for certain things, like doing the shopping.

Even economic disadvantage might prompt the child to become more considerate. One respondent reports that from the age of four years:

> 'cause of the financial difficulty . . . I wasn't able to do everything . . . I didn't feel angry; I understood that mum was alone and wouldn't have enough money and that others would have more money if they had two parents; I accepted it.

While this finding is similar to that of Wallerstein and Kelly (1980) who suggest that the adolescent becomes "money wise" and less demanding, this research found that even very young children were similarly affected. As a consequence, children became more financially independent.

"More Independent"

Some respondents reported that they became more independent and better able to express their opinions than was usual for their age. They attributed this to having to deal with distressing emotions relating to issues surrounding the parental separation process over a number of years. In the long term, children may have transcended hardship experienced in the parental separation process. Some respondents reported feeling more independent as adults, as a consequence of having dealt successfully with inter-parental conflict as well as, in some cases, economic disadvantage, in the parental separation process. This is consistent with the findings of Inglis (1982). As one respondent reports, for example:

> I'm more independent now and able to speak up for myself more; express my emotions easier and if others ask something, I'll say it whether they want to hear it or not; I'll tell the truth.

"Greater Emotional Strength"

Interviewees frequently described themselves as feeling stronger and having increased confidence as a consequence of dealing with the many issues sometimes surrounding the parental separation process during their childhood. As one respondent explains:

> When you've been through this . . . you've a much better feel for life in general 'cause nothing has been cushioned as you had to face reality; a lot of people are cushioned by their parents; I could survive a lot better in life; I'm stronger, tougher than others 'cause I had to do things . . . I'm able to deal with life a lot better.

While another explains:

> I'm lucky in a way that I had to go through something like this 'cause I know I can cope with things.

Another description of increased confidence includes one respondent's report that:

> I'm more confident now; harder, more able to cope and bounce back.

While another explains that the experience:

makes you be yourself and makes you more confident; it makes you world-wise . . . and gives you an insight into what others are thinking; hardship wises you.

NEGATIVE EMOTIONAL DIMENSIONS OF THE CHILD'S EXPERIENCE

Negative effects, including fear, damage to self-esteem and confidence, were also caused by inter-parental conflict in the marital breakdown process. One respondent reports, for example, "my confidence was really low", while another reported feeling, "low, useless and worthless". The latter respondent also reported suffering from obesity in response to her low self-worth feelings which arose in response to her parents' conflict. Other negative emotions including feelings of rejection and shock were primarily caused by parental absence, though inter-parental conflict also had some significance. Still other negative emotions, including feelings of sadness, confusion, loneliness and helplessness, were primarily caused by inter-parental conflict, while parental absence had some lesser effects also.

In my findings, anger was the most predominant negative emotional outcome in response to the parental separation process. This is consistent with Wallerstein and Kelly's (1980) findings. However, among all the studies which exist in the area, there is little consensus as to the predominant emotional effect. The present study suggests that children experience several types of anger including annoyance, bitterness and hatred. Furthermore, feelings of rejection, which commonly occurred in response to inconsistent, poor quality contact with the non-resident parent, especially where either direct or indirect inter-parental conflict existed, frequently caused the child to feel angry. Finally, anger emerged in response to parents' extra-marital relationships, economic disadvantage and, in one case, to being forced to move to a smaller home as a direct result of the parental separation.

POSITIVE BEHAVIOURAL DIMENSIONS OF THE CHILD'S EXPERIENCE

An increasing number of children are challenged by the rising rate of marital breakdown in Ireland today. The nature of childhood changes for many children, as is evident in the last section on emotions and this section on behavioural outcomes. The research undertaken provides further evidence of the possibility of the child transcending the parental separation. It indicates that many children gain from positive behavioural outcomes in response to their experience of the parental separation process. It is to this material that I will now turn.

"More Responsible"

Several respondents reported that they experienced extra responsibilities as children, causing them to become more responsible and mature than would be considered normal for their age in contemporary western society. This general trend occurred predominantly in response to parental absence in the post-separation period. Due to the absence of one parent from the home, many children had to help with the running of the household. As one respondent explains:

> The girls would do the babysitting, paying bills and shopping . . . at age ten when I'd come home from school, it would be my job to make the dinner.

While another reports:

> I had to be a lot more responsible, basic things like, at the age of ten years of age, I had to do the cooking and cleaning.

Others became more responsible in an effort to stand in for the absent parent, for the benefit of younger siblings and the resident parent. As one interviewee explains:

> I'd to work around the house and get my younger brother and sister to do things . . . myself and my older sister had the responsibility to get the younger ones to do what they were told and help mum around the house.

Similarly, another respondent reports:

> I always had to look out for mum and my sister, so I was really organised while most ten year olds were out playing.

This evidence suggests that these children coped with their parents' separation by acting in a "parental" manner (Kroll, 1994, p. 79). Further reference will be made to the phenomenon of the "parental child" later in this chapter.

The data also indicate that indirect inter-parental conflict was of some significance in causing the child to become more responsible because the resident parent discussed problems surrounding this issue with the child. For example, one respondent explains:

> I was like an adult . . . my mother used to talk to me and tell me everything about what was going on with my father at ten years of age; I had extra responsibilities.

Some evidence suggests that economic disadvantage also had some impact, making the child more responsible at a younger age than usual. One respondent explains:

> At the age of twelve or thirteen we all had part-time jobs 'cause our parents didn't have enough money to give us pocket money.

"Greater Development of Communication Skills"

Subjects reported that their childhood communication skills seemed more advanced than normal for their age. They also suggested that this effect continued through to adulthood. For example, one respondent explained that her peers:

> only had one land of conversation, I could converse with anyone, like the teachers.

While another respondent reported that in early adulthood:

> I felt different 'cause of the separation; my mind is different, like (when) I was at a funeral for example . . . and everyone was awkward, but I wasn't; I've better relations.

The data suggest that the child's ability to communicate in a more mature manner occurs in response to being involved with parents' problems relating to inter-parental conflict, parental absence and economic disadvantage throughout the marital breakdown process. However, while this effect may be considered positive, it did cause some children distress on occasion, as they were unable to form meaningful relationships or to become close friends with peers. This occurred firstly, because they felt different to other children on account of their parents' marriage being in a state of breakdown, and secondly, because they were sometimes bullied for being different in this way.

"The Parental Child"

It was also found that the child sometimes reacted by becoming "parental". The "parental child", who becomes more adult and responsible than usual for their age, standing in for the non-resident parent, is also a category identified by Kroll (1994). An example of the child taking this parental role is evident in one subject's feeling of anger in response to one of her mother's boyfriends where she states:

> He wasn't 'good' for her, not the right type of person; . . . it sounds stupid that I was telling my mother what to do when I was a child; whereas usually it's the mother telling the child; now mum says looking back, 'you were right'.

"'Extra Good' Behaviour"

A number of female respondents claimed that their behaviour as children was often better than usual for their age, as they acted in an "extra good" manner. This corresponds to the findings of Wallerstein and Kelly (1980), Kalter (1990) and Kroll (1994). However, there were no claims that boys became "extra good" similar to the findings of Kalter (1990). Becoming "extra good" occurred mainly in response to inter-parental conflict, but was also related to parental absence. Predominantly, respondents reported being "extra good" because they wanted to prevent any further distress for the resident parent, as this parent would have to deal with it alone. For example, one respondent reports:

> I was even more aware that I had to be good, 'cause if mum was on her own and if you were bold, it wouldn't be easy for her; I had a very good relationship with mum; I felt I had to be not getting in trouble all the time . . . 'cause it would have been more problems for her . . . my behaviour was more 'directionized' and better as a result.

Similarly, another respondent reports:

> I knew I couldn't do things like drink and smoke that was going to upset mum . . . she was the only one that would have to cope with it; my father didn't have to cope with anything.

Finally, subjects implied that the child became extra good because they could not sustain any further arguments and upset with the resident parent, in addition to those caused by the non-resident parent.

"Greater Academic Achievement"

Children's academic behaviour was often positively affected in the long term because they worked harder than usual, in response to several reasons relating to inter-parental conflict. These findings are in contrast to those of Cash (1995) and others who found that academic behaviour was only negatively affected by parental separation. The data suggested that children worked harder in the long term to distract themselves from inter-parental conflict and the insecurity which it brought. As one respondent explains:

> I worked to keep my mind off things, but at the same time I found it hard to study 'cause my concentration would have been much better, and maybe I wouldn't have studied as much if it hadn't happened; it was just as well though to keep out of my mum's way; it was either sit down with mum or go and study.

Similarly another respondent reports:

> I worked to distract myself.

Another child, who worked harder than usual at school to cope with the hardship brought by the insecurity of the parental separation process, states:

> I liked school and the security of nine to four o' clock.

Also of significance in explaining the child's positive long-term academic behaviour was the fact that most respondents reported receiving much support and encouragement by at least one parent or by a significant other in the child's life. The data also suggest that where there was little physical contact with a parent who was the main source of academic support and encouragement, the child continued to do well academically, provided it was good quality contact. As one respondent who had very little direct contact with his non-resident father, who was the main source of academic support, explains:

> Dad always instilled in me to read and educate myself and would say 'you have to do well in life' . . . dad always read the paper and was into current affairs . . . it was OK when my dad went away 'cause he sent a lot of mail order books and got me subscriptions to magazines; I never got low grades.

However, there was evidence that children's academic behaviour was negatively affected in the short term; for example, the child often failed examinations. This negative effect occurred due to the short-term lack of support from parents because they were "caught up" in direct and/or indirect intense conflict with each other. Rollins and Thomas (1979), Cherlin (1992) and Lanahan and Sandefur (1994) suggest that academic failure may be due to a decrease in attention from parents, whose time is devoted to conflict in the marital breakdown process. It was common for children's academic achievement to decrease as they lost interest and were unable to concentrate at school as a consequence of their experience of their parents' conflict. This study, similarly to Amato et al.'s (1995) findings, though in contrast to most research studies, found that inter-parental conflict rather than economic disadvantage was the predominant factor responsible for the child's negative academic behaviour.

NEGATIVE BEHAVIOURAL DIMENSIONS OF THE CHILD'S EXPERIENCE

While there is evidence of many positive effects in this study, some children reported being negatively affected in later years by these "positive" behaviours because they were deprived of a "normal" childhood life. This primarily occurred where the strain of extra responsibilities and extra good behaviour became too much to bear in later years. Where inter-parental conflict declined in later years in the post-separation period, it was frequently found that suppressed childhood behaviours and emotions were expressed. One respondent explained that:

> When my parents were arguing I didn't get involved; but I tend to get involved in arguments now; I try and say 'what's the story?' 'cause I felt I should have with my parents. . . I feel like shouting very loud when there are arguments because I feel lots of things are solved by disputes.

Similarly, Wallerstein and Kelly (1980) and Kroll (1994) acknowledged that "extra good" behaviour may, on occasions, be negative for the child in later life, where this behaviour is long term and where the child's needs are subsequently not met. This often occurs in response to the overwhelming nature of the resident parent's needs. In one respondent's case, the child had been "extra good" with the resident parent, but later in adulthood all ties with this parent were broken. An alternative explanation in this case might be that, while the child was "extra good" in an attempt to avoid further upset after her father left the family home, she continued to experience upset and indirect inter-parental conflict because the resident parent continued to "bad mouth" the non-resident parent, whom the child loved.

Earlier maturity and increased seriousness were found to be the most common negative behavioural effects experienced by children. Respondents reported having grown up faster and having become more mature, sensible and serious than was usual for their age, predominantly as a consequence of inter-parental conflict, which led to worry and upset on the child's part. Pre-maturity and seriousness also occurred as a consequence of being involved in adult concerns and problems relating to inter-parental conflict, parental absence and economic disadvantage, which led to the child being burdened with extra responsibilities. Interestingly, this effect was more common for females than males. It could be suggested that this occurred because more demands were made of females.

In addition, it was commonly found that the child's peer relations were negatively affected in several ways, primarily by inter-parental conflict. Generally, children were found to have few friends. Others were bullied, in addition to having few friends, and still others became "extra friendly" and/or "extra funny" with peers, thus gaining more friends than usual. Those children who were frequently exposed to inter-parental conflict where the parents failed to communicate and generally ignored each other reported having few friends. Those who were exposed to a large amount of verbal and/or physical inter-parental conflict were more likely to be bullied by peers, in addition to having few friends. However, where the child was exposed to a minimal amount of inter-parental conflict, the child's peer relations were not affected. Finally, where inter-parental conflict declined, predominantly occurring in the post-separation period, peer relations improved for most children. This supports the family conflict perspective, which notes that the adjustment of the child to the parental separation improves with the passage of time if inter-parental conflict subsides (Amato and Keith, 1991).

Aggressiveness was a further negative behavioural outcome, primarily occurring as a consequence of the child's' exposure to much inter-parental conflict. This generally occurred where anger and upset caused by parents' conflict was suppressed by the child. Where these negative emotions were later verbally expressed and where inter-parental conflict subsided, aggressiveness declined in most cases. However, the conflict did not always decline in the wake of separation. In one case, the child was exposed to much direct physical, verbal, and indirect inter-parental conflict over a number of years in the post-separation period. This was compounded by experiencing distress from a sibling who took over the role of the aggressive non-resident parent. Also, there was some evidence from this respondent and others that parental absence and economic disadvantage indirectly caused the child to become aggressive.

Some evidence in this study suggests that for children who develop a very close relationship with the resident parent of the opposite sex, gender identity is affected in the short term. This finding is similar to that of Schwarz (cited in Peterson and Zill, 1986, p. 296) who suggests that the child who becomes a stable ally of the parent of the opposite sex has problems with gender identity. Male respondents reported behaving in a more feminine manner. One respondent reports:

> First when dad left, I latched onto mum; I went everywhere with her; I was a 'mummy's boy' . . . I know it's taken awhile to get over the barrier block where you want so much to say something; to speak in a socially acceptable way; the way you've been taught; but I'd been taught and influenced by my mum, so I had a more feminine way of dealing with situations than masculine.

While another male respondent reports:

> For years I learnt a more womanly way of dealing with the world.

While male respondents had some problems with gender identity in childhood, possibly because they all lived with the parent of the opposite sex, there was no evidence to suggest that these males had problems in the long term. Indeed, it could be argued that these males benefited from acquiring what they perceived as "feminine attitudes and views", in addition to "masculine attitudes and views". Female respondents did not report problems with gender identity. This may have occurred because all female respondents lived with the parent of the same sex as themselves.

CONCLUSION

While this chapter primarily deals with the much-neglected subject of children's positive responses to parental separation, it does not deny that children are affected in a negative manner by this experience in Ireland today. It is evident that many factors contributed to the child surviving and transcending adversity within a parental separation context. Of paramount importance in the research undertaken was the finding that it is not parental separation, as such, which negatively affects the child. Rather it is the child's exposure to direct and/or indirect inter-parental conflict, occurring in the pre- and/or post-separation period of the marital breakdown process which is perceived by them as having a negative impact. While inter-parental conflict is central to the child's experience of parental separation, we have also seen that parental absence and economic disadvantage, among other factors, also play their part. Important findings show that the child's success is partly dependent on the type, frequency and extent of exposure to inter-parental conflict. When there was little conflict and the separated parents were co-operative and supportive of each other, the child transcended the short-term adversity experienced in relation to the parental marital breakdown and in the process gained useful long-term emotional and behavioural skills. Finally, while it must be stressed that the sample in this study was very small and not representative, it does, however, offer a basis for further research into this phenomenon.

References

Amato, P. and Keith, P. (1991), "Parental Divorce and the Well-being of Children: A Meta-Analysis". *Psychological Bulletin*, Vol. 110, No. 1, pp 26-46.

Amato, P. R., Loomis, L. Spencer and Booth, A. (1995), "Parental Divorce, Marital Conflict and Offspring Well-being during Early Adulthood", *Social Forces*, Vol. 73, No. 3, pp.895-915.

Arendell, T. (1986), *Mothers and Divorce*, Los Angeles: University of California Press.

Barber, B. (1992), "Family, Personality and Adolescent Problem Behaviour". *Journal of Marriage and the Family*, Vol. 54 (Feb) pp 69-79.

Cash, L. (1995), "Easy Divorce Brings High Social Costs", quoted in *The Irish Times*, 29 September 1997.

Cherlin, A. J. (1992), *Marriage, Divorce and Remarriage*, London: Sage.

Demo, D. and Acock, A. (1988), "The Impact of Divorce on Children", *Journal of Marriage and the Family*, Vol. 50, No. 3, pp. 619-648.

Emery, R. (1982), "Inter-parental Conflict and the Children of Discord and Divorce", *Psychological Bulletin*, Vol. 92, No. 2, pp 310-330.

Inglis, R. (1982), *Must Divorce Hurt the Children?* London: Temple Smith.

Kalter, N. (1990), *Growing Up With Divorce*, London: Macmillan.

Kiely, G. (1986), *Children and Marital Separation*, Dublin: Family Studies Centre.

Kroll, B. (1994), *Chasing Rainbows: Children, Divorce and Loss*, Cambridge: Russell House.

Lanahan, S. and Sandefur, G. (1994), *Growing Up With a Single Parent*, London: Harvard University Press.

McCarroll, J. (1995), "Maintaining Marriage and the Family for Richer or Poorer, For Better or for Worse", *The Irish Family*, Dublin: Irish Family Publication.

Masheter, C. (1991), "Post Divorce Relationships Between Ex-Spouses; The Roles Of Attachment and Inter-Personal Conflict", *Journal of Marriage and the Family*, Vol. 52, February, pp. 103-110.

Mitchell, A. (1985), *Children in the Middle: Living Through Divorce*, London: Tavistock.

Needle, R., Su, S. and Doherty, W. (1990), "Divorce, Remarriage and Substance Abuse". *Journal of Marriage and the Family*, Vol. 52, February, pp 157-169.

Nic Ghiolla Phádraig, M. (1992) "Marital Separation in Ireland: Situating the Results of Research on the First Three Years of Operation of the Family Mediation Service" in Kiely, G. (ed) *In and Out of Marriage: Irish and European Experiences*, Dublin: University College, Family Studies Centre.

Peterson, J. and Zill, N. (1986), "Marital Disruption, Parent-Child Relationships and Behaviour Problems In Children", *Journal of Marriage and the Family*, Vol. 48, May, pp 295-307.

Rollins, B. and Thomas, D. (1979), "Parental Support, Power and Control Techniques in the Socialization of Children" in Burr, W. Hill, R. Nye, F. and Reiss, L. (eds), *Contemporary Theories about the Family*, New York: Free Press, pp 317-364.

Rutter, M. (1979), "Maternal Deprivation: New Findings, New Concepts, New Approaches". *Child Development*, Vol. 50, pp 283-305.

Rutter, M. (1987), "Psychosocial Resilience and Protection Mechanism". *American Journal of Orthopsychiatry*, Vol. 57, pp 316-331.

Wallerstein, J. and Kelly, J. (1980), *Surviving the Breakup*, London: Grant McIntyre.

Ward, P. (1990), *Financial Consequences of Marital Breakdown*, Dublin: Combat Poverty Agency.

Notes

---

[1] Throughout this work, the use of the word "usual" and "normal" in reference to the child, refers to what the subjects considered normal in western contemporary society today.

Chapter 4

Family Fostering: Children's Experiences of Care by Relatives

Valerie O'Brien

INTRODUCTION

This chapter examines the impact of relative care on the lives of the children involved in this increasingly important child-care option. Relative care,[1] as distinct from informal care within extended families, is a care option now being used increasingly by the State. It involves the formal placement of children unable to live with their parents in their extended family networks. The focus of this chapter is primarily to examine how the relative care system impacts on the lives of children.

The chapter is drawn from a Ph.D research study carried out in Ireland between 1993-1997 (O'Brien, 1997a). It is the only study of its type conducted to date in Ireland and has contributed significantly to an understanding of this care option for children. The study used a combined qualitative and quantitative methodology. It examined the evolution of relative care networks following an emergency placement of a child in a relative home in the Eastern Health Board area.[2] It provided baseline data on a population of 92 children. The study traced the processes involved through the decision-making, assessment and post-assessment stages. It examined the ways in which current case management practices, derived primarily from an application of a traditional foster care approach, impact on the evolution of the networks. A process-oriented descriptive account of the evolution of the networks was presented. The multiple perspectives on issues offered by the birth parents, children, relatives and social workers involved was an important feature of the study. A post-Milan systemic framework, drawing principally on the "fifth province model" (Byrne, 1995; McCarthy and Byrne, 1995) was the main theoretical frame used to orientate the study.

This chapter starts by providing an overview of the emergence of this care option and the perceived advantages and potential difficulties associated with relative care practice. A snapshot is presented of the children involved and their families. This baseline data provides important markers in which the overall issues emerging from the children's experiences can be understood. The children's views of the key stages in the evolution of the placements are then presented.

The development of formal relative care in Ireland is traced in part to the Child Care Act, 1991. Relative care was introduced as a viable care option, alongside foster care, residential care and adoption. Different options are needed to meet the care needs of the approximately 3,600 children in state care at any one time in Ireland.[3] The numbers of children in care have not changed dramatically in the last 30 years, but the use of individual care options has changed.[4] Foster care has become the dominant placement of the care system. In Ireland, the percentage of children who are in foster care rose from 50 to 75 per cent of the total care population between 1977 and 1997 (Kelly and Gilligan, 2000). Prior to the publication of the Child Care Regulations in 1995 (Department of Health, 1995a) it was not possible to distinguish between children placed in foster care as distinct from relative care, as both groups of children were recorded as being in the foster care system. This lack of separation of information on the use of relative care was also a feature of many international child welfare systems (Gleeson, 1996) and made it difficult to track precisely the rate at which change was taking place.

The increased use of relative care was a trend which was evident in the agency in which the research was conducted. The numbers of placements with relatives increased from nine children placed in 1990, 20 in 1993, 145 in 1995 and 179 in

1997.[5] These figures look small when viewed against a total care population of 1,476 children in the Eastern Health Board in 1996 (Department of Health, 1999). However, when the number of new children entering the system is examined, it is evident that a quarter of all new children placed in foster care in 1996 were placed with relatives. The only national profile of children in care which contains separate profiles of the relative and foster care population is the 1996 snapshot of care trends (Department of Health, 1999). On the surface, this shows that one in every seven children in the care system is placed in relative care. However, this figure fails to indicate the rate of increase in this care option. The number of children in relative care is shown against a total care population of which 64 per cent were in the care system for two years or longer, and 40 per cent were in the system for five years or more (Department of Health, 1999). Relative care was not used to any great extent until the mid-1990s.

EMERGENCE OF RELATIVE CARE

In the 1990s, a renewed interest in family and social networks as a placement resource for children in need of formal state care occurred. Several factors account for the change in a context of major shifts in child welfare systems. These include the shift from residential care to foster care (Triseliotis, 1989; Colton, 1989). This shift is associated with the increased awareness of the negative effects of long-term institutionalisation, the importance of a family-based experience for children, especially those in long-term care, and a concern among service providers with the increased cost of residential care. Demographic trends have resulted in less availability of foster homes (Kusserow, 1992; Gilligan, 1990); at a time when family-based care is preferred. The inter-generational abuse/dysfunctional family theories that accounted for negativity towards relative placements among practitioners have been challenged, with the emergence of family therapy, systemic and strength-based approaches. The shift towards partnership in child care (Thoburn, 1994; Ryburn, 1993) opened up the previously untapped potential of family and social networks among service providers. As a result, greater emphasis was placed in practice on the process of consultation, client participation and consumer satisfaction. Principles of child care were re-appraised as people reared in alternative care began to narrate their stories, and the importance of identity and roots was reinforced. This challenged core premises previously held regarding "substitute" care. As part of this evolving thinking, many theories central to child care, e.g. the family and social networks, attachment, identity, separation and loss were re-examined. Outcome studies indicated lower disruption rates and more security for children placed within family networks (Fein et al., 1983; Rowe et al., 1984; Iglehart, 1994). These studies, though small in number, influenced practice at a time when practitioners were dealing with increasing difficulties in foster care, i.e. recruitment, breakdown etc.[6]

Relative care now accounts for an increasing number of care placements and undoubtedly this is also associated, in part, with a number of identified advantages for children placed in relative care. The advantages, identified through research and practice, are generally considered to include: the availability of familiar care in a time of crisis (Thornton, 1987); placement in a familiar ethnic and racial community (Hegar et al., 1995); avoidance of trauma of being placed with strangers (Dubowitz et al., 1994); greater facilitation of access with birth parents (Berrick et al., 1994); lower disruption rates (Iglehart, 1994); greater opportunity for sibling unity (Johnson, 1995); and greater adjustment in alternative care (Iglehart, 1994).

It is not the intention in this chapter to consider in-depth the merits of the perceived advantages for children in relative care. However, it is important that the advantages are considered against a number of concerns. The central concerns emerging in relative care are seen as protection of children, the impact on children in the event of intra-familial conflict, the level of support services, financial equity, reunification rates, and the applicability of existing case management systems (O'Brien, 1996, 1997b, 2000). The latter concerns are seen to impact more on service delivery and the support services for the relatives and the children's birth parents which, of course, indirectly impact on the children.

A "Snapshot" of Children in Relative Care and their Families

This section summarises information collected through a census of all children in relative care in the Eastern Health Board on 1 February 1995. The profile provides a "snapshot" of all the children who, on that date, were in the formal care system and placed with relatives. The "snapshot" makes available information about this relatively unknown child care population, and provides baseline information that can be developed in future studies. The disadvantage is that it provides a static and superficial view of this population at a single point in what may be one episode only during each child's care career. The information presented relates to the biographical characteristics of children and their birth families, their care careers and characteristics of the relative families they were living with.

The Children's Families

Two-thirds of the children in the study population (N=92) came from families that were headed by a single parent at the time of their admission to care. Almost two-thirds of the children (62 per cent: 54) belonged to families where their parents were married. Of this 62 per cent, 21 per cent (19) of the children's parents were still living together. The remaining children's (41 per cent: 37) parents had either separated or had died (14 per cent). One-third of the children belonged to families that were never married (38 per cent: 35) The findings in this study for families headed by a single parent are marginally higher than those presented by Richardson in her study of children in care. Her study reported that 19.2 per cent of the children's parents were married and living together while 25.8 per cent of the parents were unmarried (1985: 104).

For the two out of three children (67 per cent: 57) belonging to families headed by a single parent, half of these children lived in families whose parents had never been married (38 per cent: 35). Within this population of never-married parents, a small number of children's parents were cohabiting (5 per cent: 5), while in the case of 6 per cent (6) of the children their parents had separated and were now cohabiting. The 38 per cent of non-marital children coincide with the findings of several studies which show that this group of children is more vulnerable to placement in care in Ireland (Richardson, 1985; O'Higgins, 1996). It is noteworthy that the proportion of births to single mothers increased significantly during the interval between the two studies.

The mean age of the children was 9.7 years, and over half of the children were aged ten years and over. Over two-thirds of the children came from families that ranged from one to four children in size. Twelve (13 per cent) of the 92 children in the study were only children, 20 per cent (18) came from a family of two, 23 per cent (21) came from a family of four and the study included one family of eight children (9 per cent).

Ninety per cent of the children came from families that were dependent on social welfare for their primary source of income, and over 75 per cent of the children's parents lived in the rented housing sector. Of the remaining quarter, half of these children's parents were homeless. However, homelessness per se was not presented as the primary reason for care. Addiction featured highest as both the primary and secondary reason for care, followed by neglect. The findings relating to the families of children in relative care showed many similar characteristics to children in the general care population in Ireland. The limited research data in this area, and the small scale of the census, prevented a more thorough comparison.

This profile also shows similarities with international studies. In particular, the pattern of children in care being predominantly from single-parent families is noted, as is the prevalence of neglect and addiction as reasons for care.

CARE CAREERS OF CHILDREN

The idea of "care career" allows recognition of "child care as a process" (Millham et al., 1986, p. 11). This draws attention both to the individual's experience in the care system, and also to patterns inherent in the system into which the children are put. Pinkerton (1994), in his discussion of care career, distinguishes between care as bounded by key legal decisions, such as entering in the system, and by placement decisions. The care career of the children in the study is presented in this section according to the care status, previous care admissions, routes to relative care and age profile of children entering both care and relative care.

The care careers of the children showed that, for over half the children in relative care, their current placement was their first experience with the care system (57.6 per cent: 53). However, of the remaining 39 children who had previous care experience, 31 were moved from within the care system to their relatives. The reasons for this move were divided equally between planned moves and as a result of disrupted placements. The high numbers of teenage children placed as a result of disrupted placements has implications for the levels and type of support offered to the relatives.

A high proportion (63 per cent) of the children were in relative care on the basis of court orders. This reflects the general national trend for children in care. It is important to distinguish between those children placed in relative care when the order is already in existence, and situations where the order is taken while the children are in the relative home.

Thirty-nine per cent of children were in relative care for longer than three years. This information would be more relevant if it had been possible to examine length of time in placement against the initial care plan and placement decision making. A concern identified in international studies is the longer length of time, but with lower re-admission rates, for children in relative care compared to other care options.

The study showed that two-thirds (62) of the children had siblings placed with them or within the extended family network. Only four of the children were placed with relatives who also fostered non-related children, and this gives a picture of relative care as fostering children principally from their own families.

Fifty-four (58.7 per cent) of the children were living in relatives' homes which had been approved, while the remaining 41.3 per cent (38) of placements were awaiting approval. The average length of time to approval was between seven and twelve months, though one in five children were in homes for a year or more without being approved. The implications of failing to achieve the approval in the allotted twelve-week period as laid down in regulations (Department of Health, 1995a) is a serious issue for both the agency and the relatives who may be left awaiting support.

THE RELATIVES WHO PROVIDE CARE

The profile of the relatives in the study was similar to international studies in terms of low income levels (Thornton, 1987; Dubowitz et al.,1994; Link, 1996). While slight variation existed in the age structure compared to international trends, the relatives were, on average, older than the regular foster parents approved by the agency. The children were predominantly cared for by relatives on the maternal side of the family, with maternal aunts providing the highest level of care. Maternal aunts featured high also in international studies (Rowe et al., 1984; Thornton, 1987; Task Force, 1990; Link, 1996), but grandparents provide a greater proportion of the relative care in US (Johnson, 1995). This difference is partly explained by the different family structures.

The relatives were predominantly married, which again is at variance with the international trends. However, while taking into account the paucity of data pertaining to the general foster parent population, when compared to the Conway (1993) profile of the foster parents in the agency, the number of children (11) placed in families headed by single parents was higher. Despite the small numbers of single parents, this was a change in the agency in which the study took place.

The accommodation in which the children were living with relatives was considered. It was shown that a higher proportion of relatives were owner-occupiers compared with birth parents, but, as a group, relative carers have a higher percentage living in the rented sector compared to national figures.

The mean family size of the relative carers' family was 3.2 children, compared to a mean of 3.7 in the children's own birth family. The variation between the composition of the two types of families was limited. It is of interest, however, that eight children were placed with relatives who had no children of their own. Sixteen of the children placed came from a family size of between six and nine children, whereas only eight children were placed with families that had between six and eleven children. In light of the family composition, the trend whereby a number of the children were placed within the two year age differential usually required by the agency is significant.

The profile of children and their families has been summarised in this section. Five important trends, in particular, were identified, which warrant further attention. These include the need to track children entering relative care according to the initial care plan, and the subsequent length of time spent in the system, considering the trend recorded in America of children spending longer time periods in relative compared to non-related care. The length of the assessment process prior to final approval for the relatives' placements is also significant and has implications both for the relatives and the statutory duties of the agency. The reasons for children entering relative care also needs to be studied. Special attention should be focused on the major problem of addiction as a reason for admission to relative care.

The question of who cares and for what reason are important issues in relative care. The trend wherein care is provided predominantly on the maternal side by women needs to be further examined in terms of expectations of familial responsibilities and consequences for support services if this trend continues. In addition, the increased participation of women in the labour force may reduce the number of relatives available to provide care. The placement of children within a two years' age gap of existing children needs to be carefully considered. An exploration of the inter-familial dynamics is required, and comparison to see if high rates of disruption are evident, as is the case in regular foster care.

THE CHILDREN'S VIEWS OF KEY STAGES IN NETWORK DEVELOPMENT

The research identified five key stages in the development of relative care networks. These are the initial decision-making stage, assessment, support, access/contact and future planning. In this section the experience and views of children involved are reviewed. These views are based on interviews with children in six networks, which formed the basis for the qualitative data on which the study was based.

The basis for the interviews with children in the six networks was as follows. A sampling frame was designed to elucidate if differences existed in the networks of relationships in relative care. The sampling frame was based on the broad hypothesis that intra-familial relationships determined the overall family-state relationship in relative care. The fifth province method and the author's previous work experience informed the hypotheses and the sampling method. To ensure that a full picture of the evolving networks would be captured, it was decided to involve only those networks which had completed the process of emergency placement, assessment/home study and subsequent approval by the agency. A description of different placement types, based on the hypothesis was forwarded to the social workers involved with the networks. The six networks finally selected fitted the different network descriptions (O'Brien, 1999); all participants in the network selected agreed to co-operate with the research and the network participants had experienced all stages of the process under review.

A summary of key information on the six networks is presented below. Pseudonyms are given to the children and aspects are changed to ensure anonymity of networks.

In Network A, Aoife was a 14-year-old girl who had two siblings in informal care with other relatives. The reason for care was non-school attendance. At the time of the research, Aoife had been in the placement for 18 months. The care status was voluntary at the start of the relative placement. (Voluntary agreement was made in presence of a judge, and the child was diverted from a court-mandated placement. If co-operation was not forthcoming, grounds existed for making a court order.) The placement retained voluntary status at the time of research. The placement was recorded on the agency file as long-term care.

In Network B, Nora was a ten-year-old girl who was placed with her six-year-old sibling. The reason for care was physical and sexual abuse. She had been two years in the placement at the time of the research. The placement was the subject of a court order at the start of the placement, and this continued to the end of the period of the research. The placement was recorded on the agency file as long-term care.

In Network C, Larry was an 11-year-old boy who had no siblings. Physical abuse was the reason for care. He had been seven years in the placement at the time of research. The care was voluntary at the start and this status continued at the time of the research. The placement was recorded on the agency file as long-term care.

In Network D, Elsa was an eight-year-old girl with no siblings. She was in care due to the psychiatric problems of her parent. The placement had run for six years at the time of the research. Care was voluntary at the outset, but had become court-mandated by the time of the research. The placement was recorded on the agency file as long-term care.

Three children were placed together in Network E, 14-year-old Eilis, 11-year-old Mark, and eight-year-old Tony. Alcohol addiction was the primary reason for care. The placement had existed for nine years. Care was voluntary at the outset, but had become court-mandated by the time of the research. The placement was recorded on the agency file as long-term care.

In Network F, a 10-year old girl, Deirdre, was placed with her six-year old sibling. Ill health of the birth mother, together with marital and accommodation problems, were the reasons for care. The placement had existed for 18 months at the time of the research. The placement was voluntary at the outset and continued to be so at the time of research. The placement was recorded on the agency file as long-term care.

CHILDREN'S ACCOUNTS OF DECISION-MAKING

Children in five of the six networks had previous experiences of the care system, either in foster or residential care. The children were generally unaware of how the decision was made for them to move to live with their relatives, with the exception of the child below, who equated her move to care with her family reaching out to her:

> *Valerie*: What was your understanding of what was happening then Nora?
>
> *Nora*: They wanted me.
>
> *Valerie*: They wanted you?
>
> *Nora*: They wanted me because they loved me and because I was upset and then they wanted me to come, so I would feel a bit better. . . . Yeah, not to go on living with strangers, I wasn't getting on with them, so I went to see my uncle and auntie, some nights I slept there, and after that I lived with them.

All the children, however, understood why they were not living with their parents. The lack of insight into how the decision to place them with relatives was made may be accounted for by the children moving to relatives when they were very young or by children's concern with the immediate. It may reflect that, while social workers aim to prepare children when they are entering care or moving in the care system, the emergency nature of many of the placements reduced the potential for that preparation. It may reflect also how decision-making generally takes place amongst adults, with only minimum reference to the children. An important context marker was that many of the children did not see care with relatives as "being in care". This was particularly so for the children who had previous care experience.

> *Deirdre*: It was like when I was living with the foster parents, I did not know who I was living with, now I am just with my family.

A positive aspect identified by the birth parents at the decision-making stage was the relief that the child would remain within or return to the care of the family. This relief was also shared by the relatives who were motivated principally either to rescue the child or prevent them from entering an anonymous care system. Equally, the social workers were delighted if a suitable family placement could be found, believing that it was best if children were placed in their family, as it enhanced the chances of children staying together and it provided a resource in a time of acute shortage. The sentiments of the children were clearly expressed: for them, being with family was significantly different from being with strangers, and while they had little insight into how the decision got made, they were very clear it was their preferred care option if they could not live at home.

ASSESSMENT

Assessment refers to the process through which the suitability of the relative family to provide care and protection for a child in state care is established by the child welfare agency. A major distinction between traditional fostering and relative care is that the main assessment process takes place after placement has occurred in relative care. Prior to the relative placement, an initial risk assessment is made to ensure the child is cared for and protected in the relatives' home.

The children in the study were asked general questions only relating to how social workers should choose foster families for children who were unable to live with their own parents. The children showed little insight into the assessment process, though all had a view on the type of family with which they should be placed. Overall, the children showed an awareness of the need for the families to be checked out:

Aoife: Yes they need to find out what they are like.

The fact that the practical things should be checked was raised by one child:

Deirdre: They should make sure they are getting the right food too, or are they getting the clothes to wear and shoes and so on.

Another said it was essential that the child's view be established to ensure that:

. . . they like them. If they have good fun there. If they are a nice family.

The theme of criminal families was referenced as a determinant of suitability by one child. In the account below, the child explains the type of family children should not be left with:

> *Nora*: Bad people, like say if it's a person who robs, you shouldn't be left with them because then they probably would get you robbing when you are grown up, and when you have grown up, you will probably be put in jail.

Assessment is a central issue in relative care when the child is already in situ, and this part of the process impacts more directly on the relatives' social worker and the relatives rather than the children. Relative assessment challenges many theoretical, professional and organisational premises on which assessment practices have been organised, and in the process, confronts the agency with many practical and ethical difficulties. This is associated with the different routes to relative care, demographic differences between foster and relative carers, and the likelihood that the child is in situ.

SUPPORT

Support in general foster care is based on the premise that, when placements are made, support is required for all participants to ensure the care plan is followed through. This support is normally supplied by the agency, to the network participants, through a range of activities including training, therapeutic and financial help, and networking with peers. Providing support is seen as an essential feature of case management practices in general foster care (Aldgate and Hawley, 1986; Shaw and Hipgrave, 1989; Sellick, 1992)

The children's views of support needs to be seen against four main themes. First, children and relatives receive less services and payments than non-relative foster parents (Gleeson and Craig, 1994; Scannapieco and Hegar, 1995). Secondly, there are resource implications of providing support to the growing numbers of relatives involved in out-of-home care for children in the US (Mills and Usher, 1996). Third, is the contradictory position of holding relative care as the preferred placement option, while, at the same time, under-financing and under-supporting it (Takas, 1992; Berrick et al., 1994), and fourthly, the existence of a two-tier system serving relative and traditional foster parents (Berrick et al., 1994).

SOCIAL WORK AND SUPPORT FOR THE CHILD

In traditional foster care, the social worker's role with children in care is commonly referred to as a bridge between past and future, birth family and foster family. However in relative care, the social worker's peripheral position in the network is a key feature. The social worker's role in providing support for the child is determined by the care plan. The plan determines if reunification with parents is involved, or if the child is to remain with relatives, or is in a temporary placement until a permanent home is found. In the study, the social worker's support role to the child was determined by the reason for care, the length of time in the placement, the priority of the case in context of other demands, and the extent to which children were encouraged by their birth parents and relatives to form a relationship with the social worker.

CHILDREN'S VIEW OF SUPPORT

The children's level of awareness of the support role of the agency and its social workers varied. The children understood the role of the social worker as someone who tried to help children who cannot live with their own parents, as illustrated by this young girl's view:

> *Aoife*: They try to look after you and try to make sure you are in a good home.

Other children saw the social worker's role as mediating conflict, particularly if it was going to embarrass them, as illustrated by this young girl who wanted the social worker to attend her confirmation in case a row broke out with her mother:

> *Eilis*: I might ask the social worker to come just in case she turns up drunk on the day.

Some children knew the system very well, who provided what and what had to be negotiated with the agency, e.g. sleepovers etc. Other children had little understanding. This lack of understanding may be attributed to two reasons. Firstly, it indicates the children have a relatively "normal" upbringing, and did not see themselves as different, other than being reared by relatives. Secondly, lack of knowledge of the system left the children with certain worries, which could have been offset with a little extra knowledge. This was apparent in one situation, where the children were very concerned about the financial burdens on their relatives arising from their living in the house. This caused a level of distress, and they felt guilty, as the relative family had to move home to accommodate the extra children. They were particularly afraid that their new home might be repossessed. They were asked who they thought might help to alleviate their worries. They showed no awareness of the social worker or the agency as a potential source of help. In this comment a sense of hopelessness at finding a solution is evident:

> *Valerie*: Do you think other people should be helping Paula and Liam (relatives) more?
>
> *Mark*: Yes, but who is going to help them?

When the source of his concern was explored further with him, the concern that the house might be repossessed emerged:

> *Mark*: That they might take the house.
>
> *Valerie*: Who might take the house?
>
> *Mark*: People that own it.

On the other hand, the children in another network, though younger, were very aware that social workers were directly involved in supporting the relatives financially. They knew, for example, that social workers had to be asked for help if they wished to do extracurricular activities, obtain additional clothing or sleep over in friends' houses etc. The difference in children's knowledge of support and its availability may be explained by some families minimising the agency's role as a source of help to ensure the children have as normal a life experience as possible, or through past experience of the care system.

STIGMA OF INVOLVEMENT WITH SOCIAL WORKERS

Children in all the networks showed a level of discomfort arising from their contact with social workers, regardless of length of time, or the reason they were in care. The discomfort arose from feeling different in their neighbourhoods, and the pain associated with this difference. In these children's experience, issues arose as follows:

> *Valerie*: Well what is it like for you having a social worker coming to see you?
>
> *Eilis*: Sometimes it is all right . . . but it is not very comfortable sometimes, telling them my secrets or anything.

The comment below shows that the child's friends were her main source of support, and the social worker remained a stranger even though she has known her for years:

> *Eilis*: Well my friends are there every day like. You go down to see them for fun but they know me, and even though I know the social worker for years, she is still a stranger like.

In one situation, local children showed an acute interest in the child's background, to the point where she got into fights over it. Children going into care were not uncommon in the community in which the child lived, but there were few foster families in the area. The local perception of social workers, and the agency, was coloured with a degree of suspicion. The child went to great efforts to convince everyone that she was just like them, and refused to acknowledge that she was in care. However in doing so, she had to contend with the presence of social workers in front of friends. She got very angry when asked by her friends if the visitor was a social worker. The difficulty for children in care can be seen as they attempt to preserve a sense of privacy.

Nora: I don't really want anybody to know because I am living beside a lot of friends, so I call them Mammy and Daddy . . .

Valerie: So your friends around you . . . do your friends see them as your family ?

Nora: Yeah . . . well everybody thinks I am fostered but I'm not . . . though I am fostered but I don't want them to know and just say I'm not, so I just tell them to go and mind their own business . . . and they just say "fine, be like tha(t)" . . . and then they say "but why are the social workers hanging around?"

BARRIERS TO CHILDREN'S SUPPORT

Children's inability to trust social workers was a central theme, especially in situations where there was a level of conflict between the birth parents and the agency. The children's need for someone to help them get a greater understanding of the purpose, reasons and plan for the placement emerged in the research. This highlights the need for the support role for the children to be seen as a positive one. To be successful in working with children in relative care, the agency has to strive to provide an open, respectful service that accommodates difference, is geared towards meeting the different participants needs, and is aimed at building bridges with the different participants. This has implications for all the adult participants of the networks. Children have to be more involved in the process to prevent them feeling they cannot ask the questions. This is particularly highlighted by this ten-year old child:

Deirdre: Well I have a lot of questions, but I just don't ask anyone because no one knows the answer.

Valerie: Is it that you are afraid that people don't know the answers or you are afraid that they will get upset?

Deirdre: Well my mum would probably get upset.

The child then said that she would like to ask the questions but she did not want to talk to social workers. This was explained by the following comment:

> Well mum said here to day that she's raging with the social
> workers. In coming to see us, all they're doing is messing
> up our lives.

The child was unlikely to be able to avail of social work support services in this context. This highlights the difficulty of providing a support service in the same context in which the protection needs of the child and the agency responsibility to supervise placements are connected.

The main concerns of children in the study about the issue of support were the role of social workers in providing material supports, mediating conflicts between family members, or helping them make sense of part of the situation concerning care. The children showed various levels of understanding of the support role. This generally reflected the family's view of the agency. The children's conversations reinforced the importance of the permission granted, or encouragement given, by parents and relatives to children to develop a relationship with the social worker. The study also showed how children strive to minimise the difference from their peers in their living arrangements. The presence of social workers in their lives can draw unwelcome attention in front of peers, if it draws attention to the contact with the agency, and highlights their difference to friends. Also, the children did not see the relevance of contact with the agency as, in their view, they are in a permanent home with relatives and want "to just get on with their lives".

The type of support work conducted by the social workers varied with the children in the networks. Further research is needed to examine if the current systems of prioritising work in agencies disadvantages children in relative care. The effect of beliefs such as respect for family privacy, that children are better placed with their own relatives, and the reluctance to push the need for therapeutic work, if the relatives or birth parents are obstructive, need to be explored further.

CHILDREN'S CONTACT/ACCESS WITH THEIR PARENTS AND SIBLINGS

Access is the term used to describe arrangements made for children in the care system to have contact with their birth

families, and is the "symbolic representation of the child's relationships with two sets of parents" (Lindsey, 1996, p. 49). Under
Section 37 of the Irish Child Care Act, 1991, the health board is
required:

> . . . to facilitate reasonable access to the child by his par-
> ents, and persons acting in loco parentis, or any other per-
> son who, in the opinion of the board, has a *bone fide* interest
> in the child and such access may include allowing the child
> to reside temporarily with any such person.

Access arrangements in relative care have not been examined
in detail. Studies conducted by Thornton (1987), Iglehart (1994)
LeProhn (1994) and Johnson (1995) point to the easier access
arrangements when the child is in the relative home. The two
major differences between relative and foster care access are
connected with ease of access and its organisation within the
family. In relative care, children see their parents more frequently. In Berrick's study, one-fifth of the children saw their
parents four times a month while virtually no foster children had
this level of contact (1994, p. 51). The difference regarding more
frequent access in relative care is further captured by Johnson
where he shows that relatives tried desperately hard to encourage access. As a result, the children see their parents very often,
or else the relatives "have shut the door on the relationship" as a
result of fraught relationships and enduring difficulties over time
(1995, p. 118). This demonstration of relatives' readiness to shut
out the parental relationship challenges a certain belief among
social workers that relatives fail to exert adequate controls over
access arrangements and, as a result, may put children at risk.
Previous to Johnson's study, even though there was no evidence
to support this belief, apart from individual stories, yet the belief
remained (Task Force, 1990).

The second difference surrounding access is the relatives'
view that access is something they are responsible for organ-
ising. This further challenges the social work position, as in
foster care access is generally organised by the social worker.
Johnson (1995) captured the impact of the difference regarding
responsibility for access when he highlighted the climate of

mistrust that may emerge arising from the restrictions placed on relative carers by agencies.

While the studies of relative care and access are limited, practitioners are influenced by theoretical and research developments in the broad area of child care concerning access, which are summarised briefly below. The shift in child care philosophy, with its emphasis on partnership, continuity and identity, has propelled developments in access. In an indirect way, it may be argued that the renewed emphasis of the importance of birth family has, in part, also contributed to the emergence and increased use of relative care as a placement option in the 1990s. The following study findings have affected and influenced social work practice in terms of access/contact. Access is crucial for the development of the child's concept of self-identity and emotional development (Fanshel and Shinn, 1978; Milham et al., 1986). Greater stability is evident, resulting in less breakdown of placements when access is maintained with the family (Berridge and Cleaver, 1987). There are many routes to permanence (Triseliotis, 1989; Thoburn, 1994) and children can maintain a number of significant parental figures in a complementary rather than a competitive way (Lindsey, 1996). Regular access is the best indictor that a child will be reunified with their family (Millham et al., 1986; Bullock et al., 1993; Fanshel, Finch and Grundy, 1992). Difficulty of access was the main reason for not maintaining contact, especially in permanent placements (Rowe et al., 1984). Parental contact over time tends to wither, largely as a result of implicit barriers to access (Department of Health and Social Security, 1985). Ninety per cent of children in Bullock et al.'s 1993 study, and 79.9 per cent of Irish children leaving the care system, return to their families and communities (Department of Health, 1992). The return home will be easier and less fraught if the distance from familial relationships has not been too great.

Thoburn, however, points to the discrepancy between the research findings and practice when she states that:

> . . . despite evidence about the value of continued contact for the majority of children, social workers and systems erect unnecessary barriers to contact, and that links be-

tween children in care and members of their birth families quickly wither away (1988, p. 15).

Barriers to access are attributed to confusion over purpose, scarcity of resources, attitudes, social work practice, patterns of decision-making, and placements situated at a distance from the child's home and community (Argent, 1996; Lindsey, 1996).

CHILDREN'S VIEWS OF CONTACT

No study to date has included children's views of access, and yet the children in this research were more comfortable with discussing contact than any other topic introduced to them. Their stories reinforced the importance of frequent contact with their families, both parents and siblings. The optimum contact arrangement, where it was a positive experience, had little restrictions placed on the children, and they felt they were more generally in control of the situation. Satisfactory access arrangement was connected with a general co-operative relationship between all participants in the network. Other children's accounts of access pointed to the importance of maintaining contact. They also identified how the frequency of contact, deemed adequate by adults, may result in children feeling isolated from their family, particularly their siblings. The children saw relatives encouraging contact, more so than regular foster parents, though this would have to be verified in greater detail before a definite conclusion could be drawn. The children's perception of greater ease in relative care may also be connected with feeling a more integrated sense of self and belonging, arising out of their placement within the extended family. Difficulties were evident in the children's stories in two networks. Key issues in these placements were the disappointment experienced by the children at repeatedly failed access, and the pain of the child who could no longer sustain the level of hostility amongst the adults in the network.

The children's stories raise particular questions for the practice implications in stopping or preventing access, the frequency with which it is organised, the assumptions that exist in the absence of research, and the applicability of the model of access used in regular foster care for relative care.

CHILDREN'S VIEWS OF THEIR FUTURE

With the exception of one child, all the children in the research spoke of wishing they could live with their own parents. However, they also showed how they had come to terms with the fact that this was unlikely to happen. This did not take away the hope that the circumstances which led them to be in care would change, as illustrated through the comments below:

> *Valerie*: If you had a magic wand what would you like to say to your mother?
>
> *Mark*: Nothing . . . just to stop drinking.
>
> *Valerie*: And what about you, Tony?
>
> *Tony*: Make her stop drinking and make her back to normal and make our life okay and that we can go back and live with her again.
>
> *Valerie*: What about you Eilis?
>
> *Eilis*: Just to get her act together.

All the children saw their future with their relatives, until they were old enough to leave. On being old enough to leave, they saw a number of different paths. One child saw herself returning home with the hope that:

> *Nora*: I might be able to help her. When I am 19 or 20 I might move in with her.

Part of another child's motivation for wishing to move on from her relatives was to give her aunt more space to be with her own family:

> *Eilis*: Well when I am older if I get a job at 16 years or so, maybe I will be putting money into the bank until I reach the age when I can move away on my own. I would do it, and then I could give the house more to Paula and if I was out of there she would have more time with her own family.

The feeling of being a burden on the relatives was not a dominant theme in the children's stories, but perhaps this girl, as the eldest of a large sibling group, carried a greater sense of burden and responsibility. Another child spoke of her desire to buy her own house when she was 21. Part of the articulation of the future included a wish for an end to the conflict. One spoke of moving to England to get away from the fighting. The impact of the conflict is evident in the comments below, and though the children hope for a solution, they are nonetheless reconciled to the likelihood of this not occurring:

Elsa: They will never get better (i.e. birth parents).

Valerie: Do you think that they will never get better?

Elsa: I do.

Valerie: What would have to happen for them to get better do you think?

Elsa: It would be good news if they got better.

Valerie: Who would it be good news for?

Elsa: Me, Cath and Brendan (relatives) and also good news for my nanny and all the relations.

The one child who wanted to go home more than anything saw the adults' inability to sort out their difficulties as the major stumbling block, and advocated an end to the fighting as illustrated below:

Valerie: So what has to happen for you all to get back together again?

Deirdre: Well sort out their arguments and fights and clear everything up, parents and social workers. All the adults, they should clear every thing up and should not let children know what is going on. The less you know the better. I know things I should not know.

The children shared a realisation that, if returning home to their parents was not a reality, they would remain living with their relatives until they were grown up. This reflects a sense of their security. Those who had previous care experience said they knew the relatives wanted them because "they were family". The extent that children felt that their relatives would have had an easier life if they had not been there was a disturbing part of their stories. This was particularly an issue for children placed with siblings, where the additional work for the relatives was perhaps most obvious. This issue was also raised earlier in considering children's view of support. Its re-occurrence has implications for future services provided to children in relative care.

CONCLUSION

In this chapter, a view of relative foster care was presented which drew on children's views of the different stages of the process of care, decision-making, assessment practices, support, contact and future planning. This was set in the context of a biographical profile of the children and their families, and the children's care career. Relative care undoubtedly meets the needs of many children who cannot live with their own parents. The children spoke frankly in this research about the advantages, and while no serious protection concerns were noted, the children would prefer to live at home, would prefer adults to take more control and let them get on with "an ordinary life".

In concluding this chapter I wish to celebrate the resilience of the children who participated in this research. I also want to draw attention to some general considerations. The views expressed, about the different stages of development of relative care networks, raise serious challenges to agency policy and to social work practice. The legislation now requires that children's views are taken into account in decision-making. Relative care, if operated properly, will not be an easy (or a cheap) care option. If it is allocated a lower priority in the agency's workload, or used primarily because of perceived budgetary savings, or as a response to the shortage of other alternative care options, and good practice is not developed, then unfortunate results can be predicted for the children involved.

However, by considering the prospective benefits for the children and families and by analysing the practical, ideological, economic and social forces that both militate against and support relative care, an effective child-centred care option may be successfully developed for many children. Willingness, commitment and vision are required to embrace "this age-old tradition and new departure" in a way that is advantageous to all.

References

Aldgate, J. and Hawley, D. (1986), *Recollections of Disruption-A Study of Foster Care Breakdown*, London: National Foster Care Association.

Argent, H. (1996), *See You Soon: Contact with Children Looked After by Local Authorities*, London: BAAF.

Berrick, J.D. and Barth, R.P. (1994), "Research on Kinship Care: What Do We Know?, Where Do We Go?" *Social Service Review*, 16, 1-5.

Berrick, J.D., Barth, R.P. and Needell, B. (1994), "A Comparison of Kinship Foster Homes and Foster Family Homes — Implications for Kinship Foster-Care as Family Preservation", *Children and Youth Services Review*, 16, 33-63.

Berridge, D. and Cleaver, H. (1987), *Foster Home Breakdown*, Oxford: Basil Blackwell.

Bullock, R.; Little, M. and Milham, S. (1993), *Going Home: The Return of Children Separated from their Families*, Dartmouth: Dartmouth Social Research Unit.

Byrne, N. O.R. (1995), "Diamond Absolutes, A Daughter's Response to her Mother's Abortion", *Journal of Systemic Consultation and Management*, 255-277.

Child Care Act, The (1991), Dublin: Stationary Office.

Child Welfare League of America (1991), *A Blueprint for Fostering Infants, Children and Youth in the 1990s*, Washington DC: Child Welfare League of America.

Colton, M.J. (1989), *Dimensions of Substitute Child Care*, Gower: Aldershot.

Conway, E. (1993), "Evaluation of Fostering Campaign: October 1991", unpublished internal document, Dublin: Eastern Health Board.

Department of Health (1990), *Survey of Children in the Care of the Health Boards in 1988: Vol. 1*, Dublin: Stationary Office.

Department of Health (1992), *Survey of Children in the Care of the Health Boards*, Dublin: Stationary Office.

Department of Health (1995), *The Children's Act 1989: Residence Order Study: A Study of the Experiences of Local Authorities of Public Law Residence Orders*, London: Social Service Inspectorate.

Department of Health (1995a), Child Care Regulations (Placement of Children with Relatives) S.I. No. 130 of 1995, Dublin: Stationery Office.

Department of Health (1999), *Health Statistics 1999, Dublin: Information Management Unit*, Department of Health and Children

Department of Health and Social Security (1985), *Social Work Decisions in Child Care*, London: HMSO.

Dubowitz, H. (1994), "Suggestions for Future Research, Special Issue: A Research Agenda for Child Welfare", *Child Welfare*, 73, 553-564.

Dubowitz, H., Feigelman, S. and Zuvarim, S. (1993), "A Profile of Kinship Care", *Child Welfare*, 72, 153-169.

Dubowitz, H., Feigelman, S., Harrington, D., Starr, R., Zuvarim, S. and Sawyer, R. (1994), "Children in Kinship Care: How Do They Fare?" *Social Service Review*, 1, 85-106.

Fanshel, D. and Shinn, E. (1978), *Children in Foster Care: A Longitudinal Study*, New York: Columbia University Press.

Fanshel, D. Finch, S, and Grundy, J. (1992), *Foster Children in a Life Course Perspective*, New York: Columbia University Press.

Fein, E., Maluccio, A., Hamilton, J., Ward, D. (1983), "After Foster Care: Outcomes of Permanence Planning for Children". *Child Welfare*. 6, 485-556.

Gilligan, R. (1990), *Foster Care for Children in Ireland: Issues and challenges for the 1990s*. Occasional paper, No 2, Dublin: University of Dublin, Trinity College.

Gilligan, R. (1991), *Irish Child Care Services*, Dublin: IPA.

Gleeson, J.P. and Craig, L.C. (1994), "Kinship Care in Child Welfare: An Analysis of States Policies", *Social Service Review*, 16, 7-31.

Gleeson, J.P. (1996), "Kinship Care in Child Welfare Service: the Policy Debate in an Era of Reform", *Child Welfare* 75, 419-449.

Hegar, R. and Scannapieco, M. (1995), "From Family Duty to Family Foster Care: The Evolution of Kinship Care", *Child Welfare*, 64, 200-216.

Iglehart, A. (1994), "Kinship Foster Care: Placement, Service and Outcome Issues", *Social Service Review*, 16, 107-122.

Johnson (1995), "Traditions in a New Time: Stories of Grandmothers", Ph.D., Columbia University, New York.

Kelly, G. and Gilligan, R. (2000), *Issues in Foster Care, Policy, Practice and Research*, London: Jessica Kingsley.

Kusserow, R. (1992), *Using Relatives for Foster Care*. Washington DC., US Department. of Health and Human Services, Office of the Inspector General, OEI.16-90--2391.

LeProhn, N. (1994), "The Role of the Kinship Foster Parent: A Comparison of the Role Conceptions of Relative and Non Relative Foster Parents", *Social Service Review*, 16, 65-84.

Lindsey, C. (1996), "Systemic and Developmental Aspects of Contact", in Argent, H. *See You Soon: Contact with Children Looked after by Local Authorities*, London: BAFF

Link, M.K. (1996), "Permanancy Outcomes in Kinship Care: A Study of Children Placed in Kinship Care in Erie County, New York", *Child Welfare* 75, 509-529.

McCarthy, I. and Byrne, N. (1995), "A Spell in the Fifth Province: It's between Meself, Herself, Yerself and Your Two Imaginary Friends", in Friedman, S. (ed) *The Reflecting Team in Action*, New York: Guilford.

Millham, S., Bullock, R., Hosie, K. and Haak, M. (1986), *Lost in Care: The Problem of Maintaining Links Between Children and their Families*, Aldershot: Gower.

Mills, C. and Usher, D. (1996), "A Kinship Care Case Management Approach", *Child Welfare*, 75, 600-617.

O'Brien, V. (1996), "Relative Foster Care: An Untapped Placement Alternative for Children in the Care System? A Discussion of the Central Issues". *Journal of Child Centred Practice*. 3, 7-21.

O'Brien, V. (1997a), "Fostering the Family: A New Systemic Approach to Evolving Networks of Relative Care", Ph.D submitted to National University of Ireland.

O'Brien, V. (1997b), "Relative Foster Care — A Family/State Discourse, Feedback", the *Magazine of the Family Therapy Association*, Spring, 7, 16-23.

O'Brien, V. (1999), "Evolving Networks of Relative Care: Some Findings from an Irish Study" in Grieff, R. (ed), *Kinship Care*, Ashgate: Arena

O'Brien, V. (2000), "Relative Care: A Different Type of Foster Care — Implications for Practice" in Kelly, G. and Gilligan, R. *Issues in Foster Care, Policy, Practice and Research*, London: Jessica Kingsley.

O'Higgins, K. (1996), *Disruption, Displacement, Discontinuity: Children in Care and their Families in Ireland*, Dublin: ESRI.

Pinkerton , J. (1994), *In Care at Home, Parenting, the State and Civil Society*, Aldershot: Avebury.

Richardson, V. (1985), *Whose Children? An Analysis of Some Aspects of Child Care Policy in Ireland*, Dublin: Family Studies Unit, UCD.

Rowe, J., Cain, H., Hundelby, M. and Keane, A. (1984), *Long Term Foster Care*, London: Batsford.

Ryburn, M. (1993), "Empowering Practice in Family Placement". Paper delivered at the Eighth International Foster Care Conference, Dublin (July).

Scannapieco, M.& Hegar, R.L. (1995), "Kinship Care: A Comparison of Two Case Management Models", *Child and Adolescent Social Work*, 12, 147-156.

Sellick, C. (1992), *Supporting Foster Parents*, Avebury: Aldershot.

Shaw, M. and Hipgrave, T. (1989), "Young People and their Carers in Specialist Fostering", *Adoption and Fostering*, 13, 11-17.

Takas, M. (1992), "Kinship Care: Developing A Safe and Effective Framework for Protective Placements of Children with Relatives", *Children's Legal Rights Journal*, 13, 12-19.

Task Force on Permanency Planning for Children (1990), *Kinship Care: The Double Edged Dilemma*, Rochester: New York, Inc.

Thoburn, J. (1988), *Child Placement: Principles and Practice*, Aldershot: Gower.

Thoburn, J. (1994), *Child Placement: Principles and Practice*, 2nd Edition, Aldershot: Gower.

Thornton, J. (1987), "An Investigation into the Nature of Kinship Foster Care", unpublished doctoral dissertation, Yeshiva University, New York.

Thornton, J.L. (1991), "Permanency Planning for Children in Kinship Foster Homes", *Child Welfare*, 70, 593-601.

Triseliotis, J. (1989), "Foster Care Outcomes: A Review of key Research Findings", *Adoption and Fostering*, 13, 5-7.

Notes

---

[1] The terms relative care, relative foster care and kinship care are used interchangeably in the literature to refer to this practice. In this chapter the term relative care is used, as it reflects the common language used to describe family relationships in Ireland. Kinship is the term used predominantly in the American context.

[2] The Eastern Health Board was the largest of the eight Health Boards in Ireland. The population served by the EHB at the time of the research was 1,245,225, which represented 35 per cent of the country's population. Since the completion of the research it has been divided into three separate Health Board areas.

[3] The Department of Health and Children took the last snap shot of the total number of children in care on the 31 December 1996. Prior to this, the total number of children in the care system was taken in the 1992 snap shot.

[4] In 1988, 2,614 children were in care (Department of Health, 1990). In 1996, 3,688 children were in care (Department of Health, 1999). This reflects an increase in the care population, a trend which is also identified between 1982 and 1988. The total number of children in care increased by 10 per cent between 1982 and 1988. When a longer view is taken, there is a decrease in the number of children in care. In 1968 there were 4,834 in public care (Gilligan, 1991: 185).

[5] These figures are taken from agency records for a range of different dates. Accurate counts of total number of children in care were not readily available on a single date to show the total placement of children in the care system. The total care population, between birth and age eighteen years, in the agency in 1996 was 1,476 children.

[6] Caution is needed in drawing conclusions from outcome studies to date, as the studies tend to be predominantly American, and lack highly significant representative samples and adequate control groups.

Chapter 5

Children's Experiences in After-School Care

Eilis Hennessy[1]

INTRODUCTION

Over the course of the last two decades, the topic of day care in Ireland has moved from being of specialist concern to a minority of parents and experts in child development to a subject of national debate, legislation and controversy. This increased interest reflects the growing usage of non-parental day care for children of all ages. For example, a recent report by the ESRI (Williams and Collins, 1998) estimated that 9.6 per cent of children between the ages of six and twelve are cared for by someone other than their parents in the hours immediately after school each day. This amounts to over 46,000 children. The estimates for the numbers of younger children in day care are even greater. Thus, one survey by Hennessy and Hayes (1997) found that 76 per cent of children had spent some part of their pre-school years in regular non-parental day care. Clearly, day care is now part of the lives of very large numbers of pre-school and school-age children in Ireland.

Public debate has focused on working parents' needs for affordable day care and the importance of ensuring that the day care environment is a safe and stimulating one for children. Contributions to the debate have typically come from parents, day care providers, the media, day care professions and employers. On the whole, the views of children who spend time in day care have not been sought. This is despite the fact that Ireland has ratified the United Nations Convention on the Rights of the Child which stipulates that children should be consulted about matters which affect their lives. The potential value of consulting children is highlighted in a growing body of research evidence which suggests that children can give useful and reliable information about their experiences as service users (Hennessy, 1999).

This chapter is based on some of the findings of a research project that aimed to understand children's perspectives on after-school care. Using a combination of open-ended questions and Likert-type ratings, children were asked about the activities and facilities available to them and about their enjoyment of those activities. Background information on parental education, occupation and weekly hours in after-school care were gathered from questionnaires completed by parents. Because the children attended a range of different types of after-school care it is possible to compare the experiences of the children in the different settings. Consulting children directly about their experiences can help to give legitimacy to their points of view and to emphasise that their views may differ from those of the adults around them.

CHANGING PATTERNS OF MATERNAL EMPLOYMENT

In Ireland over the last 20 years, in line with most other European Union countries, maternal participation in the labour force has increased substantially. In the early 1980s the Report of the Working Party on Child Care Facilities for Working Parents (1983) identified a trend of increasing participation of married women in the labour force which, at the time, stood at less than 17 per cent. Estimates of maternal employment from that time were far lower. For example, a survey by Fine-Davis (1983) estimated that just 5 per cent of all women on the electoral register, with at least one child under the age of 15, were employed. In the following decade the figures increased substantially. By 1990, McKenna reported that 23 per cent of mothers with a child under the age of nine were working. In the same year, figures from the European Commission Childcare Network (1990) indicated that Ireland had one of the fastest increasing rates of maternal employment in the EU. Figures from the most recent report on day care facilities suggest that about 29 per cent of mothers with a child under the age of nine are in the labour force (Partnership 2000 Expert Working Group on Childcare, 1999).

While the figures on maternal employment show a clear upward trend, there is not a direct correspondence between maternal employment and the use of day care. Parents may work at different times of the day and may be able to share the care of their children between them, or fathers may stay at home to care for children while mothers work. Unfortunately, however, statistics are not collected from the perspective of children's lives and changes in patterns of parental employment are one of the few means available for estimating changes in the patterns of day care use. However, there is also evidence from other sources to suggest that children are now more likely to spend time in day care. For example, two expert working groups have been established in the last ten years to report on the provision of facilities for the children of working parents (Working Group on Childcare Facilities for Working Parents established in 1990 and the Partnership 2000 Expert Working Group on Childcare established in 1997). These groups were established in response to a widely held view that the absence of affordable day care was preventing many parents, and particularly mothers, from entering or returning to the labour force. National government has also identified the need for the provision of more day care places for children and, in response, has provided funding for various pilot projects including the Pilot Childcare Initiative (1994-1997) and the Equal Opportunities Childcare Programme.

Taken in combination, the figures on maternal employment and government initiatives suggest that family working practices and day care patterns have changed significantly in the last 20 years. Children of all ages in Ireland now seem to be more likely to spend part of each day in day care than they were 20 years ago.

CONSULTING CHILDREN

Although much of the debate on day care has focused on the needs of working parents, the fact that day care must meet children's needs has been acknowledged in all the major reports on day care published in Ireland to date. For example, the report of the Working Party on Child Care Facilities for Working Parents (1983) recommended that day care provisions should be of the highest possible standards "in order to promote the best interests of children" (3.10, p. 26). The report of the Working Group on Childcare Facilities for Working Parents (1994) identified children's needs as "care, safety and protection" and "an appropriate social, educational and psychological environment." (p. 8). The need for protection and an appropriate environment is also acknowledged in the Child Care (Pre-School Services) Regulations, (Department of Health, 1996) which states that:

> A person carrying on a pre-school service shall ensure that every pre-school child attending the service has suitable means of expression and development through the use of books, toys, games and other play materials, having regard to his or her age and development (Part II, para 4).

While children's needs have been identified by the authors of reports and legislation, Lynch (1998) argues that this approach is largely based on a caretaking ideology and that Ireland has done little to empower children themselves. Instead, children's needs have been discussed by parents or experts such as day care workers, service providers, child psychologists or other professionals working with them. More recently, the report of the Partnership 2000 Expert Working Group on Childcare (1999) for the first time identified the *rights* as well as the needs of each child as "the first and primary consideration in the delivery of childcare" (p. 44). Identifying children's rights is usually based within the framework of the United Nation Convention on the Rights of the Child that upholds 42 articles relating to children's rights. While many of these articles are closely linked to ensuring that children's basic needs are met, the convention goes further by upholding children's rights to be heard and to have a say in matters affecting their lives. For example, Article 13 upholds children's rights to freedom of expression. Article 12 upholds the rights of all children to be consulted about their lives in a way that is appropriate to their age and understanding.

To date there has been little emphasis in the debate on day care in Ireland on understanding children's views of their experiences or involving children in day care organisation. Other European countries have already enshrined children's rights within their day care legislation. For example, in Denmark general principles for the operation of all day care centres were laid down by the Ministry of Social Affairs which state that children should be included in the planning and execution of activities in day care, according to their age and maturity (Langsted, 1994).

Although some might argue that children's views are already expressed through their parents' decisions and choices, research from other services for children suggests that parents' and children's views on services do not always coincide. For example, Lewis et al. (1988) investigated parents' and children's perceptions of hospital ward rounds. Parents rated the bedside rounds as moderately upsetting for their children whereas the children's responses indicated that they did not find the rounds upsetting. Kvist et al. (1991) found that parents' reports of emotional closeness to their sick children was far greater than the corresponding reports from the children. Although these findings are not drawn from day care research, they indicate that parents' and children's views may diverge and they emphasise the importance of obtaining both points of view.

In addition to the fact that parents' and children's views on emotional responses are not always in agreement there is the possibility that, in evaluating services, the two groups operate within different time frames. Parents' views on what constitutes "good" or appropriate day care may be based on some long-term outcome such as improvement in the child's social or language skills. For example, a recent survey of Irish parents (Hennessy and Delaney, 1999) found that parents reported that they gave highest priority to items relating to children's lan-

guage and reasoning skills when choosing group-based services for preschool children. Children may be more likely to
value immediate enjoyment such as having particular toys to
play with or being with friends. Such differences can only be
investigated and understood if the views of children are sought
independently from the views of their parents.

Another important reason for consulting children about day
care is that they have more information about the caregivers
and the available activities in individual settings than their parents or other outside observers. Veldman and Peck (1963) argued strongly that this expertise was a valuable resource when
evaluating student teachers. They suggested that pupils have a
unique insight into their teachers' ability to react to different
problems and to attempt varied tasks and deal with different
individuals. To ignore children's views, therefore, is to ignore a
wealth of valuable information not available from any other
source.

Davie and Galloway (1996) emphasise the importance of
consulting children because of the fact that it conveys to them
that they are listened to with respect. Although everyone likes
to believe that their views are listened to, it may be particularly
important for children, who have fewer choices in their lives
than adults. Thus, it is likely to be parents and not children who
make the original decisions about the use of day care. Listening
to children's views may, therefore, help to redress the balance.

DIFFICULTIES INVOLVED IN CONSULTING CHILDREN

Although there are many good reasons for consulting children
there are also some potential difficulties. For example, there
may be ethical considerations around children's consent to
participate (Evans and Fuller, 1996) and special attention needs
to be paid to ensuring that children are aware that they can refuse to give their opinions and that they will not suffer any adverse consequences as a result of their refusal (Hill, 1998). It is
also important to ensure that children are clear about the purpose of the questions that they are asked and that they do not
develop false expectations about the outcome of the consultation process (Davie and Galloway, 1996). Children need to be

reassured that the answers they give will be treated in confidence and this should be explained to them in language that is developmentally appropriate. The researcher also needs to be alert to the possibility that children will try to give answers that they think he or she wants to hear.

A further series of concerns about consulting children rests on limitations in their cognitive abilities. For example, some authors have drawn attention to the fact that children have limited attention and memory skills (Lewis, 1992). These limitations require that the questions are developmentally appropriate and that the questioning process does not go on beyond any child's attention span. Others have suggested that children may be suggestible, likely to omit detail in description and susceptible to producing incorrect information under pressure (Hall, 1996). Russell (1996) has also highlighted the difficulties involved in consulting children with disabilities and special needs who may have communication problems.

Despite these potential difficulties, a growing body of evidence indicates that by listening to children we can gain a valuable insight into their perspectives on matters affecting their lives. Listening to children not only gives them equality of respect with other groups in society but also provides valuable information that could not be obtained from any other source.

CHILDREN'S VIEWS ON DAY CARE

A number of studies have already been published on children's views of their day care experiences. Most of these studies were conducted in the United States. For example, Driscoll et al. (1990) devised a questionnaire for four- and five-year-olds in pre-school which asked about their teachers and aspects of the pre-school environment (e.g. noise level, availability of materials). Armstrong and Sugawara (1989) focused on children's emotional reactions to their experiences and their findings indicated that the great majority of children had positive feelings about day care. Austin et al. (1996) reported that children's home circumstances were related to their evaluation of day care, such that children with more stressful life circumstances were more likely to provide a negative evaluation of day care.

However, the children in Austin et al.'s (1996) study were all under six-years-old and research with older children indicates that children's evaluations are closely related to their experiences in after-school care. For example, Rosenthal and Vandell (1996) found that children (9 to 12 years) were less likely to be positive about after-school care if the group size was larger and if there were a lot of negative interactions with the staff. Children were more likely to be positive if there was a wide range of activities available to them.

While previous studies indicate that it is possible to gather interesting and useful data from children about their experiences in day care and after-school care, the data that were collected are limited in a number of ways. For example, most of the studies focused almost exclusively on children's experiences in group care settings, thus excluding the experiences of children looked after by childminders or in the homes of relatives. Research on patterns of day care use in Ireland suggests that the latter types are much more common forms of care than group-based settings such as crèches or after-school groups (Hennessy and Hayes, 1997; Williams and Collins, 1998). Previous studies have also tended to gather data from pre-school children and children towards the upper end of primary school, providing little information on children in their first years of primary school. The present study attempts to overcome some of these limitations and to understand the experiences of children in after-school settings in Ireland.

THE PRESENT STUDY

The research findings presented in this chapter are part of a study looking at children's perceptions of their experiences in different types of after-school care in the Dublin area. Three of the study's aims will be addressed:

- To document children's perceptions of activities available to them after school in crèches, childminders' homes and relatives' homes

- To document children's enjoyment of their after-school care experiences

- To document children's reports of their emotional reactions to after-school care experiences.

The 108 children (49 boys, 59 girls) who took part were attending 11 schools in the Dublin area which had been selected. In each school, letters were sent home to the parents of children in senior infants, first class and second class giving information about the study and requesting permission to interview their child if they were currently attending after-school care. Parents were also asked to provide information about their education and current employment status as well as details of their child's current after-school care arrangements. Permission was given for 6.3 per cent of children to take part in the research and no information is available on whether the parents of the remaining children refused permission or were not using after-school care. Based on Williams and Collins' (1998) research, we know that 9.6 per cent of children in the 6 to 12-year age group are likely to have been attending after-school care. Although a small number of children in the study fall outside this age range, it can serve as a rough estimate of the numbers eligible. This suggests that our response rate was approximately 66 per cent of eligible children.

The children who took part were between 5 years and 8 years, 9 months old with an average age of 6 years, 7 months. Ten children who were looked after by nannies or au pairs in their own homes are excluded from the results presented here. The decision to exclude this group was based, primarily, on the small number of children availing of this type of care arrangement. A second reason for their exclusion from the current analysis is based on the fact that the focus of much of the questionnaire (e.g. description of available activities) would have a different meaning for children who were being cared for in their own home, albeit by someone other than their parents. A breakdown of numbers of children in the other types of after-school arrangements is given in Table 5.1. These figures may be compared with Williams and Collins' (1998) findings which indicate that approximately 30 per cent of children who attend after-school care are in childminders' homes, a further 30 per cent in the homes of relatives, 39 per cent in their own home with a caregiver and just 1 per cent in some form of group care.

Table 5.1: Details of After-School Care Arrangements

Type of Child Care	Number of Children	Mean Hours per Week in Child Care (Sd)
Childminder	31	10.9 (6.9)
Relative	30	11.0 (7.3)
Crèche	37	13.1 (8.0)

A researcher visited each school and interviewed children individually using an interview protocol that included open-ended questions, questions that could be answered dichotomously and some questions that were answered with three- or four-point Likert rating scales.[1] Each interview lasted about 12 minutes and all the interviews were tape recorded and subsequently transcribed. A previous study using the same interview schedule (Hennessy, 1998) indicated that children's reports were consistent over a two-week time period.

Available Activities

Table 5.2 presents a breakdown of the activities available to children in each type of after-school setting. Although the overall figures for each activity indicate that the majority of children have access to all activities, there were also considerable variations in the availability of activities between the types of after-school setting and many of these differences were significant when tested with a chi-square test.

Children looked after by relatives were significantly less likely to have other children to play with than children looked after by childminders or in crèches ($\chi^2 = 23.7$, df=2, p<.01). Children in crèches and in the care of relatives were less likely to be able to play outside than were children cared for by childminders ($\chi^2 = 6.4$, df=2, p<.05). Children who were looked after by childminders were less likely to have access to books that they liked than were children who attended crèches or who

---

[1] A copy of the interview schedule is available from the author on request.

went to the homes of relatives ($\chi^2 = 11.9$, df=2, p<.01). Finally, children who went to crèches after school were significantly less likely to have a television to watch than were children who were looked after by a relative or childminder ($\chi^2 = 21.2$, df=2, p<.01).

Table 5.2: Activities Available in Each Type of Care Setting

Type of Care	Other Children to Play with	Toys	Outside Area to Play	Books	TV
Childminder	31 (100%)	25 (81%)	31 (100%)	16 (52%)	30 (97%)
Relative	18 (60%)	25 (87%)	25 (83%)	22 (73%)	30 (100%)
Crèche	35 (95%)	33 (89%)	30 (81%)	33 (89%)	24 (65%)
Overall	84 (86%)	84 (86%)	86 (88%)	71 (72%)	84 (86%)

Percentages have been rounded to the nearest whole number.

Enjoyment of Experiences

A four-point Likert-type rating scale was used to assess children's enjoyment of the activities that they had access to in after-school care. For each activity (e.g. playing outside) children were asked to indicate whether they liked it "a lot", "a little", "not really" or "not at all". The children's responses indicate that almost all children enjoyed the activities "a little" or "a lot" and there were only small differences between the reports of children in the different types of after-school care, none of which were significant. A breakdown of these figures is given in Table 5.3.

Further illustrations of children's enjoyment of their after-school activities are available from children's responses to the open-ended question: "What do you like most about [name of after-school care]?". One seven-year-old girl who was looked after by her grandmother said that she enjoyed most the fact that "there's lots of toys and there's millions of books". Another seven-year-old girl had a more unusual reason for enjoying her grandparents' house:

> Well I go out into the greenhouse and there's this kind of chair and a kind of a blankety thing and I put it down on the ground and I lie down on it and sometimes I have my lunch there. It's really hot, it's nice.

A seven-year-old boy who went to a crèche every day after school said:

> Oh I think I like two things the best, going outside to play. No, I like three. Going outside to play, getting your dinner there . . . and going upstairs to play with all the toys, because upstairs there's good toys.

Table 5.3: Children's Reported Enjoyment of Available Activities

Rating	Activity			
	Toys	*Playing outside*	*Books*	*TV*
"A lot"	50 (59%)	62 (72%)	27 (38%)	55 (65%)
"A little"	29 (34%)	21 (24%)	32 (45%)	27 (32%)
"Not really"	5 (6%)	2 (2%)	9 (13%)	1 (1%)
"Not at all"	1 (1%)	1 (1%)	3 (4%)	1 (1%)

Figures vary across activities because not all children had access to all activities. Percentages have been rounded to the nearest whole number

Emotional Responses to After-School Care

In order to evaluate whether after-school care is a positive or negative experience for children they were asked a series of questions about their emotional reactions to their experiences. The children were asked to indicate how they felt (i) on arrival in the care setting (ii) when they were with the person who looks after them; (iii) when they were with other children in the care setting; and (iv) when they were collected. The children were then asked to indicate whether they felt the emotion "a lot" or "a little" so that all emotions could be rated on a four-point Likert-type scale from "very negative" to "very positive". There were no significant differences between the emotions reported by children in the different care settings and all figures are presented in Table 5.4.

From the figures reported in Table 5.4 it is clear that after-school care is a positive emotional experience for the majority of children in the study.

Table 5.4: *Children's Reported Emotions in Child Care*

Rating	Activity			
	Arriving in Child Care	*With Caregiver*	*With Other Children*	*When Collected*
Very positive	50 (52%)	59 (60%)	55 (66%)	60 (61%)
Slightly positive	37 (38%)	35 (36%)	23 (28%)	33 (34%)
Slightly negative	5 (5%)	2 (2%)	4 (5%)	5 (5%)
Very negative	4 (4%)	2 (2%)	1 (1%)	0

When asked what they most liked about after-school care many of the children made positive emotional responses. A five-year-old girl who was looked after by a childminder said, "I'm all excited because my friend C. is home at the same time as me". Another eight-year-old said, "Well I like my granny and grand-dad a lot". One six-year-old girl was also enthusiastic about the crèche she went to after school: "Well, I like that it's great fun and it's brilliant. And I love the dinner."

DISCUSSION

The present research represents a first look at the experiences of young primary school children in three of the most common types of after-school care arrangement in Ireland. The findings indicate interesting differences between the experiences of children in the different types of care and these differences warrant further consideration. For example, children who were looked after by a relative were the least likely to have someone to play with. Although details of the exact relationship between the child and the caregiver were not sought, it was clear that for the majority of children the relative who cared for them was a grandparent. It is likely that the absence of children to play with may be due to the fact that grandparents do not live in areas with large numbers of young children or that grandparents live some distance from the school so that children do not know other children in the area.

It is more difficult to explain why children looked after by a childminder should be least likely to have access to books. It should be noted, however, that childminders who care for fewer than three preschool children are not subject to the Child Care Act,1991 and therefore have no legal obligation to provide for children's developmental needs. There has been little research on childminders in Ireland so we know little about the background and training of the people providing this service. Childminders may not have given high priority to the provision of books for this age group of children, or may have provided books that were uninteresting to the children.

The fact that children going to crèches were less likely than other children to be able to play outside is surprising given that section 28 of the Child Care (Pre-School) Services Regulations, (Department of Health, 1996) requires child care providers to provide outdoor play facilities. It may be that the children's responses reflected their inability to access such facilities, rather than their absence. Rules in some crèches might prevent access to outdoor facilities during the times when these children normally attend. Because the children in this study were the only source of information on their after-school care setting it is not possible to check the reasons for children's inability to play outside.

Despite reported differences in their experiences, the findings suggest that after-school care is a positive experience for the majority of children in all types of settings. Children's responses to the open-ended questions further emphasised how much they enjoyed their time in after-school care. With any research of this kind it is possible the positive answers about after-school care were due to a bias in the selection of children to interview. Although the researcher interviewed all children whose parents gave permission, it is possible that parents who were concerned about their child's current after-school care arrangement may not have given permission for their children to take part. This possibility cannot be ruled out although the findings are consistent with research in other countries with younger children (Armstrong and Sugawara, 1989). It is also clear from the findings that some children who were not particularly happy with their after-school care arrangement were given permission to take part. This finding is also important because it suggests that children were prepared to tell the researcher if they were not satisfied with their after-school care arrangement.

Another way to judge possible bias in the sample selection is to look at the proportion of children in after-school care who were not permitted to take part in the study. Unfortunately, the majority of parents who did not want their child to take part in the research simply did not return the form so we do not know anything about their patterns of after-school care use. We know, however, that 6.3 per cent of children in the relevant classes in the schools were given permission to take part in the research and the ESRI estimates that about 9.6 per cent of children would have been in after-school care so this represents about 66 per cent of children attending after-school care (Williams and Collins, 1998). This estimate suggests that quite a high proportion of eligible children were interviewed as part of the study implying that the figures may reflect a relatively high level of satisfaction.

Although the present study included a relatively small sample of children, the findings of consistent differences in the experiences of children in different types of after-school care may be useful in guiding parents and caregivers who wish to make after-school care a more enjoyable experience for children. While no attempt was made to compare children's views with those of their parents or other caregivers, the importance of consulting children directly is highlighted by a number of the study's findings. For example, not all children in crèches reported that they had someone to play with despite the group-based structure of the crèche. It is only when children are consulted directly that it is possible to know whether services are meeting their individual needs. Finally, it is hoped that the process of consultation described in this study may encourage those involved in providing after-school care services to talk to the children in their care about their experiences so that the children's views can be taken into account when planning for change. Based on the current study's positive findings about children's emotional reactions and enjoyment of their experiences, they may also find that this is a very rewarding experience for them.

References

Armstrong, J. and Sugawara, A.I. (1989), "Children's perceptions of their day care experiences", *Early Child Development and Care*, 49, 1-15.

Austin, A.M.B., Godfrey, M.K., Larsen, J.M., Lindauer, S.L.K. and Norton, M.C. (1996), "Determinants of children's satisfaction with their child care providers", *Early Child Development and Care*, 115, 19-36.

Child Care Act, 1991, Dublin: Stationery Office.

Davie, R. and Galloway, D. (1996), "The voice of the child in education", in R. Davie, and D. Galloway (eds.) *Listening to Children in Education*, London: David Fulton, pp. 2-14.

Department of Health (1996), *Child Care (Pre-School Services) Regulations, 1996 and Explanatory Guide to Requirements and Procedures for Notification and Inspection*, Dublin: Stationery Office.

Driscoll, A., Peterson, K., Browning, M. and Stevens, D. (1990), "Teacher evaluation in early childhood education: What information can young children provide?" *Child Study Journal*, 20, (2), 67-79.

European Commission Childcare Network (1990) *Childcare in the European Communities 1985-1990*, Brussels: Commission of the European Communities.

Evans, P. and Fuller, M. (1996), "Hello. Who am I speaking to?" Communicating with preschool children in educational research settings, *Early Years*, 17, (1), 17-20.

Fine-Davis, M. (1983), "Mothers' attitudes toward child care and employment: A nation-wide survey", in *Government Working Party on Child Care Facilities for Working Parents, Report to the Minister for Labour*, Dublin: Stationery Office.

Hall, N. (1996), "Eliciting children's views: the contribution of psychologists", in R. Davie, G. Upton, and V. Varma (eds.) *The Voice of the Child. A Handbook for Professionals*, London: Falmer Press, pp. 61-78.

Hennessy, E. (1998), "Consistency in young children's reports of child care experiences", poster presented at the XVth Biennial ISSBD Meeting, Berne, Switzerland, July 1-4.

Hennessy, E. (1999), "Children as service evaluators", *Child Psychology and Psychiatry Review*, 4, 153-161.

Hennessy, E., and Delaney, P. (1999), "Using the Early Childhood Environment Rating Scale in Ireland: Do parents and service providers share its values?" *Early Years*, 19 (2), 12-25.

Hennessy, E. and Hayes, N. (1997), "Early childhood services in Ireland", *International Journal of Early Years Education*, 5, 211-224.

Hill, M. (1998), "Ethical issues in qualitative methodology with children", in D. Hogan, and R. Gilligan (eds.) *Researching Children's Experiences: Qualitative Approaches,* Dublin: The Children's Research Centre, Trinity College, pp. 11-22.

Kvist, S. B. M., Rajantie, J., Kvist, M., and Siimes, M. A. (1991), "Perceptions of problematic events and quality of care among patients and parents after successful therapy of the child's malignant disease", *Social Science and Medicine*, 33, 249-256.

Langsted, O. (1994), "Looking at quality from the child's perspective", in P. Moss and A. Pence (eds.) *Valuing Quality in Early Childhood Services*, London: Paul Chapman.

Lewis, A. (1992), "Group child interviews as a research tool", *British Educational Research Journal*, 18, (4) 413-421.

Lewis, C., Knopf, D., Chastain-Lorber, K., Ablin, A., Zoger, S., Matthay, K., Glasser, M. and Pantell, R. (1988), "Patient, parent, and physician perspectives on pediatric oncology rounds", *Journal of Pediatrics*, 112, 378-384.

Lynch, K. (1998), "The status of children and young persons: Educational and related issues", in S. Healy and B. Reynolds (eds.) *Social Policy in Ireland*, Dublin: Oak Tree Press.

McKenna, A. (1990), *Childcare in Ireland Challenge and Opportunity*, Dublin: Employment Equality Agency.

Partnership 2000 Expert Working Group on Childcare (1999), *National Childcare Strategy*, Dublin: Stationery Office.

Rosenthal, R., and Vandell, D. L. (1996), "Quality of care at school-aged child-care programs: Regulatable features, observed experiences, child perspectives, and parent perspectives", *Child Development*, 67, 2434-2445.

Russell, P. (1996), "Listening to children with disabilities and special educational needs", in R. Davie, G. Upton, and V. Varma (eds.) *The Voice of the Child. A Handbook for Professionals,* London: Falmer Press, pp. 107-119.

Veldman, D.J. and Peck, R. F. (1963), "Student teacher characteristics from the pupils' viewpoint", *Journal of Educational Psychology*, 54, 346-355.

Williams, J. and Collins, C. (1998), "Child-care arrangements in Ireland — A Report to the Commission on the Family June 1997", in *Strengthening Families for Life, Final Report of the Commission on the Family to the Minister for Social, Community and Family Affairs*, Dublin: Stationery Office.

Working Party on Child Care Facilities for Working Parents (1983), *Report to the Minister for Labour*, Dublin: Stationery Office.

Working Group on Child Care Facilities for Working Parents (1994), *Report to the Minister for Equality and Law Reform*, Dublin: Stationery Office.

Notes

[1] The author gratefully acknowledges the assistance of Elizabeth Nixon in collecting data, the President's Research Award, University College Dublin, for part funding, and the many children, parents and schools who took part in the research.

Part 2:

Challenges for Children
and Families

Chapter 6

Children's Exposure to Drug Use: Concerns of Drug-using and Non-drug-using Parents[1]

Diane Hogan and Louise Higgins

INTRODUCTION

Little is known about the social experiences of children whose parents use drugs. This chapter presents findings from an empirical study of children growing up in the care of drug-using parents, which explored the impact on family life, and especially parenting, of parents' opiate dependence.

Traditionally, the social and psychological implications for children of their parents' drug use have received scant attention. In research, attention to children of drug users has dwelled largely on medical rather than social issues, focusing mainly on the prenatal exposure of neonates to illicit substances (Keenan, Dorman, and O'Connor, 1993; O'Connor, Stafford-Johnson, and Kelly, 1988; Ryan et al. 1983), which reflects patterns of international research (Hogan, 1998; Johnson, 1991). At the levels of policy and service provision, illicit drug use has mainly been viewed in Ireland as a problem affecting individual adults, while little attention has been paid to the potential for family members other than the individual drug user to be affected (Hogan and Higgins, 2001; Murphy and Hogan, 1999). In recent years, however, there has been growing awareness in Ireland of the potential for the drug use of individuals to have implications for other family members. The need to consider the implications for the welfare and development of children, in particular, has become evident (Hogan, 1997).

The changing understanding of the social consequences of drug use for family members has emerged in the context of findings from epidemiological research and action by drug treatment agencies. First, epidemiological research indicates that, while most heroin users are male, a significant minority are female. In 1996, for example, 31 per cent of those who received treatment in Dublin were women (Moran, O'Brien and Duff, 1997). Some commentators argue that these figures might under-represent the true numbers of women drug users, and especially those with children, since fear of removal of their children from their custody is a likely obstacle to their take-up of services (Butler and Woods, 1992). These research findings challenge the stereotype of the heroin user as a single male without family roles and responsibilities. Although data are not available on whether drug users, either male or female, have children, there is no reason to believe that they differ from the general population in this respect. Second, drug treatment agencies have played a prominent role in highlighting issues for children. For example, the Ana Liffey Project and the Rialto Community Drug Team, in a series of reports (Ana Liffey Drug Project Annual Reports, 1991, 1994, 1996; Bowden, 1996, 1997) argued for more family inclusive approaches to drug treatment, and particularly for greater support for parenting and for attention to the needs of children. These ideas were, in turn, taken on board by the Eastern Health Board (1997) and were reflected in the First Report of the Ministerial Task Force on Measures to Reduce the Demand for Drugs (Rabitte, 1997). In the late 1990s, in partnership with local drugs task forces, the Eastern Health Board established the first intensive support service for chronic opiate using parents and their children in Community Care Area 5 (Murphy and Hogan, 1999).

The present empirical study was conducted with the aim of creating a better understanding of the experience and support needs of children growing up in households in the care of drug-using parents. This chapter deals specifically with the issue of children's exposure to drug use and drug paraphernalia, and describes the concerns and the parenting practices adopted by drug-using parents to protect their children from adversity in social environments with high levels of drug use. It also describes some of the concerns and practices of non-drug-using parents in relation to children's exposure to drugs in their communities.

THE IRISH HEROIN PROBLEM

The escalating problem of opiate use in Ireland over the last two decades has been well documented (Dean et al., 1985; O'Hare and O'Brien, 1992; O'Higgins, 1996; O'Higgins and Duff, 1997; O'Mahony, 1997). Health Research Board estimates indicate that more than 3,000 individuals are receiving treatment for drug dependence, and that among these, heroin is the primary drug of misuse (O'Hare and O'Brien, 1992; O'Higgins, 1996; O'Higgins and Duff, 1997). Treatment statistics do not, of course, reflect all cases of illicit drug use and the magnitude of the problem is likely to be much greater than they imply. The most recent estimates, based on "capture-recapture" methodology, suggest that there are over 13,000 opiate users in the Dublin area (Comiskey, 1998). Opiate use is a highly context-specific problem in Irish society. It is confined largely, though not exclusively, to the Dublin area (O'Higgins and Duff, 1997). Within Dublin, moreover, the problem is localised further into discrete geographical areas. It is located primarily in the North and South inner city and some suburbs, those areas most profoundly affected by unemployment (Comiskey, 1998; Cullen, 1992, 1994; Dean, Bradshaw, and Lavelle, 1983; McKeown, Fitzgerald and Deegan, 1993; O'Higgins, 1996, O'Higgins and Duff, 1997). Furthermore, visible public drug use and related activities, such as buying and selling, are highly localised into smaller areas such as blocks within flat complexes, and certain streets (McAuliffe and Fahey, 1999).

Information on the number of opiate users who are parents, or on the number of children born to opiate users, has not been routinely gathered in Ireland. The demographic characteristics of this population indicate, however, that heroin users are typically aged between 15 and 35, with the age of first drug use falling annually (Moran et al., 1997; O'Higgins, 1996; O'Higgins and Duff, 1997), an age range that includes the typical child-bearing years.

OPIATE USERS AS PARENTS

While there is a small international literature on parenting by drug users (cf Deren, 1986; Mayes, 1996; and Hogan, 1998, for reviews) it has produced largely inconclusive findings, particularly in terms of children's social development and well-being (Hogan, 1998) and the impact on children of growing up in the care of a drug-using parent remains unclear. Research has tended to rely on correlational designs that link the social problem of drug use with child outcomes such as neglect, sexual abuse and cognitive development. Far less interest has been shown in the everyday lifestyle implications for children of parents' drug-taking behaviours, the relationships between drug-using parents and their children, or the fabric of ordinary daily family life (Colten, 1982; Hogan, 1997). The specific issue of exposure of children to drug use in their homes and communities has been largely overlooked in research.

LIFESTYLE ASSOCIATED WITH DRUG USE

A good deal of research has been conducted on the lifestyle of heroin users (Agar, 1973; Fiddle, 1976; Parker, Bakx and Newcombe, 1988; Pearson; 1987; Taylor, 1993; Zinberg, 1984). This work has led to identification of patterns of daily behaviour among heroin users that suggests that daily life quickly becomes consumed by heroin use once it begins. This body of work focuses overwhelmingly on individual drug users, however, and the implications for children of parental involvement with the daily round of obtaining money for drugs, and procuring and ingesting drugs, have not been explored. Furthermore, most research on the lifestyle of heroin users has focused on men, with few exceptions (Rosenbaum, 1979; Taylor, 1993). Taylor (1993) argues that, while some studies involve women, they typically focus on issues relating to reproduction and care of children, but pay little attention to how drug use by women fits into children's daily lives. In her study of drug-using women in Glasgow, she found that women expected to adopt traditional caring roles toward children in spite of their drug involvement. Rosenbaum (1979), in her study of heroin-using women in the US, also found that child care was highly salient for women drug users, who saw caring for their children as their greatest responsibility. Their involvement with heroin, however, meant that it was difficult for women to "carve out a routine incorporating their children's needs with their own" (p. 437), and those who were successful in doing so had the advantage of receiving a steady and reliable supply of drugs of predictable quality and potency. Such women were not forced to leave the home to seek drugs or allow others to use their homes in exchange for drugs, and were less likely to accidentally overdose on high potency drugs or to experience withdrawal sickness that could hamper their capacity for competent child care.

These studies of women drug users reveal a potential discrepancy between parenting values and goals of drug-using parents on the one hand, and parenting practices on the other. While most aspire towards carrying out everyday child care tasks, and to protecting their children from harm as any non-drug-using mother might, drug dependence can place practical constraints on meeting these goals. Parental drug use *can* operate in a relatively controlled and stable fashion, where risks are low to children of parental unavailability, over-intoxication, illness through withdrawal, and presence of strangers in the home to use drugs. But changing circumstances, some of which are beyond the direct control of the drug-using parent, can rapidly lead to unstable patterns of drug use and lifestyle, which, in turn, can increase the risk to children of receiving inadequate care and protection. The fluid nature of the heroin trade and of individual addiction means that chaos can quickly replace stability in the family life of a heroin user (Rosenbaum, 1979), as can the eviction and homelessness, imprisonment, illness or death of a drug-using partner who previously provided a supply of drugs into the home. The latter, for example, may force parents, especially women, to allow their homes to be used as venues for drug use by others in exchange for drugs (Hogan, 1999). It is critical that the challenges faced by parents who use heroin, both mothers and fathers, in caring for and protecting their children, are identified, if adequate supports are to be put in place to support parents to provide ongoing care for their children. It is also important that positive parenting goals and practices are recognised. In the present study, the steps parents take to buffer their children from adversity were explored.

THE PRESENT STUDY

The present study examines the processes by which children are affected by parental opiate dependence in the context of their day-to-day lives within their families. It investigates the drug-related social experiences of children living in two locations in Dublin, in areas of profound socio-economic disadvantage and high incidence of drug use, focusing mainly on the impact of drug use on parenting processes, on children's exposure to drugs and crime, and on children's academic and social outcomes. The study compares children of drug-using parents to children who are growing up in the same general localities and in similar socio-economic circumstances. This chapter concentrates on the issue of children's exposure to drug use, primarily by exploring parents' perspectives on children's exposure to drugs and the practices they employ to mitigate risk to their children.

The study took place in two sites in the Dublin City area, one in the inner city and the other in a suburban area. Both were areas with high levels of unemployment and both had been recently identified as having among the highest prevalence rates of opiate use in the Dublin area (Comiskey, 1998). While the areas were similar in respect of drug use and socio-economic profile, they differed in other ways in terms of social ecology. Both areas had high levels of public housing, but the inner city areas had more flat complexes in which there were higher levels of visible public drug use.

Sampling Approach

Drug-using parents were contacted through a range of agencies, including drug treatment facilities and a prison. All parents who met the sampling criteria (described below) were personally approached by agency staff and researchers and asked to participate, until the quota of 50 parents had been reached. The matched comparison group was created through a process of randomly selecting children through schools. The children lived in the same geographical areas as children of drug users, and had similar social and economic backgrounds.

Matching was conducted on a group basis, and sampling was stratified on the basis of type of housing (public or private), child sex, child age, and parent sex.

Sample Characteristics

The sample consisted of 100 parents (50 drug-using and 50 non-drug-using) and their target child of school-going age. Drug users were defined as persons who were currently dependent on opiates (heroin, morphine sulphate tablets, and/or methadone) and for whom, by their own report, opiates were the primary drugs of problem use. Non-drug users were defined as persons not known to be dependent on opiates or other illicit substances either currently or at any time during the target child's lifetime. Either a mother or father was interviewed in each family. In the drug user group all parents interviewed were drug users, and some had non-drug-using partners.

In each group the target children were, for most of the year prior to data collection, in the care and control of the parent interviewed. Children were aged 4 to 12 years. The mean age of children of drug users was 8.06 (SD= 2.17), and children of non-drug users 7.91 (SD= 2.21). A total of 52 boys and 48 girls were represented in the study and equal numbers of each sex were represented, with 26 boys and 24 girls in each group.

The average age of drug-using parents was 30.5 (SD = 5.8), and of non-drug users 35 (SD = 6.4). A total of 68 female and 32 male parents participated in the study. In the drug user group, 32 women and 18 men, and in the comparison group 36 women and 14 men, participated. A breakdown of parents' age by sex and group is provided in the table below.

Table 6.1: Parents' Age by Sex and Group

Group	Sex	N	Min. Age	Max. Age	Mean Age	Std. Deviation
Non-drug Users	Male	14	29	46	35.5714	5.7071
	Female	36	24	50	34.7500	6.7544
Drug Users	Male	18	23	48	31.7895	6.0880
	Female	32	21	49	29.7097	5.5869

Education levels were low for each group of parents. The average age of school leaving was identical in the two groups, at 14.8 years. Attainment of educational qualifications was also similarly low in the two groups. In terms of housing, which was used as the main indicator of SES, in each group the majority of families (41, or 82 per cent) lived in public sector housing, while the remaining 9 families in each group (18 per cent) were in private sector housing. The housing history of drug users was more variable that of non-drug users, in that several had experienced evictions and homelessness.

Family Structure

Twice as many of the drug-using parents were single and living alone (32 per cent) compared with non-drug-using parents (16 per cent), suggesting that children of drug users were more likely to be raised in a one-parent household. Among those families with two adults living in the home there were inter-group differences in marital status. Of the 58 per cent of drug-using parents who were living with a partner, 16 per cent were married. In the comparison group, of the 78 per cent living with a partner, 58 per cent were married.

Children of drug users were more likely than children in the comparison group to spend periods of time living outside of the family home, usually with relatives. At the time of interview, 14 (28 per cent) children of drug users were not living with the drug-using parent interviewed, compared with none of the children of non-drug users. The main reasons for separation of children and parents included imprisonment of parents, residential drug treatment and hospitalisation for drug-related illness.

Table 6.2: Marital Status, by Group

Marital Status	Non-Drug Users	Drug Users
Single, living alone	8 (16%)	16 (32%)
Single, living with partner	10 (20%)	21 (42%)
Married, living with partner	29 (58%)	8 (16%)
Separated from spouse	3*(6%)	4 (8%)**
Other		1 (2%)
Total	50	50

* One mother was living alone with her child, one living with a partner, and one with her mother.

** In all cases living alone with children.

Instruments and Analyses

A multi-method, multi-informant approach was adopted for the study as a whole. Drug-using parents were interviewed, a survey was carried out with children's teachers and focus groups were conducted with professionals working with drug users and/or their children. Children were not included directly in the research process, for two reasons. First, it was believed that some children might experience distress if asked about their drug-related family experiences and would require follow-up support following their participation in the research process. Such resources were not available for the present study. Second, at the exploratory stage of the study most parents indicated that they would not be willing to consent to their child's participation, mainly because they had not told their children about their drug use and were concerned that contact with researchers might lead to them finding out. Thus, the importance for many parents of concealing their drug use from their children presented an obstacle to researching children's experiences directly.

This paper concentrates on the findings of semi-structured interviews conducted with parents. The researchers posed all questions orally, taking extensive notes on answers provided. Answers to questions were transcribed verbatim as far as possible. Qualitative analyses were conducted using full text transcriptions of interviews. Coding categories were created on the basis of previous exploratory work and on the answers in the current data set, which gave rise to new categories of responses.

DRUG USE OF PARENTS

The majority of drug-using parents (64 per cent) were receiving methadone treatment at the time of interview. A further 14 per cent were active heroin users, 2 per cent morphine tablet users, and 10 per cent were taking more than one type of opiate. More than three-quarters, however, considered themselves to be regular users of more than one type of opiate substance. Furthermore, most were using non-opiate illicit substances and prescription drugs obtained either legally or illegally, including cannabis, tranquillisers, speed, ecstasy, and LSD. It is also notable that 12 per cent of parents who were non-opiate users indicated that they too had used other illicit substances during this period. Ten per cent had used cannabis, and 2 per cent had used cocaine on at least one occasion.

The main method of heroin use for most drug users was injecting. Almost three-quarters of drug-using parents (74 per cent) had been, or were currently, regular intravenous (IV) heroin users. It was not possible to assess the frequency of injecting, as parents had difficulty recalling how often, on average, they injected. The most common response from parents was that, when actively using heroin, they were likely to have injected three, four or five times per day, but the range extended from once a day to ten times per day. Half of drug-using parents reported sharing needles on at least one occasion.

The duration of children's social exposure to parental drug use varied considerably within the sample. More than half of parents (56 per cent) had begun opiate use more than a year prior to the birth of the target child, 12 per cent began during the first year of the child's life, and 32 per cent did so when children were more than one year old. Duration of parents' involvement with treatment services also varied substantially within the sample, ranging from thirteen years before the birth of some children to eight years after the birth of others. On average, children were two years old when their parents first received treatment for their opiate dependence. Almost all parents had begun treatment programmes on several occasions, suggesting that their opiate use moved in and out of phases of greater and lesser stability over time. Clearly, then, there was considerable heterogeneity within the group of children of drug users, in terms of their parents' drug use and drug treatment histories. Even within individual families, drug patterns tended to be volatile. An additional complicating factor was the drug status of the other parent, who was not interviewed for the study. In 33 families (66 per cent) in the drug-using group the parents reported that their partner was also a drug user, and of these 28 were opiate users. In 11 cases, drug-using parents interviewed reported that they were living with a drug-using partner, indicating that 22 per cent of children in the drug-using sample were living in a household where both adult carers were dependent on opiates. In addition, in 13 families there was another (non-parental) drug user living in the home. Furthermore, these data only reflect current living circumstances. No information is available on children's previous experiences of living with drug users. It should also be noted that there was a history of heroin use in more than half of the families in the comparison group (26, or 52 per cent). In 17 families (34 per cent) the drug user was in the immediate family, that is, the child's aunt or uncle. In the next section we explore the nature of children's exposure to drug taking and equipment in the family home.

CHILDREN'S EXPOSURE TO DRUGS IN THE HOME

Most children of drug users had *not* been exposed directly to their parents' drug-related activities, but a sizeable minority had seen their parents taking drugs, according to their parents' reports. Forty per cent of children of drug users had seen at least one parent using heroin in their home, and in 16 of these cases (32 per cent of the sample) children saw their parent injecting themselves with heroin, while in four cases (8 per cent) children saw their parent smoking heroin. The comparison group was purposefully comprised of parents who had not used opiates during the lifetime of the child. While 12 per cent of parents in this group had used non-opiate illicit substances in the previous year, none of the target children had been present. The following table summarises the proportions of children in each group who had witnessed drug taking and related activities.

Table 6.3: Children's Exposure to Drugs in the Home

	Drug Users		Non-Drug Users	
	Yes	*No*	*Yes*	*No*
Child ever saw parent using drugs	17 (34%)	33 (66%)	0	50 (100%)
Child ever saw drugs equipment in the home	22 (44%)	28 (56%)	0	50 (100%)
Parents ever allowed others to use drugs in home	36 (72%)	14 (28%)	3 (6%)	47 (94%)
Child ever saw others taking drugs in home	6 (12%)	44 (88%)	0	50 (100%)

In most instances of children witnessing injecting, this was an unplanned occurrence, happening when children walked into a room unexpectedly. For example, one mother reported that her five-year-old boy had often seen her injecting and smoking heroin although she had tried to prevent it:

> I'd be in a room and he'd be in the other but he'd know what I was doing. It's over a year since he's seen that. If he walked into the room [when I was using] I'd scream and tell him to get out.

Several parents reported that their younger children were more likely to have witnessed their use of heroin. The mother of a nine-year-old girl explained that she thought her child had seen her injecting heroin:

> . . . once or twice . . . I did use in front of her when she was younger thinking she didn't cop but she did, I'm not going to lie. When she was about three or four she put a piece of string around her arm and started tapping her arm, mimicking me.

While many children saw their parents injecting and smoking heroin and possibly taking other substances, it is important to note that most parents reported that their children had *not* seen them using drugs and stated that it was not their usual practice to allow their children to witness injecting.

Another feature of drug use within the home was drug taking by other relatives, friends, acquaintances and strangers. It was common for children of drug users to be living in households where non-parental drug users had taken drugs. Almost three quarters of drug-using parents (72 per cent) said that they had allowed others to use drugs in their homes, compared with 6 per cent of non-drug users. Other drug users in the home mainly consisted of family members and friends, but also in families with drug-using parents, strangers came in to use drugs, particularly when parents' drug use was intensive. Parents were not asked how frequently others used drugs in their homes, but 12 per cent of drug users reported that their child had been present and had witnessed drug use by others in the home on at least one occasion. By contrast, no children of non-drug using parents had ever witnessed drug taking in their own homes, according to their parents. The presence of drug activity in the homes of some children of non-drug users points, however, to the difficulty in drawing a clear distinction between the exposure of children, of drug-using and non-drug using parents, to drugs in communities with high levels of drug use, and where close relatives and friends may be opiate-dependent.

DRUGS PARAPHERNALIA IN THE HOME

Children of drug-using parents were also more likely than children in the comparison group to have seen equipment used for taking drugs, such as syringes, in their own homes. Almost half of drug-using parents (44 per cent) said that their child had seen equipment used for taking drugs in their homes, while no child in the comparison group had done so. Children of drug users saw syringes and other paraphernalia in the home when in use by parents, such as when they were injecting, and when not in use, in the house. They also saw parents preparing to smoke heroin with tinfoil. Most parents reported that children were aware of the purpose for which these items were used in these contexts. One four-year-old child went to the kitchen cupboard for tinfoil as part of her morning routine, according to her mother:

> She knew what the tinfoil was for, she just knew, knew mummy smokes tinfoil in the morning. In the mornings she'd get the tinfoil for me.

Other children saw needles when their parents were injecting, as well as seeing them around the house. The mother of a twelve-year-old girl said:

> There's no use lying, she would have seen needles, if I put them away in presses . . . and they'd often find Valium.

Her daughter had seen her about to inject heroin:

> If I was in the kitchen or something and she burst in that's when she would've seen. She would've burst in when, say, the needle was in me hand, not when it was stuck in.

CHILDREN'S EXPOSURE TO DRUGS IN THE COMMUNITY

Children's exposure to drug use was not entirely restricted to the home setting. Some children were exposed to drug use, drug equipment, and conversations about drug use in the communities in which they were living, outside of their own homes. Drug-using parents were not asked questions directly about children's exposure to drugs in their communities, but 38 per cent raised the issue unprompted. Thirty-two per cent were parents living in the inner city location and 6 per cent were living in the suburban location of the study. The following comments illustrate parents' concerns about the extent of drug use in their communities and its implications for their children:

> It's a way of life around here.

> She sees a lot in the area — sometimes she says. "look at all them junkies".

> She's living in an environment where there's plenty of
> drugs.

Among non-drug-using parents over one-third stated that their
child had witnessed drug-taking in their communities, while
almost two-thirds (58 per cent) said their child had seen discarded syringes and needles. While most believed that their
child had not witnessed heroin injecting, a sizeable proportion
were concerned that their child had done so, in some cases
regularly, and worried about the potential for detrimental effects on their children's well-being. The mother of an eight-
year-old boy, for example, reported that her son had regularly
seen people using drugs in public outside the flats where they
lived.

> The girl underneath is a drug addict. [My son has] seen
> people injecting plenty of times on the stairs. . . . He found
> some [syringes] in the chute last week, he knows not to
> touch anything like that. . . . It's got worse since I moved in
> [to these flats]. I knew there was a problem but I lived in the
> area, it wasn't bad, they had it under control . . . [the kids]
> are watching it everyday, they'll watch it all. From 2.30 any
> day it's going on everywhere and maybe until 11, the kids
> are just looking at them.

Several parents were clearly distressed about the level of drug
use in areas immediately outside their homes, as the following
comments illustrate:

> . . . times she'd come up in an awful state, when the flats
> were bad they were injecting on the stairs and falling
> around, she'd be frightened. She would've seen injecting
> (father of eight-year-old girl).

> [My son has] seen needles on the stairs or out in the back
> garden, he'd see them selling, it goes on very openly.
> You'd be walking by and they'd say "are you looking?" [to
> buy heroin] (mother of eleven-year-old boy).

As well as seeing people using drugs, children were accus-
tomed to witnessing the selling and buying of drugs in the locality. Parents reported that their children knew that people

were buying drugs in the area, and recognised when some-
body was intoxicated or "stoned". Children were also accus-
tomed to seeing needles lying on the ground in areas close to
their homes. One mother, for example, said that her daughter
"sees works[2] outside on the stairs . . . they all use on our stairs."
As one drug treatment counsellor pointed out with regard to
public drug use:

> [T]he reality is that . . . it's very public . . . the reality is that
> in some areas it is a normal part of the environment.

The experience of exposure to drug taking and drug paraphernalia was highly context-specific. Visible heroin injecting and
smoking in public areas of estates was raised as a concern almost exclusively by parents living in the inner city location, and
then primarily within certain flat complexes, and indeed within
certain blocks of flats. In the suburban location, only two children were reported to have seen drug equipment, but not in
close proximity to their homes, whereas in some inner city estates parents reported that drug taking was common on stair-
wells, and that drugs were sold on the streets in the immediate
vicinity of the flats and within view of children.

PROTECTIVE PARENTING STRATEGIES

Within families with drug-using parents, children were most
likely to witness drug taking by their own parents when
younger, and if their parents were chronic drug users. High
levels of heroin use by parents also increased the likelihood
that children witnessed injecting, as parents were more likely
to reduce their efforts to conceal injecting from children under
these conditions. Furthermore, intensive heroin use was associated with greater numbers of non-parental drug users taking
drugs in the family home, and consequently an increased risk
of children's exposure.

Most drug-using parents reported striving to conceal drug
taking, both their own and others', from their children but their
strategies for doing so and their levels of vigilance varied considerably. The most common practice was to retreat to another
room in the home to inject or smoke heroin. Parents mostly re-

ported injecting in the kitchen, bathroom or bedroom. In only two cases parents said that they did not use drugs in their own home, suggesting that almost all used in the family home. Tactics used to prevent children from witnessing drug taking included encouraging children to remain outdoors, keeping doors locked when using, and issuing warnings to children to stay out of rooms parents were using in. For example:

> I would use upstairs while she was outside playing. That was one thing I always kept away from her (mother of four-year-old girl).

> I always got everything upstairs in one of the rooms. She [children's mother] would watch them . . . sometimes I locked the bedroom door while I used (father of eight-year-old child).

Many parents also said that they tried to restrict their use of drugs to times when the children were out of the home, such as when they were at school. A typical strategy was to encourage the child to go outside the home, mostly to play outside or to go to a friend's house, but several reported bribing their children by giving them money to buy sweets at the shop.

> I'd find myself bribing him a lot. . . . [I'd say] "I'll give you £2 to buy sweets", all so I could be in the kitchen . . . just so he'd be out for ten minutes.

The strain placed on parents to sustain concealment within the family was considerable, and was experienced by both mothers and fathers. For mothers of young children in need of constant supervision, however, the difficulties were greater. They experienced a direct conflict between the choice of leaving a young child unattended, or exposing them to injecting. Even when their goals were to prevent exposure to drug taking, therefore, they were not always successful in doing so. Thus, the father of an eight-year-old boy reported that his son was likely to have seen him injecting because of the high likelihood of decreased vigilance with active heroin use:

> . . . he might have spotted me once or twice. . . . I used up-
> stairs in the house, mainly when [the kids] were outside.
> When you're on drugs you always slip up. He might have
> seen me injecting once. He might have barged in to the
> room once [when I was using]. I might have been neglectful
> and forgot to lock the door. If you're using it five times daily
> of course you drop your guard.

Drug-using parents took for granted that it was unacceptable to allow their children to witness their own drug taking, and that of others, and saw it as their responsibility as parents to protect them from such experiences. As the above examples illustrate, however, they were not always successful in meeting these responsibilities.

Preventive behaviour around drug use was not restricted to drug-using parents, especially in areas where visible public drug use was common. Teaching children about the potential dangers associated with handling needles was a salient feature of parenting in most families in these locations. Parents in the comparison group taught their children to avoid physical contact with needles and syringes:

> Yeah all the kids see syringes. They're told not to be pick-
> ing them up. Some kids pick them up and bring them to
> their parents (non-drug-using mother of six-year-old girl,
> comparison group).

Drug-using parents were also likely to impart lessons to their children about personal safety in connection with drugs and needles. One drug-using father who openly communicated with his daughter about his heroin problem stated:

> I showed her the needles, said if you see them on the
> ground not to pick them up.

While parents can teach their children to avoid physical contact with needles, it is more difficult to prevent them from witnessing injecting, especially in areas used frequently by children. For all parents in these areas, drug-using and non-drug-using, protecting children from inappropriate exposure to drugs pre-

sents a stressor, adding to the considerable difficulties associated with raising children under conditions of poverty.

DISCUSSION

This paper explores one feature of the social ecology of parenting, the role of parents as buffers of stress to children in
high-risk areas. While the issue of parents as mediators of
stress has been addressed in previous studies of parenting in
communities with high levels of poverty (Bell, 1991; Dubrow
and Garbarino, 1989; Garbarino and Kostelny, 1993), the present study is unique in that it examines drug-using parents'
strategies for protecting children from adversity, that they
themselves have contributed to creating, through their engagement in a risky lifestyle.

Exposure to drug use in the home was largely confined to
children living with drug-using parents. There was considerable variation within the sample, however, in whether, and the
extent to which, children had witnessed drug taking by parents
or other individuals in their homes. The factors that shaped this
included children's age, the chronicity of parental drug use,
and the pattern of drug use and treatment. Yet, within the sample, there was considerable homogeneity in parents' attitudes
to drug use and perceptions of their responsibility to protect
children from any harm associated with their drug-related lifestyles. Almost all, whether referring to current or past heroin
use, perceived potentially negative effects on their children of
exposure to their drug use. Most employed deliberate strategies to compartmentalise their daily lives so that children were
not directly exposed to drug use, and especially injecting.
While they believed that it was important to protect children
from seeing their drug use, and from coming into contact with
any drugs paraphernalia such as syringes, many acknowledged that the constant vigilance required to do so was sometimes unachievable. In particular, parents who were injecting
several times per day, and those who had young children requiring constant supervision, found that continuous concealment within the family was unsustainable. For this reason, a
significant minority of children of drug users had seen their

parents using drugs and close to one-third saw parents injecting, some on a regular basis.

All drug-using parents shared the goal of preventing their
children from becoming drug users. A small proportion believed that allowing children to witness drug use, and openly
discussing with them the negative physiological and psychological effects it had on them, would deter their children from
modeling their behaviour. Most drug users, however, tried to
conceal not only drug taking but also related activities such as
buying and selling drugs from their children. Their investment,
in trying to shield their children from social exposure to their
drugs-related lifestyles, indicates a belief that it is potentially
harmful to children. Parents' specific beliefs about the nature of
that adversity are not well understood but a few possibilities
suggest themselves. Parents may fear that such experiences
might lead to children imitating their parents or accepting their
drug use as normal. They may fear that children will become
traumatised by witnessing an action — injecting heroin — that
is viewed by the public at large as distressing and dangerous.
On the other hand, part of the motivation to conceal drug taking
from children may be fear that children will disclose their parents' drug use publicly.

Professionals tended to believe that witnessing drug use
was not, itself, necessarily distressing to children, especially
those who had grown up with the experience and for whom it
was normalised practice. They were more concerned about the
meaning that children might attach to their parents' drug use
and the manner in which they made sense of their parents' behaviours in the light of widespread negative attitudes to drug
use and drug users. In their view, society's isolation of drug users and their families could lead children to worry about their
parents', and their own, welfare. Children might also become
distressed by their parents' intoxication and drug withdrawal if,
as a result, parents became physically or emotionally unavailable. The most pressing concern, according to professionals,
was that drug-using parents who were concerned about the impact of their lifestyle on their children were unlikely to receive
support from services to address those concerns and to devise
effective strategies for protecting their children from risk. This,

they argued, was partly because there were currently only limited opportunities for parents to discuss the impact of their drugs-related lifestyle on their parenting since most services for drug users did not offer such support, and partly because parents were inhibited by their fears about their children being removed from their care if they disclosed vulnerability in relation to their children's welfare.

Children's exposure to drugs in their communities was a phenomenon shared across the two study groups, but not by all children in these groups. In keeping with McAuliffe and Fahey's (1999) finding that visible drug use in public areas is highly localised, we discovered that children's experience of seeing drug taking and related activities in their communities was restricted mainly to the inner city area, and within that, to certain estates, and indeed to certain sub-sections of those estates. Parents in these areas encountered the challenge of protecting their children from adversity, and they largely concentrated on teaching children to avoid contact with potentially harmful discarded needles and drugs. These challenges were faced by both drug-using and non-drug-using parents. Parents in both groups also shared a concern about the potentially negative impact on children of witnessing high levels of public drug use.

The limitations of the present study must be borne in mind in reaching any conclusions about the levels of adversity and protection in the environments of children of drug users and non-drug users. The findings, regarding practices of drug users, were largely based on parents' retrospective accounts. While the majority of parents were using multiple illicit substances at the time of interview, most were receiving methadone treatment and perceived themselves to be in a stable period of their opiate dependence. We did not have any independent confirmation of the actual drug status and practices of parents, and no direct information from children about their experiences. These findings, moreover, do not represent the views of parents who are not in contact with services.

In conclusion, this paper explores the issue of children's exposure to the lifestyle associated with drugs in their homes and communities. It points to the considerable challenges faced by parents, drug users and non-drug users alike, in buffering children from risk in communities with high levels of drug use. It indicates that drug-using parents can encounter difficulties in sustaining high levels of vigilance in concealing heroin injecting when their own levels of drug use are high, but that the protection of children is highly salient for many drug users and is evident in their daily parenting practices. The findings presented here point to the need for a better understanding of the factors that deter drug-using parents from seeking professional support when their parenting is vulnerable and they are concerned about their children's safety.

References

Ana Liffey Drug Project, (1991, 1994, 1996), *Annual Reports*. Dublin: ALDP.

Agar, M. (1973), *Ripping and Running*, New York: Seminar.

Bell, C. (1991), "Traumatic stress and children in danger", *Journal of Health Care for the Poor and Undeserved*, 2, 175-188.

Bowden, M. (1997), *Report on "The Children's Project: the Ana Liffey for Children"*, Ana Liffey Drug Project Annual Report, *1996*, Dublin: ALDP.

Bowden, M. (1996), *Rialto Community Drug Team Policy Discussion Paper*, Dublin: RCDT.

Butler, S. and Woods, M. (1992), "Drugs, HIV and Ireland: Responses to Women in Dublin", in N. Dorn et al. (eds.), *AIDS: Women, Drugs, and Social Care*, London: Falmer Press.

Colten, M. E. (1982), "Attitudes, experiences and self-perceptions of heroin-addicted mothers", *Journal of Social Issues*, 38 (2), 77-92.

Comiskey, C. M. (1998), *Estimating the prevalence of opiate drug use in Dublin, Ireland 1996*, Dublin: Department of Health.

Cullen, B. (1992*)*, "Community and drugs: A case study in community conflict in the inner city of Dublin", Unpublished M. Litt thesis, Trinity College Dublin.

Cullen, B. (1994), "Community drug treatment: An untried response to drug problems in Dublin", *Irish Social Worker*, vol. 12, 2, 16-18.

Dean, G., Bradshaw, J., and Lavelle, P. (1983), *Drug misuse in Ireland, 1982-1983. Investigation in north central Dublin area and in Galway, Sligo and Cork*, Dublin: The Medico-Social Research Board.

Dean, G., O'Hare, A., O'Connor, A., Kelly, M., and Kelly, G. (1985), "The opiate epidemic in Dublin 1979-1983", *Irish Medical Journal*, 78, 108-110.

Deren, S. (1986), "Children of substance abusers: A review of the literature", *Journal of Substance Abuse Treatment*, 3, 77-94.

Dubrow, N., and Garbarino, J. (1989), "Living in the war zone: Mothers and children in public housing developments", *Child Welfare*, 68(1).

Eastern Health Board (1997), *Review of adequacy: Child care and family support services*, Dublin: Eastern Health Board.

Fiddle, G. (1976), "Sequences in addiction", *Addictive Diseases: An International Journal*, 2 (4), 553-568.

Garbarino, J. and Kostelny K. (1993), "Neighborhood and community influences on parenting", In T. Luster and L. Okagaki, *Parenting: An ecological perspective*, Hillsdale, NJ: Lawrence Erlbaum Associates, pp. 203-226.

Hogan, D. (1999), "Protecting children in high risk social environments: Parenting practices of drug-using and non-drug-using parents", paper presented at the annual meetings of the Psychological Society of Ireland.

Hogan, D. (1998), "Annotation: The psychological development and welfare of children of opiate and cocaine users: Review and research needs", *Journal of Child Psychology and Psychiatry*, 39, 5, 609-620.

Hogan, D. (1997), *The Social and Psychological Needs of Children of Drug Users: Report on Exploratory Study*, Dublin: The Children's Research Centre, Trinity College Dublin.

Hogan, D. and Higgins, L. (2001) *When Parents Use Drugs: Key Findings from a Study of Children in the Care of Drug-using Parents*. Dublin: The Children's Research Centre, Trinity College Dublin.

Johnson, J. (1991), "Forgotten no longer: An overview of research on children of chemically dependent parents", in T. M. Rivinus (ed.), *Children of Chemically-Dependent Parents*, pp. 29-54, New York: Brunner Publishers.

Keenan, E, Dorman, A., and O'Connor, J. (1993), "Six-year follow up of forty-five pregnant opiate addicts", *Irish Journal of Medical Science*, 162 (7), 252-255.

Mayes, L. C. (1996), "Substance abuse and parenting", in M. H. Bornstein (ed.), *Handbook of Parenting*, Vol. 4, Mahwah, NJ: Lawrence Erlbaum, pp. 101-125.

McAuliffe, R. and Fahey, T. (1999), "Responses to social order problems", in T. Fahey (ed.), *Social Housing in Ireland*, Dublin: Oak Tree Press, pp. 173-190.

McKeown, K., Fitzgerald, G., and Deegan, A. (1993), *The Merchant's Quay project:: A drugs/HIV service in the inner city of Dublin in 1989-1992*, Dublin: Kieran McKeown Limited, Social and Economic Research Consultants.

Moran, R., O'Brien, M., and Duff, P. (1997), *Treated drug misuse in Ireland: National Report 1996*, Dublin: Health Research Board.

Murphy, C. and Hogan, D. (1999), "Supporting families through partnership: An evaluation of the Eastern Health Board (Area 5) Community Drugs Service", unpublished research report, Dublin: Department of Health and Children.

O'Connor, J. J. Stafford-Johnson, S., and Kelly, M. G. (1988), "A review of the characteristics and treatment progress of 45 pregnant opiate addicts attending the Irish National Drug Advisory and Treatment Centre over a two year period", *Irish Journal of Medical Science*, 157 (5), 146-149.

O'Hare, A., and O'Brien, M. (1992), *Treated Drugs Misuse in the Greater Dublin Area, 1990*. Dublin: Health Research Board.

O'Higgins, K. (1996), *Treated Drugs Misuse in the Greater Dublin Area: A review of five years 1990-1994*, Dublin: Health Research Board.

O'Higgins, K. and Duff, P. (1997), *Treated Drugs Misuse in Ireland: First National Report*, 1995, Dublin: Health Research Board.

O'Mahony, P. (1997), *Criminal Chaos: Seven Crises in Irish Criminal Justice*, Dublin: Roundhall, Sweet and Maxwell.

Parker, H., Bakx, K., and Newcombe, R. (1988), *Living with Heroin: The Impact of a drugs "Epidemic" on an English community"*, Milton Keynes: Open University Press.

Pearson, G. (1987), *The New Heroin Users*, Oxford: Blackwell.

Rabitte, P. (1997), *First Report of the Ministerial Task Force on Measures to Reduce the Demand for Drugs*, Dublin: Department of An Taoiseach.

Rosenbaum, M. (1979), "Difficulties in taking care of business: Women addicts as mothers", *American Journal of Drug and Alcohol Abuse, 6(4)*, 431-446.

Ryan, A., Magee, T., Stafford-Johnson, S., Griffin, E., and Kelly, M. G. (1983), "The emergence of maternal drug addiction as a problem in Ireland 1981", *Irish Medical Journal*, 76(2), 86-89.

Taylor, A. (1993), *Women Drug Users: An Ethnography of a Female Injecting Community*, Oxford: Clarendon Press.

Zinberg, N. (1984), *Drug, Set and Setting: The Basis for Controlled Intoxicant Use*, New Haven, CT: Yale University Press.

Notes

[1] The present study was completed with the assistance of part funding from Enterprise Ireland, under the "Science and Technology against Drugs" programme. The authors gratefully acknowledge the assistance of the families, schools, and agencies that took part in the research. Correspondence should be addressed to the first author at the Department of Psychology, Aras an Phiarsaigh, Trinity College, Dublin 2. Tel: 01-608 2589, email: dmhogan@tcd.ie

[2] "Works" refers to equipment for injecting heroin.

Chapter 7

The Child, the Family
and Disability

Anne Cleary

Childhood and disability represent two areas of developing interest in sociology. Previously, as Brannen and O'Brien (1995) have said, children had remained invisible within sociological inquiry or as subsidiary within the study of other areas such as the family. Within the emerging paradigm of childhood, the world of the child is now considered worthy of analysis and there is a particular emphasis on the social construction of childhood (James and Prout, 1990). The sociological re-examination of disability has a somewhat longer history and, in the past decade, sociological inquiry has helped to produce a growing body of knowledge in this area. In particular, sociologists have contributed to the development of a "social model of disability", redefining disability as the product of a disabling society rather than in terms of individual limitations or loss (Oliver, 1990; Abberley, 1987). Yet despite these developments disability remains a significant means of social differentiation in modern societies and definitions of disability continue to be crucial in generating images and stereotypes of disabled people (Harris, 1995).

If academic attention has recently turned to topics such as childhood and disability, children with disabilities remain, as a group, academically marginalised. Yet there is some evidence of emerging interest, with a focus on disabled children as social actors, "creatively negotiating complex identities within both socially and physically disabling environments, rather than as passive and dependent" (*Childhood*, Editorial, 1998, p. 131). This approach, Priestley (1998) notes, is very different from prevailing research approaches in relation to disabled children, which tend to be dominated by narratives of dependence. The invisibility of children with disabilities may be understood in the context of hitherto dominant paradigms of childhood, especially developmentalism, which identifies specific social and biological markers on the route to adulthood. This model has contributed, as James and Prout (1990) have said, to a dependency view of children generally, while children with disabilities fare particularly badly. Similarly, functionalist accounts of the nature and process of socialisation remain problematic in relation to the disabled child. Within this framework, "children who seemed to falter in the socialisation process" (James and Prout, 1990, p. 14), were re-categorised into deviant subgroupings. Within contemporary Western culture the child, they state, occupies a paradoxical position. Children are cherished and valued and have become important signifiers for adults of hope for the future. Yet this is associated with an ideology of perfection attaching to children and childhood. In this context, the "imperfectable body" (Dutton, 1996) of the disabled child may, as Priestly (1998) notes, represent for the family a limitation on hope and meaning.

The social position of children with disabilities is also shaped by another major developmental framework, the biomedical model. The fact that disability has been constructed historically as a medical issue has, according to Middleton (1996), pathologised disabled children and further excluded them from participation in "normal" childhood. Although children in general are increasingly exposed, as Allen (1996) has said, to the scrutiny of biomedicine, children with disabilities are disproportionately subjected to medical surveillance. For disabled children "the gaze", in Foucauldian (Foucault, 1973, p. 29) terms, reaches further and has more far-reaching consequences for their life chances (Allen, 1996; Cleary, 1996). The continuing dominance of biomedical and epidemiological studies within disability research has compounded, according to Priestley (1998), assumptions about disabled children as passive rather than active social agents. Another predominant form of research in the disability area, service-based enquiry, also contributes to this view in concealing structural aspects of exclusion. Allen (1996) and Middleton (1999) have shown how disabled children are excluded from important social processes through differential mechanisms of segregation. Furthermore, within these conceptual frameworks, disabled children tend to be constructed within a unitary identity even though research evidence reveals a variety of disabled childhoods. Children with disabilities have needs and aspirations similar to nondisabled children and these are shaped less by their disability status than by other social influences such as class, gender and family relationships (Taylor, 2000; Lewis, 1995; Harris, 1995).

The dependency model of the disabled child is linked, in turn, to notions of the "handicapped family" (Glendinning, 1983). Families with disabled children, as Thomas (1978) has stated, are heavily stereotyped and pathologised either as "handicapped families" or as engaged in heroic self-sacrifice. Also, similar to prevailing views on disabled children, these families are often viewed as representing a homogeneous group defined by the existence of the disabled child in their midst. Yet such stereotyping is contrary to existing research evidence which points to the heterogeneity of these family units and to their similarity with family units generally (Lewis et al., 1999). Thus Lewis et al. (1999) suggest that the low level of labour participation by mothers of disabled children in comparison to other mothers is a consequence of the structural barriers these women face, rather than qualitatively different needs. The psychological and social benefits of such work, they contend, are similar for both groups of mothers.

A STUDY OF CHILDREN WITH DISABILITIES

Children with disabilities represent an important social grouping in Ireland yet they remain a particularly invisible and unheard group. Empirical enquiry tends to reflect the traditional approaches outlined above, although there have been some notable exceptions (Kenny et al., 2001). The following study, although limited somewhat by context and methodology, attempts to offer some insights in this area. The aim is to investigate societal perceptions of disability by examining the birth context of the child and the experiences of families with a child who has a disability. This study deals firstly with the experience of disclosure, the way in which the woman was told about her child's disability and her response to this. Relatively little attention has been given to this area yet the mother's reaction may provide a powerful reflection of societal reactions to disability and disabled people. Similarly, attitudes of hospital staff may reflect both societal values and the influence of the predominant contextual framework, the biomedical model. The second aspect of this study is an examination of the issues and concerns around surviving children and their families.

This study formed part of a large clinical research project which focused on women who had been pregnant with, or given birth to, a baby with a condition known as Neural Tube Defect (NTD). The births took place in the main Dublin maternity hospitals over a ten-year period. Neural Tube Defect is caused by failure of the neural tube to adequately develop and the two most common forms of this condition are Spina Bifida and Anencephaly. NTD results either in stillbirth or the death of the child soon after birth in 80 per cent of cases. For those children who survive beyond the first year of life (approximately 20 per cent) the condition usually implies a range of disabilities. The incidence of Neural Tube Defect, although formerly high in this country, has been declining over the past 30 years and this decline is particularly evident since the mid-1970s (Radic et al., 1988). However, it remains an important cause of neo-natal mortality in Ireland.

METHOD

The data presented in this section are based on two samples. The findings relating to birth and disclosure of the disability are based on a sample of 1,088 women who were pregnant with or gave birth to a child with an NTD condition over a ten-year period in the main Dublin maternity hospitals. Only women with a single NTD pregnancy were included. Although the study presented a number of ethical and methodological problems, a high response rate (85 per cent) was obtained. Forty-nine (4.5 per cent) of the women refused to be interviewed, 10 per cent (111) were non-contactable and seven women (0.6 per cent) had died. A total of 921 women were therefore included in the analysis. Demographic information was collected using a pre-coded questionnaire. Psychological health status was assessed using a standardised instrument (The Malaise Inventory) (Rutter et al., 1975) as well as a series of pre-coded questions. A semi-structured interview schedule was used to elicit information concerning the events surrounding pregnancy, delivery and the aftermath of the birth. The interviews were held over a four-month period and were all undertaken in the interviewee's own home. Most of the women welcomed the opportunity to talk about their children, and for those who had had a miscarriage, stillbirth or whose baby had died after birth, the interview provided a chance to address what often emerged as an important, sometimes unresolved issue in their lives.

The second sample focused on those children, born to the above mothers, who were alive at the time of the study (n=171). Seven children were excluded from the analysis either because the child was living permanently in an institution (one child) or because of missing information (six children). The total sample in the children's section of the study, therefore, was 164 children. In this section of the study, the principal aim was to examine the subsequent development and inclusion of the child within the family setting. For this purpose, a semi-structured interview was conducted with the mothers of the children. In many cases it was not known until the interview whether the child was alive or not. The mother sometimes volunteered this information when the interview appointment was made but the research team did not consider it appropriate to ask this question outside the interview setting. Children were not interviewed themselves because many were very young and also because, as the focus of the overall study was on the mothers, resources were not available to extend it directly to the children.

The Mother and the Birth of the Child

A total of 921 women were included in this part of the study. The age range of the women at the time of birth was 15 to 46 years ($\bar{x}$ = 26.5 years, sd = 5.6). Ninety-three per cent of the women were married at the time of the birth and over three-quarters (76 per cent) were living in Dublin city or county. The majority of the women (54 per cent) were from skilled or semi-skilled socio-economic categories, 11 per cent were from the unskilled grouping and 18 per cent were from the higher and lower professional/managerial categories. Fifty-nine per cent of the respondents had primary or part second level standard of education and the average school leaving age was 16 years. Twenty-four per cent had completed secondary school and four per cent had completed third level education. Almost half (48 per cent) had been engaged in intermediate non-manual occupations and 29 per cent in semi-skilled manual jobs.

For a third of the women, the index episode occurred during their first pregnancy. Thirty-seven per cent were aware of the disability prior to the birth of the child. The great majority of this group were mothers of children who died. Only 3 per cent of mothers of surviving children were aware of their child's condition prior to birth. Over half (51 per cent) learned about it during or immediately after delivery (those who experienced a miscarriage were not usually told of the condition for some time afterwards). The majority of child deaths occurred within hours of the birth and over a third of the women experienced a still-birth. Approximately 20 per cent of the children, or one child in five, survived beyond their first year. Information in relation to the disability was generally given to the women by a member of the hospital staff, usually a doctor. In the case of mothers of surviving children, the ward sister or other staff nurse frequently (31 per cent) conveyed the information. At this initial interaction, over half (57 per cent) of the women were given some information about NTD, but only a minority (14 per cent) were told the name *and* given a clear explanation of the condition. Thereafter, over a third (36 per cent) received no further information. This lack of information was an important factor in terms of the women's perceived experience of hospital care.

Although the majority (61 per cent) of the women were satisfied or fairly satisfied with the care they received, a substantial number (30 per cent) were unhappy with hospital care and among the most commonly cited reasons for dissatisfaction was a lack of adequate information. Other reasons for dissatisfaction included being denied the opportunity to see the baby and an absence of any aftercare. Furthermore, this dissatisfaction was not simply a reflection of distress or bereavement (Cleary, 2001, in preparation).

The provision of information was important because of a lack of knowledge about the condition and a general fear of disability on the part of the mothers interviewed. The type and quality of information received also influenced the mother's decision to see a baby who was stillborn or died soon after birth. For some children born with an NTD condition, quite severe fissures can be visible on their heads and this may have prompted some staff to deny access or advise the woman not to see the baby. The decision to see the deceased infant was influenced, to a considerable extent, by the information provided by hospital staff and also by the context of this communication (as, in the aftermath of the birth, the women and their partners sought to interpret the messages they were receiving). Many of the women requested to see their baby but rarely insisted when hospital staff advised against it:

> I was told the baby was too badly deformed to see and I accepted this.

Those women who did not see their babies, in general, greatly regretted this ("I would like to have seen the baby but I never got the chance") and some reported continuing fears about the child's "abnormality". In a number of cases, staff did encourage the women to see and hold their baby although the women themselves were reluctant to do so:

> I didn't want to see the baby but a nurse encouraged me and I was delighted.

> The consultant advised us to see the baby, we refused, and I regret this now.

When the focus in hospital was on impairment and accompanied by advice not to see the baby, there were two main conse- quences. Some mothers spoke of a failure on the part of hospital staff to acknowledge the child ("there was no acknowledgement of the baby"), and this contributed to their subsequent distress. Secondly, a concentration on disability confirmed for many of the women the connection between the child and "abnormality". Mothers of surviving and non-surviving children were both equally affected by the event but the distress was longer lasting for mothers of children who died. Enduring depression (i.e. lasting longer than six months) was more common in this group (35 per cent in contrast to 27 per cent).

The Children and Their Families

A total of 171 children, born to the above mothers, were still alive at the time of the study. The following analysis is confined to 164 children as information was unavailable for six children and one child was living permanently in an institution. The mean age of the children was 7.5 years (sd = 3.5) and a small majority (55 per cent) were female. Information relating to level of disability was only collected for those aged five years and over (n=136) as most of the questions were not relevant to those under five. Almost all of the children were able to eat inde- pendently and more than three-quarters were able to dress in- dependently or with some assistance. Seventeen percent of the children used wheelchairs and approximately another quarter needed some mechanical aids to assist mobility. Just over half were partly or completely incontinent. Almost two-thirds were in mainstream schooling and approximately the same number had been assessed as within the 'normal' range of intelligence. Almost a quarter were attending a special school.[1] In order to explore the impact of level of disability in the family in this study a summary measure or index of disability was con- structed consisting of five measures, mobility, I.Q., continence, ability to dress independently and ability to eat independently. Based on this categorisation 16.5% of the children were catego-

---

[1] A detailed account of the level of disability in this group of children will be presented in a forthcoming paper by Kirke, P. et al.

rised as having minimal or no disability, 67% showed mild to moderate levels and 16.5% of the children had more severe levels of disability.

CARING FOR THE CHILD

Table 7.1 illustrates the extent of care provided each day and indicates that a third of the women spent most of the day caring for the child. There was a strong and statistically significant relationship between the severity of disability and the amount of time spent caring for the child (n=56, x^2 = 41.05, df=6, p<0.001). Overall, however, 54 per cent said that caring for the child only involved part of their day and 13 per cent of the mothers said that no special care was required, that the level of care was the same as for their other children ("I'm not tied any more than with an ordinary child.") Seventy per cent said that the child's condition placed no restriction on their ability to go out during the day. Neither did it restrict holiday arrangements for most and almost a third (30 per cent) of the mothers had had a holiday in the last two years. Of the non-holiday group, only 12 per cent indicated that the lack of a holiday was linked to the child's disability. Nevertheless, almost a third of the women overall regarded themselves as quite restricted due to care responsibilities:

> I applied for a home help. . . . I feel locked in, it can go for a month before I get out.

Table 7.1: *Amount of Time Involved in Caring for the Disabled Child*

	N	%
Most of the day	53	33
Part of the day	46	28
Small part of the day	43	26
No special care needed	21	13
	163	100

Missing information = 1

This group cited the lack of suitable minders as problematic ("Babysitting is a big problem"), in particular someone who would be willing and able to assist the child with incontinence problems. Some of these women in the "high care" group were forced to give up work outside the home:

> I would have stayed working but it's difficult to get a minder.

DIFFICULTIES AND DISABLING BARRIERS

In response to a question about difficulties experienced in caring for the child with a disability, the majority of respondents cited practical problems. Eighteen per cent mentioned the physical burden of lifting the child, 15 per cent cited coping with incontinence and 6 per cent mentioned the psychological burden of constant care: ("The constant care. . . . I have to be there . . . confined to the house"). Difficulties experienced by the child were also recounted ("The incontinence is awkward for him"). Almost a third (31 per cent) referred to disabling barriers, particularly wheelchair access, transport and the difficulties of getting appropriate services and equipment ("Taking her on the bus to the hospital is an ordeal"). A number of the mothers identified the lack of equipment and access difficulties as the problem rather than the child ("There are no difficulties with the child, it is getting equipment . . . there are long waits"). A quarter of the mothers said they had experienced no particular difficulties ("He's no extra trouble; the same as for any child").

Table 7.2: Services and Benefits Required

	N	%
Increase in financial benefits	3	2
Increase in non-financial benefits	46	29
Improvement in services	28	17
Satisfied with existing services/benefits	84	52
	161	100

Missing information = 3

Just over half of the women said that they were happy with present services and benefits. The remainder felt that improvements were needed, particularly in relation to services or necessary equipment. The following quotes illustrate the difficulties some of the women experienced in obtaining necessary equipment for their children:

> I must buy a wheelchair but I just cannot afford it.

> Callipers, appliances generally are inadequate. In general services are meagre.

> The callipers have been broken for a year so (child's name) is chair-bound.

Accessing services for their children appeared to represent an area of constant struggle for many of the mothers:

> There is minimal support. She attends national school but other activities are denied her since I have no transport.

Ironically, the most difficult items to obtain, mentioned by a large group of women, were relatively small items such as nappies etc. Another, frequently mentioned, yet infrequently available service was physiotherapy, and some of the women, although untrained, were attempting to provide this for the children themselves. Four of the mothers were required to go to their child's school several times daily to assist with their toilet. The lack of services and equipment contributed to the exclusion of the child from routine life, sometimes to a significant degree and, at the same time, increased the burden of care for the mother.

> I know the way I want (child's name) life to take but the services are uncoordinated and there are obstacles in education. Services are not readily available, there are delays in all the services that should be automatic. I have to keep reapplying again and again for different services. There is a lack of information about benefits. I care for (child's name) all the time but it makes it much more difficult when I always have to seek services out.

In general, deficiencies in service provision were not related to financial circumstances. This is indicated by the fact that medical card holders expressed fewer needs for services and benefits than Voluntary Health Insurance (VHI) members.

FINANCIAL RESOURCES

The majority (73 per cent) of the families owned their own home or were in the process of buying it. The remainder, in general, rented their house from the local authority. A quarter (24 per cent) had made, or were about to make, some alternations to their home for the disabled child. Nine per cent had built an extra bedroom/bathroom and three families had had their house specially designed to suit the disabled child. In terms of medical expenses, 42 per cent had a medical card and 32 per cent had VHI cover. Table 7.3 gives their perception of the effect of the child's disability on family finances. As can be seen from this table, the majority (64 per cent) said that the child's condition had little or no effect on family finances but approximately one-fifth said that the condition had a marked or very marked effect. There were no differences between medical card and VHI groups in terms of reported effects on family finances.

Table 7.3: Effect of Child's Condition on Family Finances

	N	%
No effect	72	44
Very little effect	32	20
Some effect	26	16
Marked effect	25	15
Very marked effect	9	5
	164	100

FAMILY RELATIONSHIPS

Most (90 per cent) of the women were married and the majority appeared to be involved in close confiding relationships. Five per cent were separated and 2 per cent were widowed. Three-quarters (74 per cent) named their husband as their confidant in relation to aspects of the child's welfare, and only 12 per cent named a professional, usually a doctor. This reflected a recurring theme in the interviews, namely that the child's needs and requirements were viewed as primarily dealt with from within the family. Almost three-quarters (72 per cent) were satisfied with the general support they were receiving in relation to the child's disability. Of those who were dissatisfied (10 per cent), this dissatisfaction related to a lack of service support rather than family/confidant support. Half (51 per cent) of the families belonged to the Spina Bifida Association. However, there may be something of a social class bias in relation to membership of the association in that those with VHI cover were more likely to belong to it. Reasons given for Association membership included the support of other similar families, and also to avail of specialised services for their child. The main reason given for non-membership of this or similar type organisation was that it was felt to be unnecessary.

Table 7.4: Marital Problems Experienced

	N	%
No marital problems experienced	133	84
Problems after birth, now resolved	8	5
Some marital disharmony	15	10
Significant marital disharmony	2	1
	158	100

Missing information = 4; Single parents = 2

Table 7.4 illustrates the women's responses to a question about their marital situation. They were asked if they considered the child's condition had ever caused problems in their marriage. Eighty-four per cent indicated that the disabled child had never caused such problems. In fact, many volunteered the view that having a disabled child had had a positive effect on their relationship ("It brought us closer together"). Some of the women did acknowledge that having a disabled child in the family did affect some social activities ("While it brings a couple closer together, it puts a strain on social life") but they viewed this as related to difficulties in obtaining care or babysitting or in accessing respite services. Sixteen per cent of respondents said that the child's condition had caused some marital disharmony, but, of these, one-third said that this had been a temporary phase following the child's birth and was now resolved. The time following childbirth was acknowledged by most of the women as a difficult time psychologically:

> It can cause problems. My husband is marvellous but at first he left too much to me as if he hadn't accepted (child's name) condition . . . it reached a crisis, we discussed it and it's no longer a problem.

One per cent of the sample said that having a disabled child had caused significant marital disharmony:

> My husband did not want to know or have anything to do with (child's name) condition. His parents were, and still are, very kind to her.

There was a difference between medical card holders and the VHI group in that 25 per cent of medical card holders had experienced marital problems in comparison to 16 per cent of the VHI group. There was some indication of greater marital disharmony between parents of children with a severe disability but the numbers involved were small and therefore not statistically significant.

EMOTIONAL DIFFICULTIES AND HELP-SEEKING

The emotional impact of having a child with a disability was measured in two ways: the use of the Malaise Inventory and respondents' reports of medical help-seeking for emotional problems. A score of more than five is considered significant on the Malaise Inventory, and in this study the scores are dichotomised as either low or high on this basis. Emotional problems and help-seeking were very highly correlated, but nevertheless bore differential relationships to other factors for the reason, among others, that only 18 per cent had sought help for emotional problems while a much larger proportion reported scores greater than five on the Malaise Inventory (55 per cent).

As Table 7.5 indicates, 18 per cent of the mothers had sought help for emotional problems while over three-quarters had never required help. Help-seeking was most strongly associated with the demands of care, that is, it was most prevalent among those who spent the greater part of their time looking after their child with a disability. Twenty-five per cent of those who spent most of the day caring for their child had sought help in comparison to 9 per cent of those who spent a small part of each day caring for their child. However, help-seeking was also strongly associated with economic factors, principally the effect on family finances of the child's disability. Forty-four per cent of those whose children's conditions had had a "very marked effect" on family finances had sought medical help. The corresponding figures for "marked effect" and "no effect" were 28 per cent and 8 per cent. There also appeared to be a social class difference in that 25 per cent of those with a medical card had sought help compared to 10 per cent of those with VHI cover. In contrast, the severity of the disability was only weakly and non-significantly related to help-seeking. Help-seeking was also related to non-availability of support, and was particularly relevant in a context of marital disharmony.

Table 7.5: Help for Emotional Problems

	N	%
Presently seeking help	3	2
Sought help in past	24	16
Experienced difficulties but no help sought	3	2
No help required	131	80
	161	100

Missing information = 3

Among the group of mothers with scores of more than five on the Malaise Inventory, economic issues emerged as principal associated factors. These included non- ownership of a house (n=41, x^2 = 17.79, df=1, p< 0.001), having a medical card (n=61, x^2 = 12.8, df=1, p<0.01) and not having VHI cover (n=98, x^2 = 8.35, df=1, p<0.01). Only one other factor was significantly associated with higher Malaise Inventory scores: dissatisfaction with hospital treatment following the child's birth (n=56, x^2 = 4.39, df=1, p<0.05). While personality disposition cannot be ruled out as a cause of this finding, it does underline the importance of the context and content of disclosure.

A number of other factors were also related to higher Malaise Inventory scores, but not to a statistically significant degree. The most important of these was not belonging to a support group, but other aspects of support were also important including less availability of husband as a confidant, looking after a young (less than three years) child, and the age of the mother herself (younger age being associated with a higher Malaise Inventory score).

It is apparent, then, that the experience of emotional difficulties among the mothers of children with disabilities is not clearly or primarily associated with the direct effects of the disability. Thus, the severity of the disability was not significantly related to high levels on the malaise score. The following tables show clear progressive relationships with other mediating factors, indicating their relevance.

Table 7.6: Adverse Financial Effects and Help-Seeking

Adverse Financial Effects of Disability	Medical Help-seeking N (%)*
No effect	6 (10)
Little effect	5 (16)
Some effect	5 (19)
Marked effect	7 (28)
Very marked effect	4 (44)

* Percentage within each group

Table 7.7: Working Status and Psychological Well-being

Working Status	Malaise Score > 5 N (%)*
Full time working	5 (33)
Part time working	13 (52)
Not working	63 (59)

* Percentage within each group

Table 7.8: Maternal Age at Birth and Psychological Well-being

Maternal Age (N)	Malaise Score > 5 N (%)*
< 20 years (15)	11 (73)
21-25 years (47)	28 (58)
26-30 years (40)	20 (50)
31-35 years (30)	14 (47)
> 36 years (15)	8 (53)

* Percentage within each group

DISCUSSION

This paper addresses the impact that having a child with a disability has, both on the well-being of the mother and on family functioning. More particularly, it sets this against prevalent conceptions that tend to portray singular, homogenous accounts of disability or handicap, or of the "handicapped family". The experience of having a child with a disability is examined from two perspectives. Firstly, there are the immediate effects allied to the birth, not least of which is the high mortality rate. Secondly, issues related to the burden of caring, financial burden and the social construction of the disabled child are explored.

Since only about 20 per cent of children born with an NTD condition survive, the sample reporting birth-related experiences is much larger than the sample which reports the experience of rearing and caring for a child with a disability. The data show that giving birth to a child with a disability is a traumatic experience for a mother. A principal finding in this study is that about two-thirds of mothers who have been so affected expressed reasonable satisfaction with how the event was responded to in the hospital. There was a considerable degree of variation in the responses of health professionals, ranging from full and prompt disclosure and discussion, to what might be perceived as avoidance or postponement. It is difficult to know what determines these varying strategies, or even whether they primarily reflect staff dispositions and attitudes or, alternatively, efforts by staff to respond to their perception of the mother's needs. What emerges, however, is that about one-third of the mothers expressed dissatisfaction at the handling of their situation while in hospital. A general picture of inattention or insensitivity to their needs on the part of hospital staff is presented by this group. Some parents complied passively with procedures suggested by hospital personnel, particularly in relation to seeing their baby, then came to regret this in time.

For the mothers of those children who survived, the first notable feature of these findings is that they were not introduced to a life of hardship and unhappiness, the world of the "handicapped family". A large number of mothers of surviving and non-surviving children alike were traumatised and reported depressive rather than merely sad feelings. However, over three-quarters of these parents had recovered within six months. In fact, the rate of depression in mothers of living children was lower at six months than for the mothers of children who had not survived the birth. Instead, what becomes apparent over time is the extent to which the situation of the child with a disability becomes normalised, that is, where the disability takes second place to the child's family position and status. This can be inferred from a number of observations. Firstly, many mothers referred to and considered their children as "normal", and as being the same as their other children. This occurred particularly in cases where the disability was not so severe. Secondly, psychological distress among the mothers of children with more marked difficulties was related to certain practical implications such as restrictions on personal freedom. The severity of disability caused considerably less emotional upset than its effects upon people's use of their time. Therefore, the alleviation of this burden is not to be found within a bio-medical perspective but, instead, through the provision of certain relevant social supports. A third indicator of the way that disability becomes normalised within the family is contained in the accounts of some parents about support organisations. Parents who did not join such groups viewed their child's needs as part of the normal spectrum of family needs and issues. Mothers preferred to respond to needs in this way, for example, conferring with and confiding in their partners in preference to accessing the support of a group directed towards disability. In general, the mothers who were interviewed did not stress their child's disability, but instead frequently adverted to matters of inclusion. They referred often to the inadequacies of service and benefit provision, indicating how these deficits made inclusion a more difficult goal to attain. Another indicator of normality within these families was the low rate of marital disharmony. In fact, a number reported improved and closer relationships, and the positive effects of having a child with a disability.

Adverse financial effects emerged as an important factor in a number of families. One of the findings in relation to these financial effects was that this occurred equally across socio-economic groupings, rates showing little difference between medical card or VHI holders. Financial effects were experienced in different ways. Firstly, a desire for direct, extra financial support was expressed. Secondly, the provision of services such as physiotherapy was often lacking, and was sometimes supplied, on a private basis, at personal expense. Thirdly, there was the inconvenience of constantly negotiating services and benefits, indicating significant problems in relation to access. At a different level, financial resources were quite strongly related to emotional well-being. The latter was also influenced by the degree of available emotional support and the absence of restriction on the mother's personal time. These three influences on emotional well-being were each as significant, or more significant, than the direct effect of the child's disability.

There is no evidence from this study of the existence of "the handicapped family". The families concerned did not view themselves in a negative light, rather as ordinary families with a child who had specific difficulties that could be addressed. They did not appear to have a high level of problems, including relationship difficulties, and, as indicated, many rejected the notion of particular problems associated with the disabled child. Indeed, some of the women viewed the presence of a disabled child as a positive element within the family. The problems they experienced, in general, were related to over-coming obstacles in terms of accessing services and benefits for the child. Neither did they see themselves as similar to other families with a disabled child, although some did recognise the need for mutual support. Rather, the evidence here is that they comprised a heterogeneous grouping representing different social categories in society.

References

Abberley, P. (1987), "The concept of oppression and the development of a social theory of disability", *Disability, Handicap and Society,* 2: 5-19.

Allen, J. (1996), "Foucault and special educational needs: a 'box of tools for analysing children's experiences of mainstreaming'", *Disability and Society,* 11: 219-234.

Barnes, C. (1991), *Disabled people in Britain and discrimination: A case for anti-discrimination legislation.* London: Hurst/British Council of Organisations of Disabled People.

Brannen, J. and M. O'Brien. (1995), "Childhood and the Sociological Gaze: Paradigms and Paradoxes", *Sociology,* 29: 729-737.

Childhood, Editorial (1998), The social construction of childhood — and its limits, *Childhood,* 5: 131-132.

Cleary, A. (1996), *The Health Report,* Dublin, Report Commissioned by the Commission for the Status of People with Disabilities/Department of Law Reform.

Cleary, A. (2001), "Responding to the birth of a disabled child", in preparation.

Dutton, K. (1996), *The Perfectable Body*, London: Cassell.

Finkelstein, V. (1991), Disability: An administrative challenge? in M. Oliver (ed.) *Social Work: Disabled People and Disabling Environments*, London: Jessica Kingsley.

Foucault, M (1973), *The Birth of the Clinic*, London: Tavistock.

Gittins, D. (1998), *The Child in Question*, Basingstoke: Macmillan.

Glendinning, C. (1983), *Unshared Care: Parents and their Disabled Children.* London: Routledge and Kegan Paul.

Harris, P. (1995), "Who am I? Concepts of disability and their implications for people with learning difficulties", *Disability Studies,* 10: 341-352.

Jahoda, A., I. Markova and M. Cattermole. (1988), "Stigma and self-concept of people with a mild mental handicap", *Journal of Mental Deficiency Research,* 32: 103-115.

James, A. and A. Prout (eds.) (1990), *Constructing and Reconstructing Childhood: Contemporary Issues in the Sociological Study of the Child*, London: Falmer.

Kenny, M., NcNeela, E., Shevlin, M. and Daly, T. (2000), *Hidden Voices: Young people with disabilities speak about their second level schooling.* Report commissioned by the South-West Regional Authority, Cork: Bradshaw Books.

Lewis, A. (1995), *Children's Understandings of Disability.* London: Routledge.

Lewis, S., C. Kagan, P. Heaton, and M. Cranshaw. (1999), "Economic and psychological benefits and perspectives of mothers of disabled children", *Disability and Society,* 14: 561-575.

Low, J. (1996), "Negotiating identities, negotiating environments: an interpretation of the experiences of students with disabilities", *Disability and Society*, 11: 235-248.

Meltzer, H., M. Smyth and N. Robus (1989), *Disabled Children: Services, Transport and Education,* OPCS surveys of disability in Great Britain, Report 6, London: HMSO.

Middleton, L. (1999), "The social exclusion of disabled children: the role of the voluntary sector in the contract culture", *Disability and Society,* 14: 129-139.

Middleton, L. (1996), *Making a Difference: Social Work with Disabled Children,* Birmingham: Venture Press.

Norwich, B. (1997), "Exploring the perspectives of adolescents with moderate learning difficulties on their special schooling and themselves: Stigma and self-perceptions", *European Journal of Special Needs Education,* 12: 38-53.

Oliver, M. (1990), *The Politics of Disablement,* Basingstroke: Macmillan.

Priestley, M. (1998), "Childhood disability and disabled childhoods: Agendas for research", *Childhood,* 5: 207-223.

Qvortrup, J., M. Bardy, G,. Sgritta and H. Wintersberger (1994), *Childhood Matters: Social Theory, Practice and Politics*, Aldershot: Avebury.

Radic, A., H. Dolk and P de Wais. (1988), "Declining Rate of Neural Tube Defects in Three Eastern Counties of Ireland", *Irish Medical Journal,* 80: 226-228.

Reindal, S.M. (1999), "Independence, dependence, interdependence: some reflections on the subject and personal autonomy", *Disability and Society,* 14: 353-367.

Rutter, M., Tizard, J. and Whitmore, K. (1975), *Education, Health and Behaviour*, London: Longmans.

Stone, D. (1984), *The Disabled State,* Philadelphia, PA: Temple University Press.

Taylor, S. J. (2000), "'You're not a retard, you're just wise': Disability, social identity and family networks", *Journal of Contemporary Ethnography*, 29, 58-92.

Tomlinson, S. and R.F. Colquhoun. (1995), "The political economy of special educational needs in Britain", *Disability and Society,* 10: 191-202.

Thomas, D. (1978), *The Social Psychology of Childhood Disability,* London: Methuen.

Williams, G.H. (1999), "Bodies on a battlefield: The dialectics of disability", *Sociology of Health and Illness,* 21: 242-252.

Acknowledgements:
I would like to thank Dr. Peader Kirke and the Health Research Board for permission to use these data and Elizabeth Nixon for her assistance in the analysis of the study.

Chapter 8

Children Who Survive Cancer

Suzanne Quin

As the survival rates for many childhood cancers improve, quality of life concerns for the survivors and for their families have begun to emerge. While there is now a great deal of knowledge about the treatment of cancer and its long term effects from a medical perspective, much less is understood about the psychosocial consequences of surviving cancer. This is particularly so with children who have been relatively neglected in research on the stresses of cancer and its treatment. Those who survive this experience have achieved the desired outcome. Therefore, once treatment has been concluded, it might be assumed that the child and family resume their lives as before. However, the effects of such a profound experience are likely to have long-term effects on all who are directly affected. As Friedman and Mulhern (1991, p. 43) comment:

> . . . unfortunately, survival does not ensure adequate quality of life. In recent years, there has been growing concern about the biological and psychological late effects of childhood cancer and its treatment.

Findings from studies of childhood cancer survivors certainly give cause for concern. Research by Schroff-Pendley et at. (1997), for example, indicates that cancer survivors may be at increased risk of psychological difficulties, particularly after treatment ends. The study further found those diagnosed during middle/late childhood or adolescence to be more at risk for psychosocial difficulties than those who are diagnosed in infancy. An earlier study by Mulhern et al. (1989) found school problems and somatic complaints of undetermined origin to be prevalent. More than half of the children in their sample had scores on standardised testing which were suggestive of excessive behavioural problems and nearly as many had deficits in areas of social competence. Children from single parent households were found to be particularly vulnerable in these respects, having a two-fold increase in risk of having school-related problems and of showing fearful, inhibited or over-controlled behaviour. This study suggests that social support may be more accessible in a two-parent family that may act as a buffer to protect the child against such problems. Another explanation could relate to the socioeconomic circumstances of one-parent families which may result in the greater likelihood of a single parent having to deal with such health issues in the context of relative poverty and deprivation.

However, research on childhood cancer survivors does not indicate only negative outcomes. Lozowski (1992), reporting on research undertaken by Candlelighters Childhood Cancer Foundation, comments on the juxtaposition of its positive and negative findings. For example, survivors reported feeling more positive about things in general than their peers but their self-reported health status was more negative. In examining the latter point further it was found that, while survivors not surprisingly reported more worries surrounding cancer-related illnesses, they also reported fewer general health worries than their peers. A more recent study by Novakovic et al. (1996) supports the possibility of cancer survival in childhood and adolescence as having simultaneously positive and negative outcomes. On the negative side is the experience and memory of pain in relation to the condition and its treatment. This is coupled with the disruption of life for some time in terms of family relationships, friendships, leisure pursuits and schooling. Some will have residual physical problems arising from the condition and all face the concern about the possibility of relapse. On the positive side, survivors noted the discovery of different values in life arising from the experience and the development of a sense of tolerance and compassion for others with cancer and for people in general. Thus, while cancer can bring many negative experiences, it can also lead to the acquisition of a different value system that changes a person's life for the better.

Cincotta (1993) describes childhood cancer as a family disease as it effects everyone within the family system. For the child with cancer, the immediate family is obviously central, but it also impacts on other aspects of their total environment, principally their extended family, friends, school and neighbourhood. The child's adaptation to the illness will be largely determined by the responses of the adults and other children who are part of the child's world. This is also a two-way process in that the child's own coping abilities will, in turn, influence the responses of others.

In a study of the implications for adult relationships of cancer in childhood, Zeltzer (1993) found survivors to have slightly lower rates of marriage than the norm and to often delay marriage to a later age. This he related to parental over-protectiveness arising from the illness. Parental over-protectiveness as an issue for cancer survivors also arises in studies of the more immediate after-effects. Drotar (1997), in a review of studies on this aspect of the parent/child relationship, found parental over-protection consistently related to decreases in the child's sense of self-control and psychological distress. Madan-Swain et al. (1994) found adolescent cancer survivors to be overly compliant in family and other interpersonal relationships and to avoid interactions that involve conflict. The authors suggest that this may be due to the survivors' sense of vulnerability, because of their life threatening illness, for which they may try to compensate by being overly compliant. Another interpretation is that the experience of illness may, as already discussed, lead to the development of a different value system that results in alternative ways of relating to others.

It is clear, therefore, that research on the long-term psychosocial effects of childhood cancer must take account of its impact on all family members, including siblings. Further, it is important that children themselves are included in the research protocol rather than relying solely on parental reporting of effects. Indeed, including children as research subjects will not just enrich the data gathered but may have the indirect positive effect of combating their feelings of loss of control and exclusion reported above. However, research using children as subjects requires additional approaches to the gathering of data than one dealing with adults only. An example of this is the use of appropriate pictures to stimulate discussion and, most importantly, couching questions in ways that are accessible and meaningful to the child.

IRISH CHILDREN WITH CANCER

The limited knowledge about the after-effects of cancer diagnosis and treatment on children and their families, coupled with the lack of Irish data on this increasingly important subject, led to the creation of a research study which was based in the National Oncology/Bone Marrow Transplant Centre at Our Lady's Hospital for Sick Children, Crumlin, Dublin. Out of an initial sample of 100 families, 77 participated. Interviews were conducted with the parents, the children who had undergone treatment for cancer and were old enough to participate, their siblings and some grandparents and other members of the extended family. Both qualitative and quantitative methods were used in the research that included the use of standardised tests and in-depth interviews. The latter, when undertaken with children, incorporated the use of pictures depicting scenes from a children's hospital, drawing and the compilation of a wish list to establish the relative importance of the illness in relation to the other preoccupations or fantasies of healthy childhood. For the purposes of this chapter, the discussion will focus on the findings arising from the qualitative interviews undertaken with the children themselves and their siblings, rather than on the data gathered from the standardised tests and qualitative interviews of their parents and other adult family members.

Those included in the sample had received treatment during the years 1990 to 1994. All of the children were at least two years post-treatment and the survey sample was drawn from all four provinces with just under one-third residing in the greater Dublin area. The respondents came from all socioeconomic groups and had a varied range of types of cancers. The interviews were conducted in the family homes by arrangement. A total of 42 children who had survived cancer were interviewed. The average age of the children at the time of interview was 11.6 years. The mean duration since diagnosis was five years. While parents were willing to participate, not all wished to have their children included. Also excluded were those who had been treated most recently as infants and thus were too young to be interviewed and a few who were now adult and were away from home. The fact that some of the children were so young at the time of treatment meant that they had no real memories of the events. A surprising minority had no idea that they had had cancer, an issue likely to arise as they grew to adulthood and needed to know their medical history.

An obvious hazard in interviewing children is the possibility that they may try to respond as they think the adult will want to hear. Measures were taken to minimise this effect by giving the child plenty of time and space to get to know the researcher and to be comfortable with answering questions in an open manner. An example of the importance of giving the child time and space in the research process was illustrated in relation to memories of hospitalisation. Initially, over half of them said that they could not remember anything and this was independent of age of diagnosis. However, time and planned prompts facilitated the return of memories about their hospitalisation and treatment that had marked the beginning of a profoundly different and difficult experience for both themselves and their family.

THE TREATMENT PHASE AND ITS AFTERMATH

The key areas remembered were aspects of treatment, the staff and the playroom. Some reported very specific memories about particular times or instances:

> I felt sick and I felt horrible. . . . I remember Christmas . . . you know at Christmas you're kind of running around with all your toys. I just sat on the couch. I hardly looked at my toys.

> I was waiting around the waiting room for a long time and
> then they just said "We have a bed ready for you" and I was
> thinking "Why would I want a bed?" I thought I had the flu.

Not surprisingly, the worst parts of treatment were regarded as
being the chemotherapy, losing hair, injections and being sick.
The global effects of the experience was summed up by one
respondent:

> Most of it, nearly everything. Always being sick, never al-
> lowed to go out and play with my friends.

The children also had positive memories of the treatment
phrase. About one-third did not regard it as having been a very
bad time for them, making comments such as "It was all right",
"I think I was really lucky, I didn't really have a hard time". A
quarter of the positive responses related to specific memories
such as meeting famous people, meeting new friends, having
visitors and special treats or outings.

School plays an important part in the maintenance of some
degree of normality during the treatment process. Although
recommended by staff that the child return to school as soon as
possible, this did not tend to happen in reality. Some missed
large blocks of school ("I nearly missed a whole year") while,
for others, intermittent schooling presented problems ("I knew
nothing the days I went in"). The return to school came with its
own problems. Almost one-third specifically identified difficulties. These were not just centred on missed schoolwork; the
majority had to do with the reactions and behaviours of their
schoolmates.

> Everybody was staring at me and then I took off my hat and
> everybody said, "Oh look, she's baldy".

However, while some reported negative feelings and experiences, there were twice as many positive as there were negative comments about schooling. Children looked forward to
getting back to school, describing their feelings as "excited",
"great", "brilliant". Almost one-fifth specifically mentioned
their teacher as being helpful and encouraging. However, it

was friends who proved to be most important, mentioned in almost one-half of the responses on school.

> It was lovely going back to the friends I had.

> . . . everyone was really nice to me in school. No one really said anything, some of them even thought I was cool. I used to have loads of hats.

An aspect that seemed to invite the most comments was that of support. When asked who was there for them in terms of support, almost one-half mentioned their family with, not surprisingly, their mothers and fathers being the most frequently mentioned. Siblings and aunts were specifically selected by many of these as familial sources of support. The next largest group was friends, accounting for over one-third of responses. When asked who was there for them now at this point in time, it was friends who were identified as being of most importance, reflecting the natural shift from nuclear family to peer group with maturation.

Most of the children had something to say also about how they related to their siblings. Two-thirds referred to what they regarded as being a normal relationship describing it as "all right", "fine", "fairly well".

> My little sister sometimes wrecks my head . . . but I get on with her sometimes.

A fifth saw their relationship with their sibling(s) as having changed during their illness. These changes were described in terms of their sibling(s) being nicer to them and seeing more of them. In time, the relationship was seen as returning to the norm.

> . . . when I was in hospital she was way nicer, now I'm home and things haven't changed.

Almost all of the children commented on whether or not they felt that the experience of having had cancer had changed them in any way. Just over one-third saw it as not having made any difference, leaving just under two-thirds who felt it had altered them in some respect. Two types of changes predominated. The first related to changed appearance such as hair growing back differently, lack of energy and curtailment of activities arising from residual effects. The second and more frequently raised differences related to more personal change. The children spoke of appreciating life more, having a more relaxed approach to life, feeling that the experience had matured them and that they were better people from having had the experience and thereby having more understanding of illness and its effects.

> I learned to appreciate life more and grew up quicker.

> I think I've got a better personality. . . . I used to be real bitchy.

When the children were asked about whether they thought that their illness had changed the family overall, two-thirds felt it had not made any difference. The remaining one-third was evenly divided between those who had no view and those who considered that it had brought the family closer. While over one-half commented on the effects on their parents, few referred specifically to their siblings. In relation to either, the perceived upset was related to the time of illness and hospitalisation and was not considered to have had any lasting effects.

As regards their hopes for the future, one-third said that they did not really think about it specifically. The remainder had either general comments or else answered in terms of career aspirations and lifestyle.

> I'm going to get married and have three children.

> I'd like to live in Australia.

This sense of normality in relation to their future was also reflected in the responses to the question of what they would like if they had three wishes. Although the fact that they had had cancer did feature, it by no means predominated. What rated highest was the wish to be rich, have nice things, go on holidays, or meet famous people. Only after these did wishes in relation to being well or never being ill again arise. Of the 39 children who completed the wish list, just six put the wish for themselves or others not to be ill as their first wish, three as their second and four as their third. While this is clearly much higher than would be expected of healthy children, it is important to note that the wishes were expressed in the context of an interview about cancer. The normality of the answers overall indicated that, several years after cancer diagnosis and treatment, it is possible for children to live a normal life not permeated and directed by thoughts of illness.

RESULTS OF STANDARDISED TESTS

The findings of the standardised tests administered provided a more detailed profile of how the children were now coping with the psychosocial aspects of their everyday lives. The Loneliness/Isolation Scale (Asher and Wheeler, 1985) for younger children was completed by 38 of the sample. It examines relatedness on four scales: Friends/Social Interaction; Interests/Activities; School/Education and Isolation/Loneliness. Results showed the children to be well within the norms of well-adjusted children in each of these respects. The fact that only a very small percentage was found to score below the norm is heartening and is no more than might be expected within a general population of children. However, it was still sad to find that, within the survey population, 7.8 per cent of the children responded "always true" to the statement "I feel alone".

For older children, the Offer Self-Image Questionnaire (Offer et al., 1992) was used for the same basic purpose — that of ascertaining their self-view, relatedness to their social environment and other aspects of their psychosocial functioning. The Offer Scale is divided into a number of subsets that are measured individually and together provide a profile of the respondent. On each of the parameters, the survey respondents were well within their peer norms. The overall findings indicate a group of well-adjusted adolescents who view themselves as relating well to their peers and to their families and who, in spite of having missed some schooling, have confidence in their educational abilities.

The children's parents were also asked to rate them using the Social Skills Rating System (Gresham and Elliott, 1990) as a standardised device. This measures the parents' assessment of their children's social skills and whether they exhibit problem behaviours. On both of these parameters, the parents rated their children at levels that were well within the average range. In relation to social skills, the parents tended to rate their children highly. This could be on account of the close parent/child bond and special value placed on these children because of their illness. It is equally possible that, in general, the children had become mature, aware and sensitive to others arising from their experiences of cancer. It is also likely that their social skills would be enhanced through having to relate to a relatively large number of adults in their professional roles, such as hospital staff, their general practitioner and other community-based personnel, as well as parents and friends of other patients in the ward.

For each of the standardised tests, the data were collated to compare the population sample in relation to the established norms. In addition to the analysis of the population sample as a whole, the results of the standardised tests were further analysed in relation to gender, socioeconomic group, single/dual parent households and severity of illness. Some interesting gender differences emerged in the results of the Culture Free Self-Esteem Scale (Battle, 1990) which showed males scoring higher than females in relation to general self-esteem, social/ peer-related self-esteem and parental/home-related self-esteem. In only one aspect did females score higher than males and this was in the area of academic/school-related self-esteem. No differences were found in relation to socioeconomic background of the children, severity of the illness or children of lone parents.

SIBLINGS OF CHILDREN WITH CANCER

Even more so than is the case of children who have had cancer, research on the siblings of those affected has been very limited until relatively recently. However, research that has been undertaken has consistently identified psychosocial problems in such siblings. Rollins (1990) suggests that the siblings of children with cancer are being increasingly and correctly identified as the forgotten ones. In terms of psychosocial needs, he considers siblings to be the most isolated and neglected of all family members during the experience of serious childhood illness. Feelings of resentment, anger, anxiety, depression, fear of their own death, jealousy, guilt, psychological and physical isolation from their parents and a wide variety of behaviours aimed at obtaining parental attention have all been noted in studies of the effects of childhood cancer on siblings.

Heffernan and Zanelli (1997) identify three major stressors experienced by such siblings. The first they term "emotional realignment" which occurs when the parents become preoccupied with the ill child, resulting in the remaining children having feelings of anger, frustration, guilt and increased rivalry with the sick child. The second arises from enforced separation from the rest of the family. Practical and emotional difficulties faced by parents allows little time and space for the remaining children, thus creating feelings of sadness, loneliness, confusion, anxiety and isolation for the healthy siblings. Finally, there is the stressor of the direct effects of the condition and its treatment on the ill child where the sibling may witness, at close proximity, the physical and mental effects of anxiety, debilitation and pain which can cause feelings of guilt, anger, anxiety, embarrassment, fear and frustration.

Earlier studies had already indicated the likelihood of problems for siblings. Martinson et al. (1990) observed behavioural difficulties in a study of the impact of childhood cancer on healthy siblings. In another study, Walker (1990) found that siblings of children with cancer tried hard to become ill themselves, caused fights and arguments in their interpersonal relationships, had problems at school and took on extra chores in an effort to engage their parents' attention. Walker also reported that some siblings engrossed themselves in areas outside the family, such as leisure pursuits and schoolwork, in order to assuage feelings of guilt arising from the mistaken belief that they were the cause of the illness or because they were healthy while their sibling was ill.

The research literature, therefore, indicates the importance of taking into consideration the effects on the siblings of children who develop a life-threatening condition such as cancer. Indeed, Cincotta (1993), in reviewing studies of the effects of childhood illness on siblings, suggests that it is the siblings who may be at greater risk for psychosocial difficulties than their ill brothers or sisters. However, in common with their ill brothers and sisters, the effects on siblings are not all or always negative. Walker (1990) found that initial feelings of embarrassment were replaced by feelings of caring and empathy over time. Sargent et al.'s (1995) study supported this contention, finding that, in addition to the negative effects reported above, siblings became more compassionate and caring as a result of their brother's or sister's illness. These researchers found that older siblings coped better with the condition and its effects than did younger siblings who were more dependent on the family for support. Given the fact that many cancers such as leukaemia tend to occur in very young children, it follows that many of the healthy siblings will also be young and therefore vulnerable to its effects on family life.

SIBLINGS IN THE CRUMLIN HOSPITAL STUDY

In the current study, a total of 38 siblings were interviewed. At the time of the interview the mean age was 14 years, and the average age at time of diagnosis was nine years of age. The most salient memories they recalled about their ill siblings at the time of treatment centred on their physical appearance and the effects of the illness and treatment.

> I remember he was always in the hospital and when he came back he had a drip called "Freddy". Mum had to feed him and we all thought he was really lucky.

> . . . seeing him so white in the face and his little bits of hair, he would pull them out to annoy you.

The overwhelming memories identified by more than half of the sibling respondents were that they had missed their brother/

sister and their parents. They were frightened and they had felt
on their own at home.

> The worst part was when she came home and she was vom-
> iting all of the time. She was keeping me awake. I was
> scared because I don't like the sound of vomiting. Mam
> would be looking after her all of the time and she stayed in
> the room all of the time and she'd hardly do anything with
> us.

> It was horrible for us because we never had anyone really
> here.

There were, however, compensations for some.

> . . . he got loads of toys and you could play with them when-
> ever you wanted because he was too young to play with
> them.

> I spent a lot of time at my friend's house, which I thought
> was brilliant.

When asked about their sources of support at this time, friends
came out as being the greatest source, at under one-third of all
people mentioned. Next came parents, both holding approximately one-fifth of choices. It is interesting to note that fathers
fared slightly better than did mothers, most likely because the
latter spent more time in the hospital with the ill child. Also
identified were relatives such as aunts, uncles and grandparents. While teachers only came in for one specific mention, it
was clear from the more general comments that school was often an important source of support and normalisation for both
the siblings and the child who was ill. A small but very important minority of siblings conveyed a sense of isolation and lack
of support.

> . . . but we were lost because there was no one there for us
> to ask "Are you OK?" and we needed it, I think, just as
> much.

> (I) was scared for him and then I didn't have mam and dad
> around me because they were in Crumlin (Hospital) so it

was myself and granny. It was hard at the start because I had nobody there.

With regard to the relationship between the siblings, two-thirds described their relationship as fine/grand/OK/all right. Less than one-tenth said that they got on "really well" and the rest were non-committal. Three-fifths felt that their ill sibling tended to get preferential treatment in the family.

> Just little things, she's always getting away with little things.

> Oh yes, always special treatment from everybody. She doesn't realise it but compared to what we get . . .

A few raised the difference in their sibling since the illness.

> Since she got out of hospital, she has been very cranky, mood swings, one minute you're having a laugh with her and the next minute she'd turn around and chew you apart.

While, at one level, there was a shared perception of life returning to normal, at the same time, it was clear that it had left a residue of underlying fear and uncertainty. Two-thirds of the siblings indicated that they still had fears about their brother's/sister's health.

> I think any time he has a headache, or pains or he's feeling sick . . . the first thing that hits your mind, even though you'd never say it to him but you'd say 'Please God, don't let it be this again'. I think that's the way it's always going to be.

The fact that it could happen to one of their family also raises fears for themselves.

> Even for us, every time we get sick we are afraid something is going to happen. It started off so simple, just a little cold or whatever.

Sometimes they could carry a burden of unnecessary guilt, as was the case of one sibling who asked his mother years later:

> Was it me who caused the cancer? I knocked him.

When asked what they would choose if they had three wishes, many of the answers given by the siblings paralleled those of the children who had had cancer. Wealth, material goods and holidays proved to be the most popular choices. However, as can be seen from the table below, wishes that related to illness occurred more frequently amongst this group than it did for those who had been ill.

Table 8.1: Three Wishes

Three Wishes	Children	Siblings
First wish relating to illness	15%	13%
Second wish relating to illness	7%	32%
Third wish relating to illness	13%	19%

Table 8.2: Children's and Siblings' First Wishes

Children's First Wishes (sample in order of frequency)	Siblings' First Wishes (sample in order of frequency)
To be rich	For a million pounds
To win the lottery	For money
To meet the Spice Girls	To have a moped
To meet Boyzone	To have a Lamborghini
To play for Manchester United	To have an Escort car
That never got tumour	Good holidays for all the family
For everyone who is sick to be well	Go to Disneyland
To have a horse	That he was never sick
To have lots of friends	That he wasn't in hospital
To have roller blades	To be rid of the stuff (treatment)
	To be happy

CONCLUSION

Overall, the findings of this study are a testament to the resilience of children in the face of such adversity as the experience of a life threatening illness. It would be heartening for the parents of newly diagnosed children to learn that even the treatment stage is likely to hold some good as well as bad memories for the increasing number of children who will survive. The fact that, with hindsight, the children will evaluate the overall experience as having had some positive as well as negative outcomes is not what might be generally anticipated. This is not to negate the difficult and often very traumatic experiences that these children undergo.

It is inevitable that the development of a life-threatening condition such as cancer will impact on all members of the immediate family. Of particular concern is the effect on siblings. The interviews with parents and healthy siblings, in keeping with other research findings, indicate that siblings of seriously ill children are at risk of feeling isolated, guilty and neglected. Parents are likely to be aware of such risks but are overwhelmed by the practical and emotional demands of the sick child, particularly during the treatment phrase. This points to the need to develop appropriate supports for parents who are lacking community and family supports. It also indicates the need for services to pay particular attention to the psychosocial needs of siblings to help prevent lasting negative effects. This also holds true for a small proportion of the children who have had cancer, especially those who have residual physical effects. Some further help may be needed as this generation of children approach adulthood and have to deal with the implications of having been a child who has had cancer and survived.

·

Note: The study was funded by the Children's Research Centre and was undertaken in collaboration with the Oncology Unit, Our Lady's Hospital for Sick Children, Crumlin, Dublin. The project directors were Dr Suzanne Quin, Department of Social Policy and Social Work, University College Dublin, Dr Fin Breatnach, Dr Ann O'Meara and Mr Eddie O'Neill, Oncology Unit. The principal researcher was Ms Patricia White.

References

Asher, S.R. and Wheeler, V.A. (1985), "Children's Loneliness: A comparison of rejected and neglected peer status", *Journal of Consulting and Clinical Psychology*, Vol. 53, pp. 500-505

Battle, J. (1990), *Culture-Free Self-Esteem Inventories*, Austin, TX: Pro-Ed.

Cincotta, N. (1993), "Psychosocial Issues in the World of Children with Cancer", *Cancer Supplement*, Vol. 17, No. 10, pp. 3251-3260.

Drotar, D. (1997), "Relating Parent and Family Functioning to the Psychological Adjustment of Children with Chronic Health Conditions: Have We Learned? What Do We Need To Know?" *Journal of Pediatric Psychology*, Vol. 22, No. 2, pp. 149-165.

Friedman, A. and Mulhern, R. (1991), "Psychological Adjustment Among Children Who Are Long-Term Survivors of Cancer" in Johnson, J.A. and Johnson, S.B.(eds), *Advances in Child Health* Psychology, Tallahassee, FL: University of Florida Press.

Gresham, F.M. and Elliot, S.N. (1990), *Social Skills Rating System*, Circle Pines American Guidance Service.

Heffernan, S. and Zanelli, A. (1997), "Factors Influencing Family Participation in a Longitudinal Study: Comparison of Pediatric and Healthy Samples", *Journal of Pediatric Psychology*, Vol. 22, No. 2, pp. 245-262.

Lozowski, S. (1992), "Views of Childhood Cancer Survivors: Selected Perspectives", *Cancer Supplement*, Vol. 17, No. 10, pp. 3354-3355.

Madan-Swain, A., Brown, T., Sexton, S., Baldwin, K., Pais, R. and Ragab, A. (1994), "Adolescent Cancer Survivors, Psychological and Familial Adaptation", *Psychosomatics*, Vol. 35, No. 5, pp. 453-459.

Martinson, I., Gilliss, C., Colaizzo, D., Freeman, M. and Bossert, E. (1990), "Impact of Childhood Cancer on Healthy School-Age Siblings", *Cancer Nursing*, Vol. 13, No. 3, pp. 183-190.

Mulhern, R., Wasserman, A., Friedman, A. and Fairclough, D. (1989), "Social Competence and Behavioural Adjustment of Children who are Long-term Survivors of Cancer", *Pediatrics*, Vol. 83, No. 1., pp. 18-25.

Novakovic, B., Fears, T., Wexler, L., McClure, L., Wilson, D., McCalla, J. and Tucker, M. (1996), "Experiences of Cancer in Children and Adolescents", *Cancer Nursing*, Vol. 19, No. 1., pp. 54-59.

Offer, D., Ostrov, E., Howard, K.I. and Dolan, S. (1992), *Offer Self-Image Questionnaire Revised*, California: Western Psychological Services.

Rollins, J. (1990), "Childhood Cancer: Siblings Draw and Tell", *Pediatric Nursing*, Vol. 16, No. 1, pp. 21-27.

Sargent, J., Sahler, O., Roghmann, K., Barbarian, O., Carpenter, P., Copeland, D., Dolgin, M. and Keltzer, L. (1995), "Sibling Adaptation to Childhood Cancer Collaborative Study: Siblings' Perceptions of the Cancer Experience", *Journal of Pediatric Psychology*, Vol. 20, No. 1, pp. 151-164.

Schroff-Pendley, J., Dahlquist, L. and Dreyer, Z. (1997), "Body Image and Psychosocial Adjustment in Adolescent Cancer Survivors", *Journal of Paediatric Psychology*, Vol. 22, No. 1, pp. 29-43.

Walker, C. (1990), "Siblings of Children with Cancer", *Oncology Nursing Forum*, Vol. 17, No. 3, pp. 355-360.

Zeltzer, L. (1993), "Cancer in Adolescents and Young Adults: Psychosocial Aspects", *Cancer Supplement*, Vol. 71, No. 10, pp. 3463-3468.

Chapter 9

Resisting Daughters: Father-Daughter Child Sexual Abuse Disclosure

Imelda Colgan McCarthy and *Nollaig O'Reilly Byrne*

INTRODUCTION

In this chapter, the authors make some observations on the emergent strength of children who disclose sexual abuse by their fathers, while also considering the social and familial contexts that have supported them in their resistance of abuse. The Ireland in which these disclosures of sexual abuse were made and heard was one that was rapidly approaching its European neighbours in terms of demographic profile, women's and children's rights. During the 1970s "wife battering" and "child battering" had entered the social and professional consciousness and a development of services was commenced. In the case of the former, it was spearheaded by the women's movement in the creation of Women's Aid refuges while, in the case of the latter, child protective services became a domain of the State through its expansion of social work services, child protection mandates and guidelines.

Between the 1960s and the 1980s, Irish society transformed itself and the family was no exception. Probably the defining feature of change within the family was its democratisation. With the decreasing age gap between marital partners, the availability of contraception, decreasing family size, increased State monetary allowances for women and their employment outside of the home, women began to demand equality inside and outside of the home (Kiely, 1995; Nic Ghiolla Phádraig and Clancy, 1995). Throughout this period of increasing vocalisation in relation to women's issues, the concerns of children were also moved to the fore. One of the authors had been part of the orchestration of a national awareness of children's rights and their abuses throughout the mid-1970s (McCarthy and McQuaid, 1980). The initial social and professional focus was on the non-accidental injury of children. However, by the beginning of the 1980s a new phenomenon began to emerge. Young teenage girls began to speak out about the sexual abuse they were being subjected to by their fathers and male caretakers. These young girls began to break the taboo on talking about this silenced phenomenon in increasing numbers. These young people were now also joining a larger social movement that supported the adding of children's voices in the forging of their roles as active co-creators in family and social life.

SEXUAL ABUSE DISCLOSURE: THE EMERGENCE OF WOMEN

In relating the story of the work outlined in this chapter, some background is offered. In 1981, our team, comprising of the authors and a third colleague, Philip Kearney, undertook the study of father-daughter sexual abuse from a referral base of 30 families. We had imagined that, when these families came to the clinic, we would witness the demise of these units and seriously "damaged" members. However, what we witnessed was unexpected. We were unprepared for the strength and resources we found, particularly in these young girls and their mothers. Initially we were puzzled until we included the context of these families, an Ireland in transition, into our analysis. What we saw then was a movement within the microcosm of the "nuclear" family" which mirrored the emergence of women and children at the wider social level. It was this emergence of women and children that, we proposed, generated the disclosure of child sexual abuse within the family (McCarthy and Byrne, 1988, p. 183). In fact, it was our experience that all kinds of disclosures about the intimate abuses within families were a product of this emergence. Thus, we would strongly assert that, even today, to regard the disclosures of abuse by women and, particularly in this case, children, as cathartic, confessional and merely as a plea for protection, is to remain deaf to their desires. As social metaphors in the public domain, "abuse" and "protection" thus have the potential to become reversible shrouds in which victims are often laid out in professional and public discursive arenas.

Furthermore, descriptions of women as acquiescent to patriarchal family structure is, in our view, a caricature that does not fit with our observations of the mothers or daughters who disclose abuse. In our study, the majority are in step with their cultural contemporaries in their familiarity with women's issues. They are in tune with personal issues, for example, health, work, the questioning of a total commitment to child care and openly challenging husbands in regard to issues of status and authority. Prior to the introduction of divorce in Ireland, all held marital separation as an option. In families where sexual abuse has occurred, we reported that it was the mother's confrontation of these social issues that appeared to trigger her daughter's disclosure. This view is also resonated in Sophia McColgan's tragic and courageous account of her abuse. She, too, initially disclosed the horrendous abuse by her father when (unbeknown to her) her mother was taking steps to leave her violent and abusive husband. Tragically in this instance, both their accounts fell on deaf ears until many years later (McKay, 1998).

As we worked with these young girls and their families, in collaboration with child protection services, it became clear that an episode of disclosure is also inevitably shaped by the listening community in which it occurs. So, not only was the telling of abuse important, but the way in which it was heard is vital. Just as the context must be open for those to tell, it must also be open for those to hear.

FROM THE PRIVATE TO THE PUBLIC: THE PROCESS OF SPEAKING OUT AND LISTENING

Through our experience, we have learned that disclosure of abuse occurs in discrete or serial episodes, as an attempt to engage a listener's concern or help. Usually, it is thought about in advance and the complaint of abuse, rehearsed in one's mind, sometimes over many years (Weingarten and Cobb, 1995). As such it is a process matter, advanced with considerable internal rehearsal before the decision to speak out is made. In this process, the telling of one's abuse is just one punctuation in the discursive movement from the private domain of internal conversations to the public domain of interpersonal communications. The entire process thus can be seen to constitute a change effort, even before the actual spoken disclosure itself takes place. In this manner of thinking, the point of disclosure itself is yet another indication of major change in the life of the family and the young person. Therefore, this process from private to public utterance has many implications, both for the speaker, the complainant and for potential listeners. We deem this to be important because those in the public sphere often include representatives of the State, such as the police, social workers, residential care staff and so on, who act as gatekeepers for issues of public concern. It is important because, just as utterances are dependent on context for their initial occurrence, they are also dependent on context for their legitimation and future consequences. Let us look now at what we mean by this.

LISTENING AS A CONFESSIONAL OR WITNESSING ACTIVITY

Just as there are implications for those who disclose abuse, there are also implications for the position of those who hear the abuse account. For example, does the listener position themselves as if they are in receipt of a confession which reveals the speaker as a person in need of absolutiŏn, recuperation or correction? In professional parlance, this may translate into the need for cure, resocialisation or rehabilitation. The cathartic expression in "recovered memories" of abuse episodes may be developed as the overarching therapeutic framework for persons disclosing abuse. In other words, it might be imagined that, to "heal" themselves, those who have been abused need to re-live the abuse episodes in cathartic outpourings. This very point received comment by one victim of abuse while in the care of a religious order and the State. She said, "it is unacceptable that people should be required to go back to the source of their problems in order to seek healing" (O'Connor, 1999, p. 19). However, the question we would thus pose in this chapter is, do we, as professionals, in our listening, bring premature closure to the intentions of the speaker? In a move such as this, practitioner and theoretical discourses are privileged over lived accounts. When this occurs, the account of abuse is fitted into a prefigured frame for understanding the experiences, and thus the professional is in danger of removing themselves from dialogue and constituting a process of colonisation of the young person's narrative. As an antidote, therefore, a more important question should arise, namely, is the client's story the privileged account in the constitution of therapeutic encounters in the aftermath of abuse disclosures? In other words, does the client, who is a child in this instance, speak for herself, or are they spoken for by others who claim to know better and more? The dis-position[1] we have attempted in our work is to situate ourselves as witnesses to testimonies of abuse in acknowledgement of the courage to speak out and to resist further abuse.

We might illustrate the above dilemmas and questions as shown on Figure 9.1.

In the diamond-shaped figure, we have juxtaposed two sets of contrasting themes — those of "subject" and "object, dialogue and monologue. These terms are chosen, in this particular instance, to create a discursive field that might re-present the dilemmas of disclosure that we have mentioned previously. These are: does the subject who has been abused speak to another in dialogue about what matters most to them, or do they become an object of concern who is subjected to a professional account of their experiences through diagnosis and prefixed treatment regimes? In this latter scenario, dialogue fails before the monologic expertise of a professional who "knows better" what is called for in these instances. In this latter scenario, the young girl is "spoken for" and there is a danger that she becomes a passive receptor and listener within the drama of her life. In the former scenario, the young girl has the potential to become a co-participant in actively shaping her own "treatment" and her future life — a life without abuse.

Figure 9.1: The Disclosing Speaker as Subject or Object?

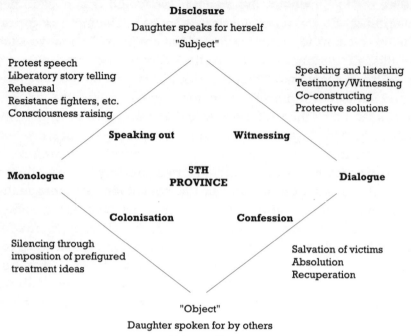

We would also suggest that this diamond figure can act as a holding frame, not only for therapeutic conversations at the micro level of clinical interaction, but also include discourses which are privileged at any one time in the society in which the particular disclosure is taking place. We have witnessed since the 1980s many shifts in what is deemed appropriate in terms of abuse disclosure and child protection. Initial knee jerk reactions have given way to more measured and collaborative approaches towards those who have been abused and non-abusing parents. The attitude to those who have abused has also changed. When we began our work at the outset of the 1980s, fathers who abused were not treated, but were deemed to be in need of psychiatric treatment or imprisonment. Today, discourses utilising "addiction metaphors", cognitive distortions and therapeutic milieus are considered in addition to, or instead of, penal custody. Therefore, if we focus on the lower part of the diamond, we, as professionals, in co-operation with our clients and their families, may begin to deconstruct ideas about their life situations that are unhelpful and construct ideas that they would find helpful. If ideas about treatment are introduced over which clients do not have a say, then one could deem this to be a situation of professional monologue, where societal or professional ideas are privileged and the voices of clients are drowned out. Where societal and professional ideas are introduced for discussion with clients, then a dialogue ensues where participants have the possibility of having their own accounts matter.

Therefore, if one acknowledges and witnesses the courage, resilience and strength in a child's efforts to speak out, resist and refuse abuse, then the process of disclosure of sexual abuse by a young child challenges traditions that previously have privatised and silenced this issue. However, as we have said, how these issues are "treated" within professional and public domains is of serious import. This is important because, nowadays, significant silencing strategies are no longer that of societal indifference or lack of permission to speak, but are often of a much more insidious institutional and professional filtering, which may usurp the disclosure. For example, a disclosure may be usurped or co-opted by way of acknowledgement and response such that it increases another source of potential domination — protection by State services.

What we mean by this is that disclosure is not an unmediated event between a speaker and a listener or listeners. The child making the disclosure enters into a significantly asymmetric relationship and often must submit to the opinion, advice, classification and action of a higher authority. As we have seen on many occasions, it is an unfortunate parallel that institutional practices challenge personal lives as contexts of oppression without a matching analysis of their own power structures. It is here, in this unequal relationship between a child, family and State representatives, that confessional speech is likely to be exacted.

In a confessional disclosure, the speaker inscribes herself in a self-descriptive discourse of an existing biographical genre of victimisation. In opposition, Alcoff and Gray (1993) connote speaking out as "survivor discourse", a political tactic that subverts the dominant order, thus eschewing projects of personal salvation or recuperation. Protest speech and confession are oppositional couplets, signifying consciousness raising on the one hand and recuperation on the other hand. The former promotes female solidarity and political change, while the latter, all too often, ensures the isolation of victims and the proliferation of treatment services.

> Too often the excavation of the buried injured child became the all consuming central drama and the effort to reject victim status and move towards maturity (sic) was largely side lined (Alcoff and Gray, 1993, p. 382).

What is overlooked in the confessional process is that, in the courageous telling of their abuses outside of the family, children are part of a protest movement about the previously sanctioned privacy of the patriarchal nuclear family. Their protest repoliticises and demystifies the privacy of the family and involves a questioning of wider social forms and values impacting on the family, which constitute contexts of oppression. Abuses are generally silenced events. Therefore, when the silence is broken, it matters much how the child and her personal story is "treated". As a complaint, disclosure can be reduced to a litany of personal hurts and resentments, privatised through therapeutic procedures and often in a way that accentuates an emotional display of shame and helplessness. This happens when rebels against abuse, co-opted into a confessional system, become classified as victims and individual sufferers. In this tragic scenario, they pose no threat to the prevailing "patriarchal" orders. Instead they become objects of a paternalistic concern. Feminists such as Alcoff and Gray (1993) and Faludi (1991) have pointed out that dominant cultures have long been known to move from a strategy of outright silencing and indifference to a strategy of recuperation. In such movements, victims emerge at the expense of "heroines", "rebels", "resistance fighters" and "rights activists" in the fight for freedom and liberation from abuse.

It is in this light that we highlight the potential of child protection procedures to colonise the protest intent in children speaking out.

CHILD PROTECTION — A PATERNALISTIC ACTIVITY, OR A FORCE FOR CHANGE?

The discourse of protection, particularly in relation to civil and human rights, almost inevitably beckons affirmation from a majority of citizens in the Western World. As the manifest concern for vulnerable members of society, it is a significant achievement of the modern state. This is particularly so in the case of children, where failures and transgressions arouse public concern and anxiety, together with heightened efforts at social control. The protection of children is a highly emotive issue.

Likewise, the protection of children's rights arouses strong emotions of espousal in most of us. It soothes professional anxieties in relation to other functions of social control. This is so, especially with those who are under State-mandated vigilance for a "failure" to meet socially designated standards of living and caring. Child protection thus becomes that motivating and mobilising emblem in an otherwise highly ambivalent professional response to mandatory expectations implicated in social control. As O'Donovan (1984, p. 80) points out:

> Protection is a concept which must be carefully analysed. Protection — for whom, from what, from whom?

If we take children, the notion of their rights is, by and large, specified by the adult community in which they live. The adult world is taken as the norm. Their rights are accorded and adjudicated by adults along the highly ritualised parameters of the law, the courts, therapeutic and welfare services. How often do we listen to the wishes and desires of children, freely given and not fitted within some dramatised ritual? Therefore, as professionals to whom children are likely to disclose abuse, we must never forget that, while it may be necessary at times to speak out and seek protection from abuse, in doing so one is also confirming one's weaker status. Every conversation we have with children around their abuse is saturated with power — how we ask questions, to whom we address questions, what we ask questions about. All such questions include certain subjects while excluding others. Where the exclusions refer to the lived experiences of the child and are not incorporated within normative considerations, we are in danger of generating situations of domination and constituting relationships of power in our practice.

TWO CASES OF PROTECTION AND RESISTANCE TO ABUSE: JULIA AND THERESA

Julia

Julia is the eldest in a family of five children ranging in age from 15 to 7 years. At the time of her disclosure of abuse, she lived with her paternal grandmother, father, mother and siblings in her grandmother's home. Julia disclosed that she had been sexually abused by her father from the age of 9 years. She reported that she disclosed the abuse in a bid to stop it and to get help for her father. Here are her words in response to her parents' report that she had been taken away from them by the social workers:

> *Nollaig*: (to Julia) and what is your belief about that?
>
> *Julia*: I believe they can take me?
>
> *Nollaig*: They can take you . . . and is it that they (the social workers) took you or that you went and they helped you to go, because there is a difference . . . did they actually take you or did you want to go and they gave you help?
>
> *Julia*: I wanted to go and they helped.
>
> *Nollaig*: They gave you help but they didn't actually take you, is that right, from your point of view?
>
> *Julia*: Yeh.

In a conversation where views are contested, Nollaig here reflects with Julia the view that, in her efforts to be free from abuse by her father, the social workers she spoke with were acting in a helpful manner, from her point of view. As the interview proceeds, Nollaig goes on to ask Julia the reasons, from her point of view, why she disclosed the abuse when she did. Again we see Julia's clearly articulating her refusal of abuse and the necessity for her to disclose it in order to end it and to get help for her father.

> *Julia*: Because, I couldn't stand what was going on . . . it was going on all the time and I couldn't stand it . . . I just couldn't put up with it anymore.
>
> *Nollaig*: Did you think he (father) wouldn't stop if you said it to him?
>
> *Julia*: It would not have made any difference.
>
> *Nollaig*: He wouldn't have listened to you . . . so your talking wouldn't have made a difference? . . . what do you think Julia? Do you think your parents understand that it was very necessary for you to share this confidence with the teacher, that that was a good thing for you to do . . . that it was helpful to you?
>
> *Julia*: Well, I think it was anyway.
>
> *Nollaig*: You think it was anyway . . . helpful just for you or for everyone?
>
> *Julia*: Well, for myself mostly.
>
> *Nollaig*: For yourself mostly? . . . I heard you saying that you wanted something done about him? What is it you want done for him?
>
> *Julia*: I don't really know what could be done.
>
> *Nollaig*: Do you think he should be helped or do you think he should be punished for having done this to his daughter?

Many children and young people who have disclosed abuse in our project have not only wanted their father to be helped, but also to be punished for his actions. In Julia's case, after her father has acknowledged the abuse, she is not sure what can be done. However, when the options are placed before her, she does not opt for punishment at this time but goes on to consider the concept of "help".

> *Julia*: Well . . . after all the years ... (pause) . . . everything can be left the way it is. He doesn't need to be punished.
>
> *Nollaig*: He doesn't need to be punished?

Julia: No, just me staying where I am, that is all.

Nollaig: Does he need to be helped?

Julia: I would say he might.

Nollaig: What would be better for him (father) . . .? What do you think the social workers who came in to help you would wish to see happen to your Dad, like (social worker's names)? What do you think they would like for your father?

Julia: I don't know because they never . . . they did mention what should be done to a person who does that but it's only an expression.

Nollaig: An expression?

Julia: They should be put behind bars.

The remainder of the session was devoted to what might happen for Julia and the rest of her family, together with what might happen to her father. Julia continued to live apart from her family, while the social workers visited her and her family on a regular basis. The family went on to have family therapy and both mother and father entered therapy for themselves with the help of the health board for a period of some years.

Theresa

Theresa is also the eldest of a family of seven children ranging in age from 15 years to 9 months. When she was eight years old, she disclosed sexual abuse by her maternal grandfather for which he subsequently served a prison sentence. When she was eleven, she disclosed that her father also sexually abused her. Subsequent to this disclosure, her father stood trial and served two years in prison. From the time of disclosure to the father's release from prison, a period of four years, the family had continuous involvement with Social Services and Child Psychiatric Services. Permission was granted by the prison governor for the father to attend family therapy with his family at the child psychiatric clinic. The social worker with a protection brief also attended these meetings. During this period, a detailed discussion of the abuse, including its effects on all family members and Theresa in particular, was addressed. Also addressed was the meaning of the father's imprisonment for Theresa, her mother and siblings. Throughout the sessions over the years, Theresa did not add anything further to her initial disclosure and was very unhappy at times that her father was sent to trial and then to prison. She did what she did to stop the abuse. After her disclosure, her father agreed to leave the family home, attended a treatment group for abusers and AA on a regular basis in the period prior to sentencing. Because of this and to protect her father, Theresa attempted to withdraw her allegation before the court case, but her father was adamant that he had committed offences against her and wished to make amends. From that time, Theresa maintained a silence throughout, which she insisted was her choice.

The excerpts that follow were taken from a planning session for the father's return to the family home prior to his release from prison. The reader will see the task of child protection illustrated through the, often challenging, words of the senior social worker. She was the professional charged with primary responsibility, not only for Theresa's safety but also that of her siblings. Earlier in the interview, she had carefully explained to the father and mother that, because of her statutory responsibilities, she would have to ask them difficult questions in relation to the future safety of their children. The parents stated they understood this and expressed gratitude to her for "being straight with them and not going behind their backs". The opening excerpt addresses the idea that it would be desirable for Theresa to continue to talk with a therapist individually about the ongoing family situation and her experiences of abuse. Here is her reply to an expectation that she should attend a therapist to speak more about the abuse, which she claimed ended with her disclosure, her father's acknowledgement of it and her mother's supportive stance.

> *Theresa*: Why do I have to be talking to someone about it?
>
> *Father*: Would you like to talk to someone?
>
> *Theresa*: Would you sit down and tell some stranger how you are feeling?

Nollaig accepting Theresa's word offers an alternative to talking to "some stranger" realising that, in her opposition,
Theresa also leaves an opening by only specifying one category of person, namely, "some stranger".

> *Nollaig*: Would you sit down and talk to some trusted pro-
> fessional person? You know professional people pretty
> good now, don't you? If you had a trusted professional per-
> son, would you speak to her?
>
> *Theresa*: (nods in the affirmative)
>
> *Nollaig*: You would? And trust doesn't happen in the first
> session.
>
> *Theresa*: True.

The senior social worker, having to ensure Theresa's safety
along with that of her siblings, follows Nollaig's introduction of
the word "trust" and asks an open question, exploring
Theresa's own views about her future safety. She then goes on
to address her own professional anxieties for Theresa's ongoing freedom and safety in the new situation where the father is
again residing in the family home. Theresa makes an interesting reply that might be open to many interpretations but makes
it clear that her words are her own and no one else's. She
speaks for herself.

> *Senior Social Worker*: What would help you to feel safe?
>
> *Theresa*: I do feel safe.
>
> *Senior Social Worker*: Do you? I am a bit anxious. . . . I just
> wonder how free Theresa is to say what she feels.
>
> *Theresa*: I am as free as I want to be. What I am saying here
> is coming from me, nobody else.

Later in the interview. the issue of the children's ongoing safety
after their father's release from prison is raised again by the
senior social worker. In a context where the mother's valiant
efforts at maintaining the family during the father's absence
from the home have been recognised, she had this to say:

Mother: We don't feel that, just because (father's) prison sentence has come to an end, that we are saying, "that's it, forget about everything else". We have to be constantly, I'm not saying on the alert, but we have to remember. It is not something that you can just forget and say, "well, that could never happen again". But I know too, that once (father) keeps up the support he gets from AA with his sponsor, that we'll be grand. If (father) was to stop that . . . it's addictive . . . it's . . . can you understand what I am trying to say?

Senior Social Worker: Yes, I do.

Mother: We really don't think it is over now, "forget about this", like it never happened.

Senior Social Worker: Life does go on and has a right to go on and within that these children have a right to be safe.

Mother: Yes. What I'm saying is I think we can see danger-posts. For us to think, "this will never happen again", would be wrong. We hope it won't happen again and once we can continue . . .

The senior social worker recognises the mother's position but stresses that the primary responsibility for safety lies with the father.

Senior Social Worker: But you do realise that (father) can make sure it will never happen again?

Mother: Yes. Once (father) continues what he has been do-ing.

Senior Social Worker: He can make sure it never happens.

Father: (to SSW) It will never happen again. I'm not just saying that. I really want it, really want it.

Senior Social Worker: Yes, I would have that feedback from (therapist and key social worker) that you do want to make sure that this doesn't happen again.

Father: I do really.

Senior Social Worker: (to mother) But I do hope that if something did happen again that you would mind your children and that (father) would be out of the house.

Father: There is no chance of that (the abuse) happening.

Mother: I wouldn't take even one bit of what went on before. (father) knows that. AA is keeping (father) right and if (father) was to stop that, that's it, "good-bye".

Senior Social Worker: I know, but sometimes . . .

Mother: But no, (SSW's name), listen . . .

Senior Social Worker: It is very difficult. You have put a lot into keeping your family together. You have been doing it really well while (father) was in jail. You have a lot invested in it.

Mother: Yes I do. And it looks now that it was worth it. If something was to go wrong again, I wouldn't wait to give it a chance, not this time.

Father: I don't want to sound complacent, but it is not going to go wrong, because I'm going to make sure it is not going to go wrong.

At this juncture, perhaps the most difficult moment comes. On the one hand, there are family members who have been through many traumatic years, each in their own way. For their part, they want to move on with their life where abuse will have no part. Over the past four years, they have shown an enormous commitment to this, starting with Theresa's disclosure; her mother's support of her; her father's acknowledgement of the abuse; his subsequent attendance at groups for sexual and alcohol abuse, both before and during his prison term; his guilty plea; and the family's ongoing co-operation with social services and the child psychiatric clinic. On the other hand are the concerns of society and the mandates for protection which social workers carry. In the face of the family's hope, the senior social worker must place the experience of professionals in this area and the concerns of society before the family and those who have been working with them. Her words are hard, but her tone is gentle.

Senior Social Worker: Well I have sat in rooms with men who have abused in the past, who swore they would never do it again and went out and did it.

Father: Yes.

Senior Social Worker: So, I have to reserve judgement, and so the work to be done is to make sure that you (mother) are very aware how these things happen.

All professionals working with children who have been abused must hold in mind the possibility of re-abuse, alongside that of hope and belief in the efforts of the abuser to change. After the senior social worker left and the other professionals were saying goodbye to the family, Theresa asked if she could speak with Nollaig, the key social worker, and Imelda alone. She again reiterated that she did not want to speak with a therapist at this point but realised that, in the future, she might want to do that and would do it in her own time. She said that she would continue to see Nollaig and so could let her know if she changed her mind. After the father's release from prison social services continued to visit the family as planned. Theresa keeps irregular contact with Nollaig. Her father has continued with AA and remains committed to non-abusive relationships. Theresa and her family, at this point, are progressing well with their lives. With her mother's support, she can claim credit for resisting and refusing abuse by speaking out, which, in turn, led to enormous positive change in the network of family relationships.

In these two cases, we witness two young girls who have bravely refused to be abused further through their disclosure of that abuse. In these particular instances, the girls did not want punishment for their offending father, even where one of the fathers went to jail. However, this is not the position of all children. Many who disclose feel strongly that their fathers and other abusers ought to "pay" for their crimes. In fact, they may see prison as a small price to pay for the robbery of their childhood and their right to care and protection.

Both Julia and Theresa, who are not atypical, presented as strong, independent-minded young women who had sought the assistance of trusted professionals to help them make sure that their abuse did not continue. It is clear that these positions echo the demands by women for freedom from abuse and achievement of equality. In doing so, these young girls are taking an active part, in their small world, of making the larger world a safer place for women and children. They are proactive social actors in the constitution of more caring relational experiences. Seeing them merely as "victims" or "survivors" *after* they have disclosed and thus refused and resisted their abuse, is to hide their strengths, resources and heroism. In honouring strengths and resources, subjects become active participants in creating more positive outcomes.

CHERISHING BRAVERY AND RESISTANCE

The question emerges then as to how child protection, as a social practice, reflexively reproduces itself as a credible, non-coercive and child-sensitive practice. Under what circumstances can children validate their own subject matter from the mess and entanglement of intimate ties — still not reduced by an "expert culture" to an edited, punctuated, corrected or completely rewritten version?

An example of the rewritten lives of children is frequently seen in texts which describe children as not resisting their abuse, not knowing that there was anything wrong but thinking that it was normal and went on in all families. However, if one begins to ask the child to describe exactly what they did when they were being abused, we hear another story. As Wade (1997) has so vividly demonstrated in his work, children will detail all the tiny and not so tiny ways in which they did not like what was happening, were afraid and how they responded. Many responses detailed how they might have slept with their clothes on, avoided situations when they might be alone with their abuser, lying on their stomachs, "playing dead", pretending to be asleep, leaving their bodies, not looking at their perpetrators, not calling him "dad" and so on. These are what Wade refers to as those "small acts of living" (Wade, 1997) which outline a child's resistance to abuse when they are in no position to alter the course of events at the time. How much more is to be gained from listening to these stories in helping children to feel that they were not passive in their abuse but were actively resisting. One need only think of Sophia McColgan's internal dialogue when her father was forcing himself and his opinions on her — "he could make me say yes but in my own mind I was saying, 'That is what you think but I think differently'" (McKay, 1998, p. 115). The acknowledgement of resistance is a discursive turn that discloses to the subject her role in the creation of safety for herself and other family members and proposes pathways to exit from a victim status. As Alice Walker states: "Resistance is the secret of joy" (1992, p. 264).

Acknowledgements

We wish to thank all the social workers and family members who have worked with us and who have taught us invaluable wisdom over the years. We also thank our dear colleague, Philip Kearney, Clanwilliam Institute, who was with us in developing many of the ideas in this chapter.

References

Alcoff, L. and Gray, L. (1993), "Survivor Discourse: Transgression or Recuperation?" *Signs: Journal of Women in Culture and Society*, 18: 260-290.

Byrne, N.O'R. and McCarthy, I.C. (1995), "Abuse, Risk and Protection" in Burck, C. and Speed, B. (eds.) *Gender, Power and Relationships*. London: Routledge.

Faludi, S. (1991), *Backlash: The Undeclared War against Women*. London: Chatto and Windus.

Hydén, M and McCarthy, I. (1994), "Woman Battering and Father-Daughter Incest Disclosure: Discourses of Denial and Acknowledgement", *Discourse and Society*, 5: 543-565.

Kiely, G. (1995), "Family Policy in Ireland" in McCarthy, I.C. (ed.) *Irish Family Studies: Collected Papers*. Dublin: Family Studies Centre, UCD.

McCarthy, I. and McQuaid, P.E. (1980), "Suspected Non-Accidental Injury to Children — A Comparative Study" *Irish Journal of Medical Science*, 150: 1-5.

McCarthy, I.C. and Byrne, N.O'R. (1988), "Mist-Taken Love: Conversations on the Problem of Incest in an Irish Context" *Family Process*, 27: 181-199.

Nic Ghiolla Phádraig, M. and Clancy, P. (1995), "Marital Fertility and Family Planning" in McCarthy, I.C. (ed.) *Irish Family Studies: Collected Papers*. Dublin: Family Studies Centre, UCD.

McKay, S. (1998), *Sophia's Story*. Dublin: Gill and Macmillan.

O'Connor, B. (1999), "Childhoods of Fear: Disgraced orders should disband", *Sunday Independent*, 16 May 1999.

O'Donovan, K. (1984), "Protection and Paternalism", in Freeman, M.D.A. (ed.) *The State, the Law and the Family: Critical Perspectives*. London: Tavistock Publications/Sweet and Maxwell.

Salamon, E. (1994), "Who is a customer for Social Services?" in McCarthy, I.C. (ed.) *Poverty and Social Exclusion: A special issue of Human Systems*, 5: (3/4) 305-318.

Wade, A. (1997), "Small Acts of Living: Everyday Resistance to Violence and Other Forms of Oppression" *Contemporary Family Therapy*, 19: 23-39.

Walker, A. (1992), *Possessing the Secret of Joy*, London: Jonathan Cape.

Weingarten, K and Cobb, S. (1995), "Timing Disclosure Sessions: Adding a Narrative Perspective to Clinical Work with Adult Survivors of Childhood Sexual Abuse", *Family Process*, 34: 257-269.

Notes

---

[1] Dis-position: This word is hyphenated to draw attention to its non-fixed meaning. We do not refer to a static internal state or position in conversation but to a dynamic processual positioning which is open to the many diverse accounts being heard.

Part 3:
Children of Cultural Minorities

Chapter 10

"Out of the Mouths of Babes and Innocents" — Children's Attitudes towards Travellers

Brendan O'Keeffe and Pat O'Connor

INTRODUCTION

This chapter looks at children's attitudes towards Travellers. It focuses on children in fourth class in primary school (i.e. aged 9-11 years) since it is at this stage that they are likely to be aware of socially and culturally constructed differences, and most likely to reflect parental and community attitudes towards such groups. Racist attitudes are increasingly topical since, although Ireland remains one of the more racially and ethnically homogeneous societies in Europe, this situation is changing rapidly. The arrival of refugees, asylum seekers, guest-workers and others in the mid-1990s has added in a new way to the ethnic diversity of a country where, in 1996, just under 7 per cent of the population were born outside Ireland (CSO, 1998). However, despite newspaper headlines referring to an "influx" of asylum seekers, according to the Department of Justice, Equality and Law Reform, Ireland received just 25,000 refugees and asylum seekers in 1999; among the smallest numerically and per capita in the EU. The anecdotal evidence of many of these recent arrivals suggests that racist attitudes and behaviour are prevalent here. At an individual level many have experienced verbal and sometimes physical attacks; organised opposition to them has been mounted by some communities; while their treatment by the State has been severely criticised by senior legal figures.

Research on Travellers, an indigenous ethnic minority group of approximately 25,000 people (less than 1 per cent of the total population), suggests that these new arrivals are not the sole targets of racist attitudes. Thus, in a recent national study, 93 per cent of the respondents said that they would not accept a Traveller into their family; 73 per cent would not accept a Traveller as a friend and 44 per cent would not accept them as a member of their community (Drury Communications, 2000). Over 70 per cent of the respondents in Mac Gréil's (1996) study said that they would not be willing to allow a Traveller into their family, and 59 per cent were not willing to accept Travellers as close neighbours; such attitudes showing "the extent of their lower caste, if not outcaste status" (1996, p. 319). An earlier ESRI study (ESRI, 1984), carried out by Davis, Grube and Morgan, also found widespread stereotyping of Travellers, this being associated with a readiness to engage in racist behaviour.

Mac Gréil (1996, p. 318) has observed that Irish government policy towards Travellers "seems to be more one of assimilation than pluralism". Traveller organisations, such as the Irish Traveller Movement; Dublin Travellers Education and Development Group and Pavee Point Travellers Centre, have seen this as a failure to recognise or respect Traveller culture (DTEDG, 1992; Pavee Point, 1999). The European Parliamentary Inquiry on Racism and Xenophobia (European Parliament, 1991) and the Department of Justice Task Force (1995) have recognised their experience of social exclusion and discrimination. In Ireland today Travellers are generally easily identified by their accent and are frequently blamed for social ills. For a variety of reasons, including the inability of the mainstream school curriculum to recognise Traveller culture, only 20 per cent of Traveller children attend secondary school (INTO, 1992, p. 24). Of the 4,000 or so travelling families in Ireland, it is estimated that almost 1,100 live on the roadside (Department of Justice, 1995, p. 107). In all, over 40 per cent of Irish Travellers do not have access to electricity, and over one-quarter do not have access to running water. Their current life expectancy is twelve years below the Irish mean; a level which was achieved by the rest of the Irish population in 1940 (Department of Justice, 1995). Thus, structurally and numerically they are in a weak position.

LITERATURE REVIEW

Racism can be defined as an ideology and/or as a set of practices. As an ideology, it involves a set of beliefs or prejudices, which legitimate discriminatory behaviour and which stereotype and devalue the other on the basis of their (presumed) biological, ethnic or cultural background. It reflects an ethnically homogenous construction of Irishness combined with a lack of acceptance of "otherness". The main identifiable targets for racism are Travellers, black Irish people and (in the 1990s) asylum seekers and refugees. The Harmony Report (1992) identified racism as the attribution of negative qualities to a race or nationality and the acting upon such beliefs. In his classic study of Irish prejudice, Mac Gréil (1977) describes prejudice as the ascription to a group of generalised negative beliefs derived from pre-judging them. The United Nations Report (1980, p. 3) warned that:

> Stereotypes which become fixed in the public mind, are repeated, are resistant to factual evidence to disprove them, and can become dangerous when they are used to justify and reinforce prejudice, discrimination and the persecution of vulnerable minorities.

Scapegoating is frequently associated with such stereotypical attitudes. Mac Gréil identified the characteristics of a scapegoat as its relative weakness, ease of identification, and association with popular problems in society. Elias and Scottson went further and noted that:

> An established group tends to attribute to its outsider group as a whole the "bad" characteristics of that group's worst section.

In contrast, the self-image of the established group tends to be modelled on the minority of its best or exemplary members

(1994, p. xix). Brief (1998) described such stereotypes as "devaluations . . . transmitted to the members of a society, through the various socialisation processes" (1998, p. 122).

Racist attitudes are classically seen as multidimensional, incorporating cognitive, affective and behavioural dimensions (Allport, 1954). The cognitive attitudinal element includes stereotyping, scapegoating, and the ascribing of generalised negative qualities to an ethnic or racial group. The affective dimension of racist attitudes is particularly concerned with the existence of prejudice, defined as "a predisposition to think, feel and act in ways that are against or away from rather than for or toward other persons" (Newcomb, cited in Ehrlich, 1973). The behavioural dimension is expressed in actual discrimination and social exclusion. In many studies (Bringham and Weissbach, 1972; Mac Gréil, 1996) the Bogardus Social Distance Scale is used as a proximate indicator of such behavioural attitudes. It looks at people's willingness to admit members of an ethnic or racial group to each of the following degrees of social intimacy: close kinship or marriage (1); club as personal friends (2); as neighbours (3); into employment in their occupation or in their country (4); as a citizen of their country (5); as a visitor to their country (6); exclusion from their country (7). Thus the higher the score, the more racist the subject. Using this scale, Mac Gréil found that Irish social distance scores, as regards Travellers, had increased since the early 1970s from 2.9 to 3.6 (see Table 10.1 below). Hence it seemed useful to focus on children's attitudes to having Travellers as neighbours (i.e. number three on the Bogardus Social Distance Scale; just around the limit of acceptance in Mac Gréil, 1996).

Mac Gréil's (1977) earlier work found that women were consistently more racist than men; a pattern which was consistent with Wilson's observations (cited in Bagley, 1979, p. 22) that, as women were more prone to feelings of insecurity, they were more likely to be racist. Hannan et al. (1996) noted that girls still have lower levels of self-esteem than boys. Hence one might expect that girls would be more racist than boys. However, Mac Gréil's (1996) later survey found that there had been a convergence in the prejudice scores of males and females. It is difficult to make sense of these apparently contradictory trends. However it is possible that the key factor is that an underlying lack of respect towards Travellers is expressed rather differently by men and women, and that this is what underlies the inconsistent findings as regards gender differences. Thus it seemed useful to explore the impact of gender in this study. It also seemed important to explore the relevance of social class. In Ireland, children in working class areas are more likely to have personal contact with Travellers, since accommodation for Travellers is generally provided in working class areas. Such personal ties have been thought likely to bring about better race relations, although Deegan (1996) concluded, on the basis of a review of that evidence, that in order to eliminate racist attitudes, inter-ethnic contact had to be accompanied by an elimination of competition between racial groups. It is by no means clear that this occurs in working class areas.

Table 10.1 : Overall Social Distance Scores — Percentage Willing to Accept a Traveller in the Following Categories

Category	1973	1989
Kinship (1)	29.0	13.5
Friendship (2)	51.1	26.7
Neighbour (3)	64.3	41.0
Co-worker (4)	75.5	63.7
Citizen (5)	93.4	90.0
Visitor (6)	2.8	7.0
Exclude (7)	3.8	3.0
Mean Social Distance	2.904	3.681
N	2,302	1,000

Source: Mac Gréil (1996)

To date, there have been very few sociological studies of children's views, although it is increasingly recognised that children have the potential to engage in the research process (Morrow, 1998). Childhood has long been seen as a critical time for the internalisation of parental ethnic attitudes (Allport, 1954); a view that has been recently restated by the United Nations High Commissioner for Human Rights, Mary Robinson (Anti-Racism Teacher's Pack TCD, 1999). Bee (1995) found that there was widespread agreement on the importance of the behaviour and the attitudes of family and peers, while Brief (1998) observed an association between children's attitudes and those of their parents in a number of studies. He concluded that:

> . . . children learn not only from what their parents say, but from observing how their parents behave towards members of various groups (1998, p. 122).

METHODOLOGY

It is difficult to gain access to groups of children outside the school context (Morrow, 1998). Hence, it was decided to approach children through their schools. Segregated housing in Dublin made it possible to identify an all-girls and all-boys suburban middle class school, and similar working class inner city schools for boys and girls. The location of each of the four schools proved to be an accurate indicator of an individual child's class position (crudely assessed in terms of their father's occupation: see Drudy, 1995, for a critique). Thus in the middle class school, the fathers of the children in the study were in professional or managerial occupations, and in the working class schools all but one of the fathers were either employed in unskilled manual work or were unemployed.

Co-operation was sought and obtained from the principal teacher in each school and exactly the same procedure was used in each case as regards selecting the children. Thus roughly one in three children from each fourth class in each school (i.e. 9-11 year olds) were randomly selected and invited to participate in a group discussion for 30 minutes in a spare room. Each group participant was given a page with a brief description of six individuals of the same gender and age group as themselves, but each from different ethnic backgrounds, namely Bosnian, British, Japanese, Traveller, Irish and French. Each group was told:

> The house/flat next door to you is for sale. Each of these people is thinking of moving in. Discuss if you would like each one to be your new next door neighbour.

These group discussions, involving a total of 23 children, were recorded and transcribed. Most of the discussion in fact focused on the Traveller children and this is the focus in this article. Pseudonyms are used in the text to ensure confidentiality.

At the same time, the other children in the class remained in their classroom with their individual teacher and spent the 30 minutes drawing and writing in response to the stimulus, "What I think of Travellers". These drawings and individual written work were also collected and analysed. The methodology used thus allowed attitudes to be revealed in both an individual context (by analysing what they drew or wrote under the open-ended heading, "What I think of Travellers"); and in a collective context (by analysing the text of the four taped transcribed group discussions). In total 69 children took part in the study: 23 children took part in the group discussion and 46 completed drawings and wrote down individually what they thought of Travellers.

Other studies have noted that each of these approaches are particularly suited to children (Morrow, 1998). The use of vignettes of various kinds is common in studies of children's attitudes (O'Brien et al., 1996; Morrow, 1998). Drawing is seen as fun and it "deflects the adult gaze" although such drawings can be difficult to interpret (Morrow, 1998). Cox (1992) has seen drawings as a kind of writing that the child employs when they cannot express their ideas and feelings as they come in contact with their environment. Replying to an open-ended question is seen as an equally appropriate method for children since it means that they are not privy to any biases the researcher may have and are invited to say what they think. All of these approaches are seen as much more suitable for children than formal individual interviews since the latter are associated in children's minds with being reprimanded (Morrow, 1998).

Racist attitudes were measured at both an individual and group level. Thus the cognitive dimension was assessed by quantifying the stereotypical statements which were made about Travellers in the individual written work in reply to the stimulus, "What I think of Travellers" in group discussions or deduced from their drawings. In the two former cases this involved classifying each statement (i.e. sentence or clause) using Laffal's 14-item dictionary for classifying ethnic descriptive words and stereotypes (Ehrlich, 1973). For the drawings each item or scene was classified using the same dictionary. For example, a drawing of a horse and caravan was classified as an "economic characteristic", while a drawing of Travellers involved in an assault was classified as a "negative moral quality". Similarly, the affective dimension was operationalised by quantifying the frequency of positive and negative dispositions towards Travellers as reflected in the group discussion, in individual written statements or as deduced from the drawings. Every expression (statement, item or scene drawn) was also assessed and classified as expressing a positive, negative or neutral disposition towards Travellers. At both the cognitive and affective level, the degree of racism was defined on the basis of the proportion of negative statements within the total number of statements. The behavioural dimension was operationalised at group level only, using item three of the Bogardus Scale of Social Distance, that is, looking at the children's willingness to have Travellers live next door. Thus the study uses material collected in three different ways to explore these children's attitudes towards Travellers.

FINDINGS

The results show that racist attitudes exist towards Travellers at both the individual and group levels and at the cognitive, affective and behavioural dimensions. Firstly, then, at an individual cognitive level, there was widespread evidence of negative stereotyping and scapegoating in all the children's written statements and drawings. Individual written expressions of negative stereotyping included: "They leave loads of rubbish and mess behind"; "they spend it all [money] on drink"; "they hit the horses"; "they rob"; "they kill"; "they break into peoples' houses." Many of the children said that Travellers were "dishonest", "dirty" "have too much money", and "are cruel". It seems plausible to suggest that children repeat what they have heard at home, so that their views reflect those in the wider society. The numbers are small and the conclusions necessarily tentative, but it was striking that negative stereotypes were most frequently expressed individually by the working class boys, with relatively little difference in the cognitive attitudes expressed by the other children (See Figure 10.1).

Figure 10.1: Negative Cognitive Stereotypical Expressions as a Percentage of the Total Expressions at Individual Level, Combining Drawings and Written Statements

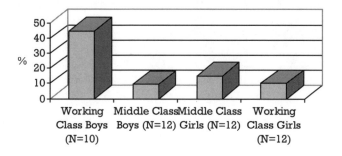

The affective attitudinal element involves the extent and depth of prejudice: it refers to attitudes based on pre-judgements, and is generally expressed by demonstrating negative dispositions towards a group based on its ethnicity. Again, there was a suggestion in the data that the working class boys, in their individual written statements and drawings, were the most negative in their affective disposition towards Travellers. Their prejudiced attitudes were reflected in individual written statements such as: "Knackers should be put away". In their drawings, 45 per cent identified Travellers with crime, 18 per cent with drunkenness, and 54 per cent with forms of dirt and squalor. Most drew campfires, surrounded by litter and vermin. Begging also emerged as a common theme in the drawings, and was referred to by over 50 per cent of the middle class girls in their individual statements. Almost one-quarter of the drawings of middle class boys showed Travellers with new vans, while many of them in their individual statements also noted this and said that "they spend their money on drink" (the implication being that their wealth was not acquired honestly). Such attitudes are clearly prejudiced, and indicative of negative affective dispositions (See Figure 10.2).

*Figure 10.2: Negative Affective Dispositions towards Trav-
ellers as a Percentage of Total Expressions at Individual
Level, Combining Drawings and Written Statements*

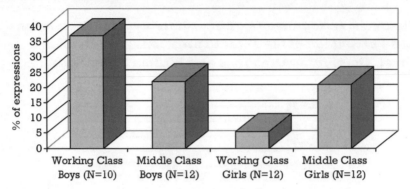

The girls also stereotyped Travellers, describing them as "smelly", "dirty", "brought up badly", saying that they "make the place look dirty" and that they "leave rubbish all over the place". However their individual statements also displayed pity towards them: "I feel sorry for them because they have no clean clothes"; "You couldn't make any friends because you would be moving around all the time." Such statements can be seen as reflecting a kind of patronising pity involving a degree of compassion but also a kind of moral superiority. These kinds of sentiments were peculiar to the girls, and as will be shown later, they also emerged in the girls' group discussions. Such attitudes were not included in the quantitative analysis. They can be seen as reflecting a lack of respect for Travellers, albeit one which is rather different from the boys' racist attitudes. It is possible that they underlie apparent conflicts in the literature as regards the existence of gender differences in this area.

In each of the four group discussions, at a cognitive level, Travellers were stereotyped as dishonest, drunken, dirty, and selfish. In all cases the number of negative qualities ascribed to Travellers far exceeded the positive qualities and there was also widespread scapegoating of Travellers. Travellers were seen as the ones to blame for social ills such as stealing cars, vandalism, violence and cruelty to animals. In the group context, negative stereotypes were most commonly used by the middle class boys. They referred to the Travellers as "doing bad things . . . like robbing . . . messing at the church . . . I think they done some damage to it"; "they rip the licence plates off them"[cars]; "they do be up to all sorts of trouble and all . . . you invite them in and that's it . . . your house is gone in the morning"; "they never get themselves in trouble, always other people." It was implied that they were responsible for even more serious things — "having bonfires by throwing petrol over cars, and there was a man burned inside a car".

Figure 10.3: Cognitive Positive and Negative Stereotypes Ascribed to Travellers in the Group Context

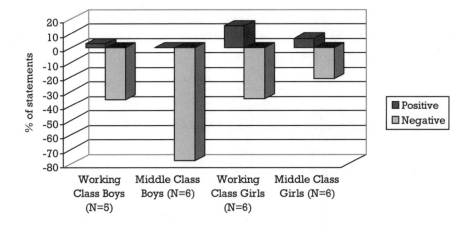

Cognitive negative stereotypes accounted for, on average, 28 per cent of the total comments made by both groups of girls, while for the boys, the average level was 57 per cent. However, the level of negative stereotyping among the middle class boys was more than twice as high as that of the working class boys. Furthermore, the frequency of negative stereotypes, expressed by the middle class boys within the group context, was over eight times higher than at the individual level, rising from 9 per cent of cognitive expressions in reply to the stimulus, "What I think of Travellers", to over three-quarters (78 per cent) of the cognitive expressions in the group context.

Similarly at an affective level, negative dispositions towards Travellers constituted a much higher proportion of the total statements made by boys than girls. Thus, negative dispositions in the group data were expressed by girls only half as often as the boys. Furthermore, only a tiny minority of the statements of the working class and middle class boys reflected a positive disposition with a slightly larger proportion of such statements being made by the girls — especially the working class girls (see Figure 10.3). The numbers are very small but it was striking that at a behavioural level both groups of girls expressed a willingness to accept the Traveller girl as a neighbour in the vignette. The boys were much less willing to accept a Traveller into their neighbourhood, with the middle class boys being least willing to allow Travellers into their neighbourhood.

Figure 10.4: Frequency of Negative Affective Dispositions to Travellers, as a Percentage of the Total Statements Expressed by Each Group

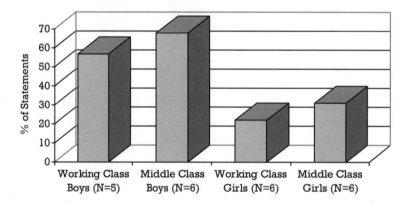

Since there are only four transcripts available, it is impossible to generalise since idiosyncratic factors may be involved. It was striking, however, that a very clear leader emerged within the middle class boys group (Nicky) who led the hostility towards and cognitive stereotyping of Jimmy, the Traveller, in the group discussion. His very first comment about Jimmy indicated his disapproval of the Traveller life style: "It would be better if he stayed in one place". When asked directly if he would like to live near a Traveller he laughed and said that he would not: "They might rob you", and "They'd be kicking your bins and say the dog done it or something." Shortly afterwards he said that Jimmy should be the last one to get the house. At this early stage in the group discussion two of the other boys in the group who had previously spoken up for Jimmy twice said that Jimmy should be the last one of those in the vignettes to get the house. Even when reminded of their earlier positions by the facilitator, they simply said "changed my mind". Nicky asserted his position of power by repeating his own decision to put Jimmy last, and asking, "Who do you pick?" Four of the five middle class boys in the group, including both those who had previously supported Jimmy, said "Jimmy last". Shortly afterwards Nicky took an even more overtly authoritative role in the group: "Don't all talk at the same time. If everyone talks at the same time it won't record."

Thus in the middle class boys group, Nicky's position of dominance was established early on, and his views were influential in the group discussion. In quantitative terms his position was reflected in the number of interventions he made as compared with the other children (72 as compared with an average of 40; the range being from 9-72). The difference in the level of cognitive racist attitudes expressed by the middle class boys at the individual and group level dramatically illustrates the impact of his leadership in this setting (see Figure 10.5).

It was striking that in the three other group discussions no clear leader emerged. In the working class group, two boys contributed almost equally to the group discussion (average of 24 inputs: range from 10-38). Initially they started from very different positions. Thus, at the start of the group discussion, one of these boys (Danny) said "I like Jimmy. I'd like to have him [live near me]" with the second one (Joe) saying that "We don't like 'em [Travellers] at all". Shortly afterwards Danny named a friend "who is a knacker" prompting Joe to say, "I do be playing with him and if anyone call him a knacker I'll beat him up". This suggests that realistic knowledge of a Traveller lifestyle may be negatively associated with the attribution of negative qualities to Travellers — a trend which was supported across the study as a whole (Spearman's correlation co-efficient: -.5, sig.006). In Dublin, working class children are more likely to have contact with Travellers. The numbers are small, but the trends bear out suggestions that opportunities for co-operation challenge stereotypes and reduce racism (Ehrlich, 1973; Brief, 1998). However this appeared only in the male group context and only influenced the cognitive dimension. Thus, arguably because of Danny and Joe's own experiences with Traveller children, the cognitive racism, expressed by these working class boys in a group context, was lower than their individual expression.

Figure 10.5: Comparison of Cognitive and Affective Racist Attitudes at Individual and Group Level

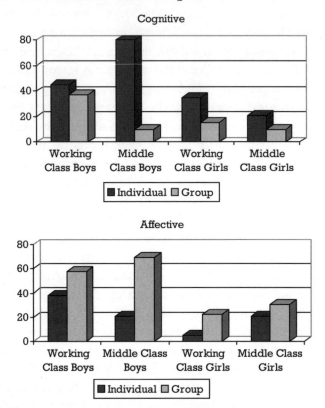

Working Class Boys: Individual, 10, Group, 5; Middle Class Boys: Individual, 12, Group, 6; Working Class Girls: Individual, 12, Group, 6; Middle Class Girls: Individual, 12, Group, 6.

No clear leader emerged in either of the girls' group discussions. Amongst the middle class girls there was no clear leader although Jane made slightly more interventions than Anne or Sally (46 as compared with 41 and 38 respectively: average across this group being 29 and the range 9-46). Jane was the first to refer to Travellers (after some initial hesitation) in a negative stereotypical way:

> The only thing I don't like about Travellers . . . they are . . . you know . . . dirty.

She was faced with an immediate challenge by Anne to this position ("Not all of them"), and modified her view ("Well, some people"). Shortly afterwards however, it was Anne who expressed such stereotypical views:

> When the children go to school, they can't afford to pay. They have spent it all on drink.

These stereotypical views were also articulated by Sally, the third contender for group leadership:

> Whenever they want money they pretend to hurt themselves. . . . If the women get money they keep it for themselves. They don't buy something for their child.

The silences in the transcript suggest a degree of unease with the direction of the discussion and/or with what appears to be a competition for leadership amongst these three girls. However, in contrast to the boys' groups, a different discourse then begins to emerge, initially characterised by concern and justice and later by a kind of patronising pity.

> *Anne*: I suppose it's not fair. They've nowhere to go. They should build a few things for them . . .

> *Jane*: Some Travellers and their parents don't have any jobs, but am, they rob money, they shoplift and things. They don't get any help out I know but it's their own fault for doing it, but am they can't help it. Their Mom and Dad have no money.

> *Laura*: They might have no food.

> *Jane*: And sometimes their caravan gets burned down . . .

> *Sally:* Some people like, they might talk common or dress common, but they are nice.

At the end of the group discussion the three contenders for leadership chose Katie (the Traveller vignette) as a neighbour; with Jane articulating their feelings of patronising pity:

> I feel sorry for Katie. That is why I picked her. . . . And you could tell her what's right and wrong. . . .

Thus, one might suggest that the articulation of a kind of moral superiority is an acceptable discourse amongst these middle class girls.

In the working class girls' group no clear leader emerged either and it was much more difficult to keep the discussion focused on the issue than in the other groups. Helen is one of the three children who effectively dominated the group discussion (48 interventions as compared with Lorna's 31 and Liz with 28: the average being 22; range 6-48). In contrast to the middle class boys' group, Helen was unsuccessful in getting her leadership accepted. She had a stereotypical view of Travellers: "You can get anything off them. You can get nits off them". It is clear from the other girls' response (giggles and "I'm telling the teacher") that this is not a socially acceptable view in their classroom. However it is one that is very clearly repeated by Helen: "They're very dangerous, cause they might rape you or anything". However as in the middle class girls group, negative stereotyping of Travellers competes with concern. Thus, right at the start in the working class girls' group discussion, Lorna, one of the contenders for group leadership, says that:

> No matter what she [Katie, the Traveller child] is, she is still a person, even if she is a Traveller.

Later on she says:

> They are not monsters or anything that you can hate them or something. A Traveller is good to play with cause you can learn things about them.

Liz, the third contender for leadership endorses a similar view: "like we are all the same". As in the working class boys' group, she mentions that she knows one and "she is all right". Nevertheless, negative cognitive references continue to occur in the discussion ("They're dangerous, they do things for food"; "If you say you have no bread around you they'd hit you or something."). However a more compassionate tone also emerges, with Lorna saying:

> Some people say they [Travellers] want a beating but that's mean. I wouldn't mind playing with them.

> It's not fair us having food and leaving the gypsies going to the dumps and looking for food because they will get rubbish food.

Faced with both Lorna and Liz's tenacity in insisting that "I think that we should help the gypsies more", Helen, who has consistently expressed negative stereotypical views, capitulates at the end of the discussion saying, "I think we should help them cause it is not fair on gypsies", reflecting a similar kind of patronising pity to that which emerges amongst the middle class girls. This kind of pattern is very different to that which emerges in the boys' group discussions.

One might suggest that, in our particular social and cultural context, girls are comfortable with a discourse of pity:

> I feel sorry for them because they have no clean clothes, just smelly clothes, and not that nice houses (middle class girl)

> I'd give them food and money (working class girl).

This can be seen as reflecting a kind of compassion, but one which simultaneously asserts a degree of moral superiority. In the girls' group discussions it was associated with an unwillingness to accept a leader. This is compatible with Connell's (1995) view that the kind of domination that is acceptable in male contexts is more muted in female ones (not least because the whole construction of femininity is in a context of male hegemony). This would certainly help one to make sense both of the leadership struggles in the girls' groups, as well as the importance of a kind of moral superiority towards Travellers. Such attitudes, disguised as pity or compassion, are compatible with the dominant conception of femininity that focuses on caring, service etc (O'Connor, 1998). This discourse of femininity legitimates the group expression of patronising pity in a way that a discourse of masculinity does not. Such attitudes, although ostensibly less noxious than racism, are ultimately not, however, any more respectful of Travellers and their life style.

Conclusion

This research into 9 to 11-year-old children's racist attitudes to Travellers has differentiated between cognitive, affective and behaviour dimensions, and has explored these in their individual written statements and drawings, as well as in the content of their taped group discussions. The results demonstrate the existence of racist attitudes towards Travellers (at cognitive, affective and behavioural levels) amongst the children in this study — thus suggesting the need for a three-pronged approach to tackle such racism.

The numbers are small and hence any conclusions are extremely tentative. This caveat is even more important since quite a complex picture emerged as regards the relationship between racist attitudes, gender and social class. In this small study, working class boys expressed the highest proportion of negative cognitive and affective racist attitudes in their individual written statements and drawings. However, in the group discussion context, it was the middle class boys who expressed the most negative cognitive stereotypes and behaviours. It is not clear to what extent this simply reflected the strong leadership exerted within that group. However, there was some suggestion that the negative cognitive stereotypes, expressed by the working class boys in an individual context, were modified in the group context — a context where one of the leadership contenders drew on his own experiences of Travellers to challenge the others' cognitive stereotyping of them. This raises interesting questions about the conditions which are associated with the emergence of a strong leader; about middle class boys' needs for group acceptance and leadership; about the impact of the leader on group behaviour; and the extent to which stereotyping can be offset by actual contact with Travellers. Overall, the proportion of negative affective dispositions expressed in the group context was larger amongst the boys than girls; with the boys being less willing than the girls to have a Traveller living next door. The interaction between boys, during the group discussions, suggests that change in racist attitudes amongst them will only occur if such group phenomena are tackled.

In looking more closely at the girls' group transcripts it was striking that attempts to establish leadership in these groups were unsuccessful, so that the impact of the group context was less obvious amongst them. It was also striking that a kind of patronising pity was much more likely to occur amongst them than amongst the boys. One might suggest that this reflected a kind of compassion, but one which simultaneously asserted a degree of moral superiority towards Travellers. It can be seen as less noxious than racism, but it is ultimately not any more respectful of Travellers and their life style. It is, of course, not possible to generalise from this study since it is based on a sample of 9 to 11-year-old children in fourth class within two single sex middle class and two working class schools in Dublin. However, it does provide an interesting insight into the extent and nature of racist attitudes amongst such children.

References

Allport, G.W. (1954), *The Nature of Prejudice*, Cambridge, MA: Addison-Wesley

Bagley, C. and Verma G. (1979), *Racial Prejudice, The Individual and Society*, Hampshire: Saxon House

Bagley, J. (1979), *Personality, Self-Esteem and Prejudice*, Hampshire: Saxon House

Bee, H. (1995), *The Developing Child*, 7th edition, New York: Harper Collins

Brief, A.P. (1998), *Attitudes in and around Organisations*, London: Sage

Bringham, J. and Weissbach, T. (1972), *Racial Attitudes in America: Analysis and Findings of Social Psychology*, New York: Harper and Brace Publications

Central Statistics Office (1998), *Census of Population*, Dublin: Government Publications (2000)

Cohen, A.P. (1985), *The Symbolic Construction of Community*, UK: Ellis Horwood

Connell, R.W. (1995) *Masculinities,* Cambridge, UK: Polity Press.

Cox, M. (1992), *Children's Drawings*, New York: Penguin

Davis, E.E., Grube, J.W. and Morgan, M. (1984), *Attitudes towards Poverty and Related Social Issues in Ireland, Paper No. 117*, Dublin: Economic and Social Research Institute

Deegan, J.S. (1996), *Children's Friendships in Culturally Diverse Classrooms*, London: Falmer Press.

Department of Justice (1995), *Report of the Task Force on the Travelling Community*, Dublin: Government Publications.

Drudy, S. (1995) "Class, Society, Inequality and the 'Declassed'", in P. Clancy, S. Drudy, K. Lynch and L. O'Dowd (eds), *Irish Society: Sociological Perspectives*. Dublin: Institute of Public Administration.

Drury Communications (2000), *Citizen Traveller Survey*, Dublin: Drury Communications.

DTEDG (1992), *Irish Travellers — New Analysis and New Initiatives*, Dublin: Pavee Point Travellers Centre.

Ehrlich, H. J. (1973), *The Social Psychology of Prejudice*, London: Wiley and Sons.

Elias, N and Scottson, J.L. (1994), *The Established and the Outsiders*, London: Sage.

European Parliament Committee on Racism and Xenophobia (1991*), Report No. 160/85, Findings of the Committee on Racism and Xenophobia*, Luxembourg: European Parliament.

Greenstein, F.I (1965), *Children and Politics*, New Haven and London: Yale University Press.

Hannan, D., Smyth, E., McCullagh, J., O'Leary R., and McMahon, D. (1996), *Co-Education and Gender Equality*, Dublin: Oak Tree Press.

Harmony Report (1992), *Racial Discrimination in Ireland — Realities and Remedies*, Dublin: Harmony.

Irish National Co-ordinating Committee Department of Justice, Equality and Law Reform (1998), *1997 European Year Against Racism: Ireland Report*, Dublin: Stationary Office.

Irish National Teachers Organisation (1992), *Travellers in Education*, Dublin: Irish National Teachers Organisation.

Mac Gréil, M. (1977), *Prejudice and Tolerance in Ireland*, Dublin: College of Industrial Relations.

Mac Gréil, M. (1996), *Prejudice in Ireland Revisited*, Dublin: College of Industrial Relations.

McVeigh, (1997), *The Racialization of Irishness: Racism and anti-racism in Ireland*, Belfast: Centre for Research and Documentation.

Morrow, V. (1998), "If you were a Teacher, it would be harder to talk to you: Reflections on Qualitative Research with Children in School", *International Journal of Social Research Methodology*, Vol. 1, No. 4, pp. 297-314.

O'Brien, M., Alldred, P. and Jones, D. (1996), "Children's Construction of Family and Kinship" in J. Brannen and M. O'Brien (eds), *Children in Families: Research and Policy*, London: Falmer Press.

O'Connor, P. (1998), *Emerging Voices: Women in Contemporary Irish Society*, Dublin: Institute of Public Administration.

Pavee Point Anti-Racist Code of Practice (1999), Dublin: Pavee Point Travellers Centre.

Trinity College Dublin (1999), *Anti-Racism Teachers Pack, Section C3: Recognising and Respecting Differences*, http://www.tcd.ie/Education/Teachers_Pack /Text_Only/C3/Base.html.

United Nations Minority Rights Group (1980), *Roma Europe's Gypsies, Report No. 14*, London: UN.

Chapter 11

Traveller Childhood in Ireland

Máirín Kenny

INTRODUCTION

Traveller children are increasingly attending school, where they face daily reminders that their settled peers have problems with them. As O'Keeffe and O'Connor (Chapter 10, this volume) have identified, settled children of the majority population display racist attitudes to Travellers. Only if they are not listened to can they be presumed to be "innocent". Anti-Traveller racism is rooted in settled society's perception of them as powerfully representing "ideological and symbolic disorder" (Okely, 1983, p. 2) and a threat to sedentary order and fixity (Liégeois, 1994). This old children's rhyme says as much:

> My mother said I never should/Play with the Gypsies in the wood.
>
> If I did she would say/Naughty girl to disobey.
>
> Your hair shan't curl, your shoes shan't shine,/You Gypsy girl, you shan't be mine.
>
> And my father said that if I did/He'd rap my head with the teapot lid.
>
> The wood was dark, the grass was green,/In came Sally with a tambourine.

I went to the sea — no ships to get across,/I paid ten shillings for a blind white horse.

I jumped on his back and was off in a crack,/Sally tell your[/my] mother I shall never come back.

So children can play skilfully with sedentary constructs of order and power, insiders and outsiders (and patriarchy: mother does the work, teaches stereotypes and sanctions, while father's input is violent but minimal). The narrator will effectively become a gypsy if she goes to that exotic underworld. She goes anyway but finds limit, not freedom, there. In the last line of this rhyme in *The Book of a Thousand Poems* (Murray MacBain, unrevised since 1942), the settled narrator rejects this world in her diktat to Sally, as she speeds back to her own mother's order. Recent editors, replacing the pronoun "your" with "my", reverse this option. While this upends a stereotype of settled child victim of Gypsy kidnappers, it minimises the unequal power relation between the two worlds by implying that Sally can move as freely as the narrator. But dominance is not so easily erased: the settled child still gives the orders. Generations of playing children passing on this rhyme demonstrate how racism is rooted not in its targets but in its practitioners, and how even very young children in a racist society can be racist. Antiracist education of the majority from the earliest age is essential to the inclusion of minorised groups (Epstein, 1993). O'Keeffe and O'Connor (2001) have demonstrated this in relation to Irish settled children and Travellers.

Travellers, Ireland's largest and arguably most excluded ethnic minority, comprise less than one per cent of the population. Settled society's constructions of Travellers inform its constructions of Traveller childhood, and powerfully delimit how Travellers and their children live. Helleiner (1998) cites the section on Traveller women in the 1995 Task Force Report as showing how gender, class, ethnicity and age intersect in their experience. Their children's experience equally could usefully be addressed. Both settled and Traveller society are patriarchal, but differences in how they manage this power relation can contribute to the dominant group's readings of Travellers' child-rearing practices. So the children are often seen as multiple victims — as the weakest members of a presumed inadequate group and as children of doubly inadequate (Traveller and "uneducated") mothers (Crickley, 1992; Helleiner, 1998).

This chapter will review the context in which Traveller children live, as evidenced in studies of historical and ongoing settled-Traveller relations, and policy regarding their accommodation and health status in the Republic of Ireland. Discussion of Travellers' management of childhood will set the context for the review of policy and practice regarding their formal schooling, and of how it and the Travellers' traditions regarding childhood and youth intersect with each other. Finally, linkages will be indicated between the experiences of, and possibilities for, formal childhood education for Travellers and other minorised groups in this increasingly diverse society.

HISTORICAL AND POLICY CONTEXT

In its dealings with Travellers, Ireland substantially follows the European pattern identified by Liégeois (1994). Gypsies/ Travellers were historically seen as exotic/dangerous, and their annihilation was attempted by strategies ranging from outlawing nomadic trading to popular and official pogroms. In Irish official records "Tynkeres" first appear in the twelfth century. However, Travellers escaped specific anti-nomadic persecutions because the colonial powers targeted the native Irish as a whole (to the relief of Irish Travellers in England finding that they "only" have to face anti-Irish racism, unless their lifestyle betrays them). Evidence in folklore and in the 1835 Poor Law Commission Reports indicates that Travellers in agrarian Ireland were economically necessary but socially unwanted, and kept themselves or were kept apart (Gmelch, 1977).

In modern Europe, officialdom adopted policies of humanitarian integration/absorption. Interventions could be draconian: in some countries, for example, Gypsy/Traveller children were institutionalised or fostered out to settled families at birth (the 1960 Government Commission on Itinerancy forcefully rejected a similar policy for Ireland). But less severe policies were also absorptionist. The modern policy era in Ireland began with police censuses of Travellers in 1944, 1952 and 1956, taken for the Department of Justice — a location of official concern indicating that Travellers were seen as actual or potential criminals. In the 1960s there was slow progress towards a broader vision. The Report of the Commission on Itinerancy was published in 1963. Two subsequent Government committees published Reports, the Review Body in 1983 and the Task Force in 1995.

O'Connell (1992) identified "models of Travellers" informing policy and practice. If Travellers are perceived as inadequates, deviants, or even "normal" but in crisis, the policy response is compensatory and reformist, to facilitate their eventual absorption into mainstream society and provision. If they are seen as an ethnic group, majority-oriented monocultural policies and practices are challenged. In the 1960s and 1970s, statutory and voluntary bodies focused on answering dominant assertions and assumptions regarding Travellers' deviancy by protesting Travellers' honesty, decency, and care for their children and pleading for their acceptance. They portrayed Travellers as in crisis, or inadequate. Policies were validated by applications of subculture of poverty theory or similar frameworks to the Traveller case (McCarthy, 1971; Gmelch, 1975). Gmelch (1990) and McCarthy (1994) strongly argue for Travellers' nomadic ethnic identity. Since the 1970s, official discourse has ostensibly progressed from absorption to inclusion, from pleas for an ending of wrongs to calls for recognition of rights to assertions of Travellers' identity and equal status in a diverse society. But old theories persist in the rationale for service provision. Portrayal of Traveller children and parents illustrate these developments and contradictions.

Travellers are increasingly involving themselves in policy development. There were no Travellers in the 11-member Commission which reported in 1963; three of the 23 Review Body members were Traveller representatives of the National Council (1983, pp. 1, 2); and three of the 18 Task Force members were Travellers, representing two all-Traveller organisations (the Irish Traveller Movement and the National Federation of Travelling People) and a mixed Traveller and settled organisation, Pavee Point (Task Force, 1995, p. 8). Though the term "ethnic group" only appears in quotations, the ethnic model substantially informs the Task Force Report (1995). It is most fully articulated in Sections B (Culture) and C (Discrimination). In sum, a move is identifiable in official discourse, from treating Travellers as silent objects of concern and correction, to letting them speak, and to recognising them as self-determining agents.

Children have been a key focus for and tool in the debate about Traveller welfare. Helleiner's (1998) analysis of media and policy texts relating to them reveals a steady flow of discourse of inadequacy and normalisation. Popular stereotyping is expressed and reinforced in media indictments of Traveller parents and their "wild" children and the threat they pose, especially to vulnerable settled women and children. The intent of hostile and sympathetic texts converge when officialdom attributes their difficulties to personal and familial deficits, thereby validating the criticisms of the dominant society. Starting with the Commission Report (1963), official texts challenge this, noting that Travellers love their children and want the best for them. But these texts identify Traveller parents as "inadequate socialisers of their children" (Helleiner, 1998, p. 306), and invoke their children's distress (often illustrated with photographs, as on the cover of the 1983 Review Body Report) to promote pro-settlement policies. When Travellers themselves cite their children's plight to activate their patrons' generosity (Gmelch, 1977, p. 77) or challenge exclusion (Bewley, 1974, p. 29), officialdom can validate these policies by citing them. But a common assumption is that their plight is generated, not by anti-nomadic prejudice, but by nomadism itself; and that the life chances of these marginalised children require adoption of pro-settlement accommodation policies and ethnocentric intervention in cultural practices around marriage, child care, education and family structures (Crickley, 1992; Helleiner, 1998). However, nuanced critique is required. For instance, the 1963 Report (echoing the rhyme "my mother said") states that Traveller parents "have little regard for their [children's] appearance, cleanliness, health, and none for their education or future" (p. 81). Helleiner notes that here, "invocations of Traveller children's 'needs' were marshalled on the basis of little evidence beyond normative models of childhood" (1998, p. 307).

But this Report in 1963 is the first official document of the misery of Travellers' lives. In a section on health (laced with criticism of Travellers and nomadism) it publishes appalling infant mortality statistics. While challenging the analysis it is necessary also to register the validity of the data.

TRAVELLERS' ACCOMMODATION AND HEALTH STATUS

Statistics on Travellers, drawn mainly from annual local authority counts, are problematic data sources.[1] Enumerators, or their employing authorities, must decide who is a Traveller and Travellers must decide whether or not to declare their identity. Accommodation policies have had effect, though vitiated by inadequacy and cultural bias: in 1960 nearly all were living in appalling destitution in roadside camps; in 1995 under one-third were on the roadside. In 1963, improvement was equated with housing, but pro-nomadic arguments are shifting the focus from type towards quality of accommodation (Review Body, 1983; Task Force, 1995). However, as O'Keeffe and O'Connor (2001) note in their paper, access to adequate accommodation is still a major problem for many. It has particular impact on children's health and education status.

Data on Traveller children's health status, though drawn from more reliable public health records, is also unevenly collected and presented. The 1963 Commission Report gives figures for infant mortality, but qualifies its comparative data with a note as to lack of clarity in the methods used to identify Traveller infant mortality. The 1961 national infant mortality rate was 30.5 per 1,000, and for a lower income urban group it was 60 per 1,000. In respect of all Traveller children born since 1944, the infant mortality rate was 113 per 1,000, and in respect of all born since 1950 it was 76 per 1,000 (1963, p. 47). Though these figures indicate some improvement over time, they were a shocking indicator of Traveller children's quality of life. Data in Barry, Herity and Solan (1989) show a continuing lag behind the national norm. They separate stillbirths, perinatal, and infant mortality.

Table 11.1: Mortality Rate per 1,000 in Early Life: National and Traveller Figures, 1987

	Ireland	Travellers
Stillbirth rate	6.9	19.5
Perinatal mortality rate	9.9	29.3*
Infant mortality rate	7.4	18.1**

* Equal to the national rate for 1966
** Equal to the national rate for 1971

Source: Barry, Herity and Solan (1989, pp. 14-15)

The average family size of Travellers is falling but the population age profile is still youthful: over 50 per cent were under 15 years in 1986 (Barry and Daly, 1988). Travellers' life expectancy, an indicator of community health, rose from 30 years in 1961 to about 60 in 1987 — the level for the settled population in the 1940s. Compared to the same-sex settled population, male Travellers were more than twice as likely, and female Travellers more than three times as likely, to die in a given year. The accidental death ratio was far higher, particularly for women (over six times that for settled women), and most such deaths occurred to women in roadside camps. Take-up of ante- and post-natal care remains low. A number of health boards provide outreach services to improve access, particularly for site-bound young families, but much more needs to be done to ensure health care service delivery at anything like the level for the majority population. Though often called for, a thorough study of Traveller morbidity and mortality has not been done (Task Force, 1995).

Once more, readings can be problematic. Barry, Herity and Solan (1989) attribute child mortality from metabolic disorders solely to close kin marriages and they read the campsite accidental death rate as indicating a need for safety education. But further research is needed into the effects of consanguinity (Task Force, 1995, p. 144), and it is logical to suggest that the primary cause of accidental deaths on illegal camps lies not in ignorance but in the anti-nomadism which pushes families into living on road margins — a metaphor for and outcome of settled society's attitudes to Travellers and their lifestyle. Environmental, social and personal factors affecting Travellers' health vary both between and within types of accommodation. In the author's experience the relation between this cluster and health or education status is complex.

CHILDHOOD IN TRAVELLER SOCIETY

Liégeois (1994, pp. 85-87) describes childhood among Gypsy/Travellers across Europe. McCarthy (1971, pp. 72 ff.), Barnes (1975, pp. 242 ff.) and Gmelch (1975, pp. 74 ff.) present similar, but harsher, pictures of Irish Traveller childhood. Liégeois (1994) notes that Travellers live in small family groups to maintain their nomadism and socio-economic activities, so the extended family network does not dominate everyday life as it can in traditional settled societies. This distinction apart, Traveller family structure and child socialisation processes identified in these studies resemble those in pre-industrial European societies (Aries, 1960; Mitterauer, 1992), or in "traditional" societies in the contemporary world (Whiting and Edwards, 1988). Three aspects of this will be commented on here: the family setting, vocational education and values transmission.

Family identity takes priority over individual identity. There are common spaces for work, home and children and times for work and recreation are not segregated. Patriarchal rankings are maintained: girls are trained to serve men though they often resist this, and demanding, aggressive behaviour is welcomed in boys. Controls are lessened for boys as they move into mid-childhood and travel far from the home site, but they increase for girls who are restricted by home making and child-rearing. They are also carefully chaperoned once they enter adolescence. Children are fully part of adult society and their child-like activities do not attract much notice. Rough play is accepted, tolerance for pain is cultivated and tantrums are tolerated provided they are appropriately sited (not inside the trailer for instance). "Reluctance to obey commands continues right through the life cycle, and is extremely striking" (McCarthy, 1971, p. 74). These practices constitute not inadequate socialisation, but logical preparation for the hardships of nomadic life and the management of relations with the hostile dominant society. Since these studies, Travellers have modified their management of childhood but, as will be seen, Traveller parents hold to many of their traditional principles in their management of childhood.

Vocational education is by apprenticeship. From the earliest age children are integrated into the family work unit, in both the nurturance and economic domains. Sons work with men, daughters with women. Such apprenticeship-based education systems can powerfully promote children's security and self-worth. Traveller children are not just wanted, they are needed. Their work is not just a valuable training opportunity for them, it is essential to the family's operations. But home-based training is no longer enough and Travellers are turning to schools, their oppressors' institutions, to acquire the tools to take on the challenges of modern settled society and its institutions (Liégeois, 1994). This has been difficult. McCarthy (1971) observed Travellers' desperate hunger for literacy clashing with the tension that could arise when less tactful children displayed new skills (1971, p. 76). At a minimum, mothers often assert in interviews that they want their children to "read and write, what I never got", but they also want them to have the same chances as anyone else (Kenny, 1997a). It can be argued that school places a double burden on the children, particularly the girls who must face accumulated chores in the evening which, had they not been in school, they could have done over the day at a slower pace. This is not quite true. Laundry and cleaning can pile up, but attending to a hungry infant or wandering toddler must be done as the need arises. To quote Nan Joyce, "since you were nine or ten you were holding the youngest child in your arms, you were sort of weighed down with them" (Joyce and Farmar, 1985, p. 16). Mothers and female pupils talk of valuing the break from child minding that the girls get during their time in school (Kenny, 1997a).

A rich addition to an otherwise limiting picture of traditional Traveller childhood is indicated by Gmelch's portrayal of campsite story-telling (1978). Mac Gréine (1932) vividly depicts a Traveller woman in a dilapidated campsite, enthralling him with stories. This tradition fed the spirits of the adults and

they opened it up to their children. Mac Aongusa (1992) out-
lines how Travellers transmitted values through story. In their
versions of folk tales, values relating to relationships, roles,
property, nomadism, time, are all shaped by their basic termi-
nal value — survival. This is one way in which, as Liégeois
(1994) notes, Travellers turn seeming evidence of their failure
to prosper into cause for celebrating their success in surviving.
But modernisation is posing challenges to this tradition and the
values it enshrines. The media can fuel adolescents' resentment
of the limits imposed on them by majority society, by their parents and by their family roles (McCarthy, 1971). On the other
hand, the role and potential of the story-telling heritage is being recovered by contemporary socio-political Traveller organisations, recording their traditions in heritage projects (Ó
Riain, ed., 1992, Ó Floinn, 1995). The children, not surprisingly,
look mainly for popular child entertainment (Gmelch, 1978, p.
36) and Travellers are increasingly incorporating contemporary childhood practices into their way of life. Schools and
other settled statutory and voluntary service agencies, not to
speak of the media, have played a part but it would be difficult
to separate settled impositions from Travellers' choices. However, the children still feel the pull of the old stories (Mac Aongusa, 1992), and heritage projects offer rich seams for exploration by and with children, in and out of schools. By borrowing,
reclaiming and reworking cultural practices, the minority culture engages with the dominant one and with its own future,
and struggles to shape the elements to its own ends (Okely,
1983; Liégeois, 1994). Included in this borrowing and engagement with the dominant sector is Travellers' adoption of
schooling.

School Provision

Counting Traveller pupils is problematic. Some schools do not
count housed Travellers as Travellers, perhaps to forestall settled parents' opposition to Traveller enrolment. Others count all
they can to make a case for additional staffing and resources.
Others balk at forcing pupils who, with good cause, are hiding
their ethnic identity to "come out" simply to ascertain what the

system is doing for them. Yet quantitative indicators are needed. Only 700 out of about 2,000 children have access to pre-school provision for Travellers (Coolahan, 1998, p. 23), but it is very popular where offered and community-based provision offers a great opportunity for parents and other adults to become service providers (Murray, 1997). At all other levels, parental involvement is weak and, for many providing home support, is difficult due to their living conditions. Over 80 per cent of the 5,000+ primary-age children are enrolled in school; their average attendance rate is about 70 per cent. About a third are in special classes, a third in mainstream classes with support from a resource teacher for Travellers and the remainder are fully integrated. Only about 20 per cent of the 2,000 young adolescents are enrolled, most of them in 11 separate post-primary units called Junior Education Centres for Travellers (JECs). But numbers in mainstream second level are growing (Task Force, 1995). So school provision and supports reflect uneven progression in policy. Enrolment was initially the prime concern, but provision is more problematic.

The school system, with its unwieldy structures and its taught and hidden curricula, developed without reference to Traveller culture, so schooling for them usually means immersion in the dominant culture (Review Body, 1983; Drudy and Lynch, 1993; Task Force, 1995; Kenny, 1997a). Traveller children were initially identified as targets of a kind of educational search and rescue mission. Separate classes or schools for them were opened with the aim of socialising them and bringing their academic skills up to par, so that they could be absorbed into the "normal" classes. Their parents were perceived as inadequate so, besides funding educational materials and transport, the Department of Education grant-aided hygiene facilities. Schools that provided meals were lauded (Commission, 1963; Department of Education, 1970; Review Body, 1983). Travellers accepted this (some thought all children were treated thus) but now recall it with shame and anger (Kenny, 1997a). Gradually, officialdom moved towards a more cultural model of Travellers and now the education partners promote principles of equal access and cultural recognition (ITM, 1992; INTO, 1992; Department of Education, 1994). The Task Force

(1995) advocates student and parent empowerment in integrated schools that adopt an inclusive ethos and anti-racist, intercultural curricula and policies for all.

Provision and practice in relation to Travellers in school developed on an ad hoc basis, becoming increasingly varied. At primary level, classes for Travellers were nearly all located in mainstream buildings which facilitated integration. But preschool provision for Travellers "is 'bewildering' in its variety . . . of accommodation, staffing, programmes and accountability" (Coolahan, 1998, p. 83). This will be difficult to remedy until such provision is nested in comprehensive provision for all. Junior Educational Centres are also isolated from local mainstream provision. Besides impeding progress towards integrating Traveller and settled students, this isolation inhibits improvements in quality of provision and in pedagogic and theoretical development (Task Force, 1995; Kenny, 1996). For instance, strategies to avoid the development of a dual system can prove counterproductive. To preclude competition with local second level schools, JECs offer only the modified Junior Certificate programme. But this strategy channels JEC students out of third level and into "further education", mainly in FÁS Training Centres for Travellers. This issue, the impact of second level structures on adult education options (Drudy and Lynch, 1993), marks the cut-off point of this paper. The provision for young adult Travellers is currently being reassessed (Pavee Point, 1999).

Whatever the system, poor pupil performance and readings of it can bespeak under-theorised or even questionable constructs of the child and parent population. Systematic data has not been collected but teacher evaluations suggest that many Travellers in both mainstream and separate school provision still underachieve, falling one to three years behind the norm for their age (Kenny, 1997a). Poor attendance is often blamed and is attributed mainly to more urgent priorities at home and to racism in school. Personal and family difficulties are also cited. It is arguable that as regards attendance, family demands do not pose the same difficulty as racism. For some minority children, racism also provokes structurally produced learning difficulties — difficulties rooted, not in personal or familial deficits, but in historic and ongoing experience of oppression (Kenny, 1993). But if poor performance is read through the lens of client deficit theories, that feeds back into the system, reinforcing deficit-based policies and pedagogic responses. Fortunately, some education partners read the evidence in the light of structural factors and so there is movement forward, albeit uneven.

CULTURAL ISSUES AND SCHOOLING

Cultural difficulties arise in relation to discussing adolescent Travellers or their education under the heading of childhood. The period Travellers allocate to childhood is lengthening, but it is still something of a settled imposition to call Travellers aged over 12 "children". In student-teacher relations at post-primary level, this adult status of young teenagers intersects problematically with other cultural factors — a desire for schooling, the legacy of racism, and concerns regarding adolescence. A study of Traveller students' resistance practices in a JEC (field work conducted in 1986) reveals some of the complexities involved (Kenny, 1997a).

Students struggled constantly against the school's controls and demands and underachieved to a remarkable degree. This contrasted with their stated positions in interviews, which would seem to indicate a teacher's paradise. Students and parents alike approved of authoritative teaching and discipline and resented liberal, facilitative teaching styles. Softness at primary level was associated with segregated provision, strictness with integration. One parent said, "the teacher loses interest, doesn't make them"; another that "it's 'God help you, you're a Traveller you're not able', but they're well able". One student said, "you'd have to stay quiet [in a mixed[2] school so] I'd put my mind down to it". The Task Force (1995) lists irrelevant cultural and curricular aspirations in second level as key factors in Travellers' low participation in second-level schooling (similar criticisms can be levelled at primary schools, but the more child-centred regime there softens the impact). It calls both for appropriate programmes and for enforcement of school attendance laws. But in the field, internal contradictions informed discourse and performance. A number of students said they were in the JEC because they had not learned to read in primary school; if they had, they could have stopped after Confirmation. They and their parents were concerned solely with achieving functional literacy, an aim that does not require the elaborateness of even a modified second-level programme. Yet these students' near chronic opposition melted on one memorable occasion when they celebrated their culture in the classroom, in an explosion of enthusiastic work that was far broader than their stated minimal agenda required.

Several students said they preferred being among their own because they were free of anti-Traveller hostility, they could learn better and the teachers liked them. However, cultural conflicts and the impact of historic and current experiences of racism distorted relationships and performance remarkably. The students' multi-layered performance reflected the impact of centuries of dominance by and mistrust of settled people, Travellers' traditional management of authority, and these adolescents' self-perception and aspirations. School, in a sense, was retaining them in childhood, but these young people had made their Confirmation, a rite marking transition from childhood. Unmarried young boys and girls have a special position of advanced apprenticeship combined with freedom from both children's lower-order chores and the full obligations of adulthood (Mitterauer, 1992). Their struggle was arguably a discourse in action, related to being a Traveller in school at that age and for what or for whose purposes (Kenny, 1995a, 1997a).

Segregation played a role, but not a simple one. In second level schools, parents and children preferred separate provision, mainly for cultural reasons. Travellers' reservations about second-level schooling in part relate to their effort to control the rate of change, to maintain the cohesion of their social fabric (Kenny, 1995a). Nearly every student interviewed said they would marry a Traveller, stay "with their own". A key concern among parents and older youth was that if Traveller girls went to secondary school they would marry settled boys and "Travellers would be gone then". They would have found their concern validated by a female interviewee (age 16) who had attended a comprehensive school: "When I came [to the Training

Centre] they were all saying 'I wouldn't marry a country (settled) boy'. Well *I would*." The others were just afraid, she said, because they had not mixed.

Again, things are changing. Travellers are increasingly keeping their children in school until at least age 14, lengthening their childhood. Sometimes parents seek and children reject continued schooling; sometimes the opposite. Boys usually oppose by leaving to join their fathers or older youths, socialising and trading with them or starting up their own projects. Girls, traditionally the ones expected to acquire literacy skills for form filling, letter writing and so on, are now more likely to express interest in gaining jobs skills. However, most of them still join in the child-rearing work of their mothers by age 15, often with what can best be described as an air of deep job satisfaction. These activities and roles are not unique to Traveller youth, but they give them specific Traveller dimensions, positive or negative. Some may be retreating from modernisation into old, reified practices (Liégeois, 1994). Or, through their options, they can declare their identity by helping to maintain the Travellers' traditionally flexible, resilient socioeconomic networks. A synthesis is also being reached by some. Research data collected to date (Kenny, for Pavee Point, ongoing) seems to validate informal perceptions in the field that increasingly Traveller parents are confident of their children's ability to retain their group allegiance and attend second level school, and that the young people are encouraged to socialise and choose their own marriage partner, Traveller or settled.

Harris (1995) rejects the idea of ethnic identity and ethnic self-hatred as fixed, all-defining entities, noting that individual and group identities form distinct yet intersecting domains. People constantly rework their various identities, but puberty and adolescence are intense periods of exploration and ambivalence. Persistent racism can erode self-concept. Only insiders can ascertain if this affects members' performance within Traveller society, but it is often strongly in evidence in interface situations such as school. Ethnic minority young people require space to reclaim and build cultural pride, to face these explorations with confidence. Otherwise there is danger of foreclosure, of turning in on reified old practices, or of alienation as

they reject their traditions (Liégeois, 1994). Travellers are incorporating second level schooling into a rapidly changing
culture. Many young Travellers do well on their own terms
without further schooling; they have taken what they wanted of
the skills and experiences the system offered. Many in each
succeeding cohort range more widely within it than their older
siblings. Their management of this change is crucial to their
future as a self-determining people. In the process, what settled
people regard as fulfilment of personal potential is seemingly
overlooked. But the individual who sacrifices community con-
nections for the sake of personal progress also pays a great
price.

CONCLUSION

A cross-cultural challenge is being negotiated by Travellers
and formal education providers, but it is usually not overtly
named. The partners are working with issues relating to man-
aging change in how Traveller children live their childhood, in
Traveller society within the wider Irish "world". Currently, small
but growing numbers of Travellers are following Intermediate
and Leaving Certificate programmes in mainstream schools. For
its part, the system uses carrot and stick to entice Traveller youth
into second level. But the crucial context for this is an education
for the children of the majority, informed by principles of anti-
racism and inclusion. O'Keeffe and O'Connor's (2001) work reveals the need for this.

Discussion of childhood in this society requires discussion of
schooling, perhaps most importantly because, in school, children from all sectors do, or should, interact constantly over
years. Schools should promote equality, enabling all children to
develop fully as individuals and members of society (Department of Education, 1995, p. 10). But even in schools that try to
do so, countering racism and exclusion can only be a successful
schools' project if it is also a societal one (Giroux, 1983). Minority children and parents know this well. Travellers' experience compares with that of other minorities such as refugees
(Kenny, ed., 1995b; McVeigh and Binchy, 1998). There are also
parallels with class-based exclusion processes. As noted

above, sound, visionary policy is needed to challenge the source of the problem — the dominant majority and its children. In this hitherto relatively homogenous society, the concept of social "normality" must be transformed to denote an expectation of diversity. The core task of education is not so much personal growth as exploration of identities, the pursuit of rich, flexible, happily unfinished answers to the questions "Who am I?/you?/we?/they? (Kenny, 1997b). Then, diverse groups might come to dance at the crossroads rather than trip over each other, the stronger walking on the weak. In learning to hear and to honour the needs and aspirations of Traveller children, adult society and its institutions might learn to hear and honour the children of all minorities.

Bibliography

Anthologies

Harrison, M. and Stuart-Clark, C. (eds), (1988), *The Oxford Treasury of Children's Verse*, Oxford: Oxford University Press.

Morgan, G. (ed.) (1998), *Read Me . . .A Poem a Day for the National Year of Reading*, London: MacMillan Children's Books.

Mullins, T. (ed.), (1997), *Run Lightly . . . Poems for Young People*, Cork: Mercier Press.

Murray MacBain, J. (ed.) (1942), *The Book of a Thousand Poems*, London: Evans Brothers Ltd

References

Aries, P. (1960), *Centuries of Childhood*, London: Penguin.

Barnes, B. (1975), "Irish Travelling People", in F. Rehfisch (ed.), *Gypsies, Tinkers and other Travellers*, London: Academic Press.

Barry, J and Daly, L. (1988), *The Travellers' Health Status Study: Census of Travelling People*, Dublin: Health Research Board.

Barry, J. Herity, B. and Solan, J. (1989), *Travellers Vital Statistics, 1987*, Dublin: HRB.

Bewley, V. (1974) "The Travelling People in Ireland", in V. Bewley (ed.), *Travelling People*, Dublin: Veritas Publications.

Coolahan, J. (1998), *see Forum Secretariat below.*

Crickley, A (1992) "Feminism and Ethnicity", in *DTEDG File. Irish Travellers: New Analysis, New Initiatives*, Dublin: Pavee Point Publications.

Department of Education (1970), *Committee Report on Educational Facilities for Children of Itinerants*, Dublin: Stationery Office.

Department of Education (1994), *The Education of Traveller Children in National Schools: Guidelines*, Dublin: Stationery Office.

Department of Education (1995), *Charting our Education Future. White Paper on Education*, Dublin: Stationery Office.

Drudy, S. and Lynch, K. (1993), *Schools and Society in Ireland*, Dublin: Gill and MacMillan.

Epstein, D. (1993), *Changing classroom cultures: anti-racism, politics and schools*, Stoke on Trent: Trentham Books.

Forum Secretariat, J. Coolahan (ed.) (1998), *Report of the National Forum for Early Childhood Education*, Dublin: Stationery Office.

Giroux, H.A. (1983), *Theory and Resistance in Education: A Pedagogy of Opposition*, London: Heinemann.

Gmelch, G. (1977), *Tinkers and Travellers: The Urbanisation of an Itinerant People*, California: Cummings.

Gmelch, G. (1978), "The Folktales and the Collectors", in G. Gmelch and B. Kroup (eds.), *To Shorten thè Road: Travellers' Tales from Ireland. Essays and Biographies by George Gmelch; Folktales edited by Ben Kroup*, Dublin: O'Brien Press.

Gmelch, S.B. (1975), *Tinkers and Travellers: Ireland's Nomads*, Dublin: O'Brien Press.

Gmelch, S.B. (1990), "From Poverty Subculture to Political Lobby: The Traveller Rights Movement in Ireland", in C. Curtin and T.M. Wilson (eds), *Ireland from Below: Social Change in Local Communities*, Galway: University Press.

Harris, H.W. (1995), "Introduction: A Conceptual Overview of Race, Ethnicity and Identity" in H.W. Harris, H.C. Blue and E.E.H. Griffith (eds), *Racial and Ethnic Identity: Psychological Development and Creative Expression*, London: Routledge.

Helleiner, J. (1998), "Contested Childhood: The discourse and politics of Traveller childhood in Ireland", *Childhood*, Vol. 5, No. 3, pp. 303-324.

Ireland, Commission on Itinerancy (1963), *Report of the Commission on Itinerancy*, Dublin: Stationery Office.

Ireland, Travelling People Review Body (1983), *Report of the Travelling People Review Body*, Dublin: Stationery Office.

Ireland, Task Force on the Travelling Community (1995), *Report of the Task Force on the Travelling Community*, Dublin: Stationery Office.

Irish National Teachers Organisation (1992), *Travellers in Education*, Dublin: INTO.

Irish Traveller Movement (1992), *Travellers and Education*, Dublin: ITM.

Joyce, N. and Farmar, A. (1985) *Traveller*, Dublin: Gill and MacMillan.

Kenny, M. (1993), "Travellers at School: A Teacher's Perspective", *The Irish Times Education and Living Supplement*, 13 December 1993, S8.

Kenny, M. (1995a), "Understanding what we see and hear: Travellers and second-level schooling", *Glocklai, The Journal of the Association of Teachers of Traveller People*, Vol. 2, No. 3, pp. 10-16.

Kenny, M., (1995b), "Educational Provision for Traveller and Refugee Children: Promoting Achievement", unpublished Report on a Council of Europe seminar.

Kenny, M. (1997a), *The Routes of Resistance: Travellers and Second Level Schooling*, Aldershot: Ashgate Publishing.

Kenny, M. (1997b), "Who are They, Who are We?", in E. Crowley & J. Mac Laughlin (eds), *Under the Belly of the Tiger: Class, Race, Identity and Culture in Global Ireland*. Dublin: Irish Reporter Press.

Liégeois, J-P. (1994), *Roma, Gypsies, Travellers*, Strasbourg: Council of Europe Press.

Mac Aongusa, M. (1992), *The Alienation of Travellers from the Educational System*, Dublin: Sociological Association monograph.

Mac Gréine, P. (1932), "Irish Tinkers or 'Travellers'", *Béaloideas*, Vol 3, pp. 170-186.

McCarthy, P. (1971), "Itinerancy and Poverty: A Study in the sub-culture of poverty", unpublished MSoc.Sc Thesis, University College, Dublin.

McCarthy, P. (1994) "The Sub-Culture of Poverty Reconsidered" in M. McCann and J. Ruane (eds), *Irish Travellers: Culture and Ethnicity*, Belfast: Institute of Irish Studies, Queen's University.

McVeigh, R. and Binchy, A. (1998), *Travellers, Refugees & Racism in Tallaght*, Dublin: West Tallaght Resource Centre.

Mitterauer, M. (1992), *A History of Youth*, Oxford: Blackwell Publishers.

Murray, C. (1997), *Pavee Children: A Study on Childcare Issues for Travellers*, Dublin: Pavee Point Publications.

O'Connell, J. (1992), "Working with Irish Travellers", in *DTEDG File. Irish Travellers: New Analysis, New Initiatives*, Dublin: Pavee Point Publications.

Ó Floinn, B. (1995), "Travellers and the Oral Tradition", in N. Ní Laodhóg (ed.), *A Heritage Ahead: Cultural Action and Travellers*, Dublin: Pavee Point Publications.

O'Keefe, B and O'Connor, P. (2001) "'Out of the Mouths of Babes and Innocents': Children's Attitudes Towards Travellers", in Cleary A, Nic Ghiolla Phádraig, M and Quin, S. (eds), *Understanding Children: Volume 2*, Dublin: Oak Tree Press.

Okely, J. (1983), *The Traveller Gypsies*, Cambridge University Press.

Ó Riain, G. (ed.) (1992), *Traveller Ways, Traveller Words*, Dublin: Pavee Point Publications.

Pavee Point (1999), *Bridges to the Future: A Report on Future Roles for the Senior Traveller Training Centres*, Dublin: Pavee Point Publications.

Whiting, B.B. and Edwards, C.P. (1988), *Children of Different Worlds: The Formation of Social Behaviour*, Harvard University Publications.

Notes

[1] The author is indebted to her late friend and colleague, John O'Connell, in general for his pioneering vision in the field of action-research relating to Travellers; and in particular, for an incisive discussion (1999) of the pitfalls attending attempts to provide comprehensive statistical picture of the Traveller population.

[2] The term "mixed school" in this chapter denotes a school, whether co-educational or not, in which Traveller and settled pupils are integrated.

Chapter 12

A Foreshortened Childhood: Refugee and Asylum-seeking Children in Ireland

Geraldine Nolan

Ireland is a relative newcomer to the field of refugee resettlement. The number of refugees and asylum seekers[1] entering the country since it became a signatory to the Geneva Convention in 1956 has been relatively small. This can be attributed to reluctance at Government level to admit refugees coupled with an apparent lack of awareness of Ireland as a possible destination for asylum seekers. Consequently until 1985 there was no established procedure for processing an application for asylum in Ireland. The 1990s saw a significant change. In response to war in the former Yugoslavia, Ireland has since 1992 admitted in excess of 1,300 Bosnian refugees (Department of Justice, Equality and Law Reform, 1999). More recently the Irish Government has undertaken a resettlement programme for Kosovar refugees. In addition to these "invited refugees" there has been a dramatic rise in the number of asylum seekers coming to the country. Increasingly the latter group includes children.

In response to these refugee influxes there has been a growing involvement by various Government departments and State agencies. The 1990s saw three bills relating to refugees brought before the Oireachtas culminating in the passing of the 1996 Refugee Act. The debate surrounding this legislation and other refugee issues led to unprecedented media coverage and wider public interest in the " refugee question". This has not

always been positive and the experiences of many refugees
would call into question the notion of Ireland as a place of welcome.

While the number of refugees as a percentage of population
remains small, they have become increasingly visible in urban
centres. The Bosnians, most of whom have settled in Dublin,
now constitute the largest refugee community in Ireland. The
next largest is that of the Vietnamese. From the original group
of 212 refugees who came to Ireland in 1979, the Irish Vietnamese community has grown to over 800 (Department of Justice,
Equality and Law Reform, 1999). In addition to these programme refugees there are smaller groups of asylum seekers.
Of these, Nigerians comprise the largest single group representing 31.1 per cent of applications last year, followed by Ro-
manians with 21.8 per cent.

REFUGEE CHILDREN IN IRELAND

Refugee children now form a small but distinct group within
Irish society. They are unique in terms of the trauma and up-
heaval which they have experienced and the way in which they
must then adapt to life in a new country. As a result they are a
particularly vulnerable group whose world is different from that
of other children. Their status as children and as refugees
means that they are in a sense doubly disadvantaged. As children they are more vulnerable than adult refugees. Yet they are
also more flexible and have the potential to adapt more easily.

Refugee children can be divided into two categories: those
who are directly refugees and those who are indirectly refugees. The former are children who came to Ireland as refugees;
the latter, children born to refugees living here. There are
many parallels between the two, such as likely difficulties in
relation to cultural alienation and language. This has been the
experience with Vietnamese children born in Ireland who often
have no English on starting school and are as much in need of
language support as a newly arrived refugee child. As the first
generation of Irish-born Bosnian children reach school going
age, a similar pattern is emerging (Refugee Agency, 1999).

As yet policies in relation to refugee children are far from clear-cut and the allocation of resources often inequitable. While all refugee children share characteristics and circumstances in common arising from their experiences in their home countries and their subsequent flight, there is considerable variety in the way they experience being a refugee in Ireland. Their status on entering the country (asylum seeker or programme refugee) impacts on their subsequent lifestyle in many ways, determining where they can live, the quality of their housing, access to particular schools and additional support within those schools, the presence of a community support network and access to mother tongue teaching.

The children of asylum seekers are in a more vulnerable position than other refugee children. While the families of programme refugees may begin to rebuild their lives, attend language classes and seek employment, asylum seekers are in a state of limbo. Their future is uncertain as their families await a decision on their status. This places additional strains on the children.

The likelihood of experiencing racism and discrimination is in accordance with the principle of propinquity whereby preference is given to those closest in terms of racial appearance, religious belief and ethnic origin (Mac Gréil, 1996). How a Bosnian child experiences being a refugee in Ireland might then be different in many ways to the child of a Somali asylum seeker. Similarly, within a particular refugee community the experiences of children will differ.

It is difficult to get data on the number of refugee children in Ireland. At the end of 1998, there were 117 Bosnian and 70 Vietnamese children of primary school age registered with the Refugee Support Service (Refugee Agency, 1999). A survey carried out by the Department of Education and Science in the same year showed that there were 1,641 non-national pupils from 104 countries attending 288 schools at primary level. The numbers have increased considerably since then (Department of Justice, Equality and Law Reform, 1999).

There is, as yet, little research or literature relating to refugees in the Irish context and even less on the subject of refugee children.[2] In 1994, the Department of Education established the

Refugee Support Service, a visiting teacher service to support
the children of programme refugees in primary schools in
Dublin. The service operated on a temporary basis from 1994
until 1999. The observations made in this chapter are based on
the author's experience as a support teacher working with Bosnian and Vietnamese children during that period.

THE REFUGEE EXPERIENCE

All refugee children have experienced loss. They have lost a
way of life, country, home, relatives, neighbours, friends and
belongings — all that was familiar and represented security.
The enormity of the change is captured succinctly in the words
of one Bosnian girl: "One plane, one journey took me away
from my life" (Lodge, 1995). While all refugee children share
the experience of loss, they differ in the extent of their loss and
trauma and in their coping strategies.

Children are most at risk if they have witnessed or suffered
direct violence themselves or if they have experienced bereavement and lack family or community support (Richman,
1993). There is a proven link between the level of exposure to a
stressor and the subsequent adjustment. Thus children can
come to accept ongoing low intensity conflicts such as the
Northern Ireland "troubles" whereas the suddenness of the
Bosnian or more recently the Kosovar conflicts intensifies their
traumatic impact. Ireland has admitted Bosnian refugees at
various stages since 1992. Differences have been noted between earlier groups and those arriving more recently. The
latter's experience of war would have been longer and more
intense. They have had many experiences that are beyond the
realm of normal childhood experience. Children who lived
through the siege of Sarajevo, for example, experienced terrible cold and hunger and the very real fear that they would die
of starvation.

Such experiences influence children's perceptions of the
world and their social construct of reality. This may impact in
small ways. A teacher in a Dublin primary school described an
art class where her pupils were making salt dough models. A

Bosnian boy in the class refused to join in because he said that this was a waste of good food.

While the impact of traumatic experiences must be acknowledged this does not necessarily mean that all refugee children are psychologically harmed, although some are. International research has tended to focus on the psychological problems of refugee children and consequently there is a dearth of anthropological literature (Vrečer, 1996). As a result, refugee children's ability to cope and function satisfactorily has been largely underestimated and the need for therapeutic interventions overestimated.

In their work with refugee children from Bosnia–Herzegovina over a four-year period, Kos and Derviškadić–Jovanić (1998) found that the majority functioned well and that the manifestation of symptoms of trauma as found in various psychological checklists was remarkably infrequent. Instead they suggest that the following comment by a Bosnian teacher comes closer to highlighting the impact of war on most children:

> Our children are not disturbed. There is a deep sorrow for losses and anguish for native land in their souls (cited in Kos and Derviškadić–Jovanić, 1998).

The reality of refugee children's lives is a combination of ordinary childhood experiences interspersed with the extraordinary as the following description illustrates. Here a refugee child now living in Dublin remembers her first day in school, an experience shared by children the world over. This was in 1993, at a time when refugees were fleeing to her village from other parts of Bosnia.

> The first time I went to school I was surprised because the school was so full. We had two classes in the one classroom. We all had to share chairs; on two chairs there were four children. While we were playing in the playground we were really scared that there might be grenades. During the winter we sledged. One day the food and salt ran out. Some children were coming to my village asking for food and winter clothes. We gave them stuff when we had it to give. . . . One day we had no food and people ate what they could find. During the

> war lots of people died from grenades and some lost limbs.
> Lots of children are orphans now (The Future, 1998, p. 19).

More than anything, refugee children need time and space to adjust to loss. They need an environment where they can feel safe again, and where they have an opportunity to talk about and share their experiences with others when they are ready to do so. In this way they may come to realise that they are not alone and that their reactions are normal.

COPING STRATEGIES

Children adopt different coping strategies at different stages. Withdrawal, where the child becomes introspective and will not engage with those around them, is one of the most frequent responses to trauma noted by teachers working with Bosnian children in Irish primary schools (INTO, 1998). The extent and pattern of withdrawal varies. Where this is prolonged, it may militate against the child's social and educational progress compounding the difficulties of learning English and increasing the child's sense of isolation.

Some refugee children exhibit aggression towards their peers; others appear emotionally upset, or overly sensitive. Many children express their experiences non-verbally through drawing or play. Younger children in particular may act out war games in the yard or play corner. One group of Bosnian children repeatedly chose to paint and draw war scenes for the first few months in their new school in Dublin. For children who had recently arrived from a war zone and did not have sufficient English to communicate, this was a means of expressing and sharing their experiences. It is not uncommon for children to continue to incorporate past experiences in their drawings for some time. The teacher of an 11-year-old Bosnian boy who had spent two years in school in Ireland commented that it was only at the end of the second year that he had stopped drawing pictures of weapons. Apart from this, the boy had adjusted well to school and appeared happy and outgoing.

For some refugee children previous experiences may impact sporadically and unexpectedly. Seemingly ordinary sounds such as a banging door, a siren in the street, the rumbling of the school heating system or a voice on the school intercom may prompt memories of past traumas causing the child to become upset. Others suffer from sleep problems, increased anxiety and depression, poor concentration or impaired memory.

Children appear to cope best when they can give a meaning to their experiences. A strong sense of pride in their homeland and a longing to return are common feelings among refugee children. While they appreciate the advantages of living in Ireland — no war, employment and educational opportunities — they miss a sense of belonging.

> This is not our country. In Bosnia you have your own house, all your family and friends. You know everyone and everyone knows you.

Memories of home are kept alive in different ways.

> Very often, I dream about my house and those days near the river. I have a videotape about the river and the city, which I often watch. That's the story about my city and one day I hope I will go back there (The Future, 1998, p. 18).

Since the Dayton Accord, many Bosnians living in Ireland have returned to Bosnia, a small number permanently, others for holidays. There are many who can never return to their old homes, which are now in occupied territory. The following passage written by a Bosnian boy, now a refugee in Dublin, illustrates how he has come to terms with this loss:

> Everyone should be proud to live in their hometown, wherever that town may be. Unfortunately the memories I have of my hometown are getting less, as it is so long since I left with my family. They wanted to destroy everything which was non-Serbian in my town. No one knows who is living in my house now. I'm wondering about it and whether the people have a son of my age. I wonder if he's playing with the toys which I couldn't bring with me because my bag was too small to carry many things. I wonder if he's happy and if he is able to sleep peacefully in my bed? No, I don't think so.

Now I am living a long way from my town and I'm not as happy in the place I'm living in now as I was in Bosnia. But I'm sure I'm happier than the boy who is living in my house now. Perhaps he isn't guilty because he's a child like me and nobody expects anything of children. Perhaps he will be aware of where he grew up, what his father or relatives did in the war. Maybe he'll be ashamed, but I know that I am going to be proud of my father who was in the army of Bosnia-Herzegovina defending my people (The Future, 1998, p. p. 18).

THE FAMILY

The family constitutes a central context in which most refugee children must forge a new way of life. While the presence of their family provides stability for the refugee child, the functioning of the family in exile is often impaired. It is easy to forget sometimes that refugees are ordinary people who once led ordinary lives. Most enjoyed a good standard of living, their own homes, personal possessions, jobs, cars, holidays, choices — a stark contrast to life on social welfare in Ireland. The effort required to come to terms with their changed status often makes parents less effective in their parental role leaving children to their own devices.

Racial harassment and abuse is a further stressor. For most refugees, encountering racism is a new experience and consequently one for which they do not have coping strategies. From talking to children from both communities it appears that Vietnamese families were more often victims of racism, Bosnians less so. In a recent survey of Bosnian and Vietnamese refugees 32 per cent of the Vietnamese and 10 per cent of the Bosnians surveyed indicated that they had experienced racial abuse, primarily verbal (O'Regan, 1998). As refugee numbers have grown there has been an increase in incidents of racism although this is difficult to quantify in the absence of an effective monitoring system (Faughnan, 1999; Boyle, 1999).

Refugee children have lost the safe context of childhood and as a result are often mature beyond their years (Povrzanović, 1997), Some refugee parents seek to protect their children by avoiding discussion of the problems. Others are so overwhelmed by their situation that they fail to recognise their children's trauma. Children frequently repress their own feelings in an attempt to protect their parents. In an Irish context, the difficulties of refugee children were commented on as follows:

> Refugee children not only experience the isolation generated by lack of fluency in the language which surrounds them, but may be withdrawn and mistrustful as a result of the events or circumstances which made them refugees in the first place. The result is that they are likely to find integration with their Irish peers extremely difficult. They are a soft target for bullying both within the environs of the school and in their local neighbourhood. However they are frequently obliged to keep such serious problems to themselves because their parents are experiencing problems of their own (Little and Lazenby Simpson, 1996).

When children successfully adapt to a new life and culture, their success may ironically be a source of further problems. Adult refugees' time perspectives tend to be more focused on the past and society of origin, whereas children adjust more rapidly to a new language and customs (Westermeyer, 1991). This facilitates their resettlement but it may also be a source of additional stresses where there is an adaptation lag between young and old.

When a child acculturates more rapidly than their parents they may have to assume adult roles. This is particularly likely when parents are not competent in the language of the host country and responsibility for liaising with public agencies then falls to the child. A 12-year-old Bosnian girl described how she acted as an interpreter accompanying her father to his driving test — a task which she had not relished, particularly when her father wished to express his displeasure to the tester on learning that he had failed. An 11-year-old Vietnamese girl regularly places orders with suppliers for her grandmother's business, as she is the most competent English speaker in her family.

These are some of the more innocuous interpretative tasks which children perform. At times these can be a positive experience for adult and child, however they are more often a source of resentment and frustration. Parental language de-

pendency and increased child responsibility alter the parent/
child relationship. Acting as interpreters may expose children
to adult problems, further encroaching on an already foreshortened childhood. This may have practical consequences such as
absenteeism from school, which in turn compounds the problems of a child who is already struggling academically.

SCHOOL

Schools have the potential to promote children's recovery by
helping them to become effective learners as quickly as possible. Returning to school is an important step in restoring a
sense of normality to the refugee child's life. The establishment
of a structured daily routine with normal developmental tasks
provides a respite and facilitates the recovery process. The
school can provide a strong and protective sense of community.
This is particularly important for children whose families are in
crisis and cannot adequately support them.

It is widely acknowledged that the greater the compatibility
between the culture of the school and home, the greater the
likelihood of the child experiencing success at school. This is
particularly significant in a country such as Ireland where life
chances are largely determined by educational achievement
(Drudy and Lynch, 1993).

It has been suggested that while many refugee parents are
in crude socio-economic terms "working class", their aspirations for their children approximate more to "middle class"
views (Tomlinson, 1984). However, such parents require more
help than those generally deemed "disadvantaged" since they
lack first-hand experience of the education system. Difficulties
arise where parents do not understand the approaches to
learning which schools and teachers take and cannot therefore
support their children's learning (Gregory, 1993). For cultural
reasons they may feel that education is the job of the school and
that they must not interfere. Others are so preoccupied with the
struggle of day-to-day living that they do not have the energy to
involve themselves in their children's school life.

Language often proves to be a significant barrier to communication. As a result, many refugee children in Irish schools are

the primary means of communication between their home and school. As such they regularly have the responsibility of conveying information about themselves or their siblings from the school to their parents and vice versa.

Undoubtedly the first weeks and months in school are the most difficult for refugee children. Many remember an overwhelming feeling of sadness. Two years after arriving in Ireland, a Bosnian girl described what it was like:

> You feel terrible, really sad and when you go home from school you just want to cry and you never want to go back.

Children are particularly vulnerable and isolated at this stage as their parents are often having similar difficulties coming to terms with a new language and culture. Furthermore, being the new child and unable to speak English, the refugee child cannot draw on the support of their peers.

Some refugee parents underestimate the difficulties that their children face in adjusting to a new education system and may be disappointed that they are no longer top of the class as they were in their home country. Unrealistic expectations (their own or those of a parent) can be a source of unnecessary stress for refugee children. It is easy for children to feel disheartened when their best efforts seem to achieve poor results. This is especially hard for those who, in the past, have been high achievers.

In contrast to earlier groups, Bosnian children coming to Ireland in recent years have suffered considerable disruption to their education. For these children, adapting to school not only involves learning a new language but also catching up on years of missed schooling. This is particularly difficult for children at the upper end of primary school, many of whom lack basic literacy and numeracy skills. Without intensive intervention, it is unlikely that they will achieve their full potential.

Asked what they found difficult about starting school in Ireland, apart from the obvious language problem, many children comment on the phenomenon of "killing with kindness", where in the early days they were constantly surrounded by other children asking them questions which they did not understand. In contrast, some then found themselves left friendless once the novelty wore off. For older children, play and social interaction is more language-based, further compounding the difficulties for a child in the early stages of learning English. One girl described the loneliness of long lunchtimes in the schoolyard surrounded by groups of children in whose conversations she could not participate. Her brother, a keen footballer, had fared better as he could join in the lunchtime football games. The perception that it is easier for boys than for girls to integrate with their Irish peers was shared by a number of older refugee girls.

Many refugee children remark on how tiring the school day can be, particularly for recently arrived children. The high level of concentration which is required to operate through a second language is often underestimated. As children progress, it is easy to forget the ongoing effort required to sustain that progress. Even when a child has passed the initial stages of learning English and appears fairly fluent in social situations, they must still bridge the considerable gap between what has been termed the "language of the playground" (Gibbons, 1996) and the considerably more demanding level of English required for academic tasks.

The fact that refugees are not a homogenous group was noted earlier. One cannot assume that just because children come from the same country they will have the same background or be friends. A Bosnian boy recalled starting in a new school where his teacher, with the best will in the world, had introduced him to another Bosnian boy assuming that they would be friends. In fact the two families did not associate with each other. The principal of another primary school recounted a similar experience where she had unwittingly offended a Bosnian parent by sending a message about her child through another Bosnian. The parent of the child in question pointed out that all Bosnians were not the same and that she was entitled to privacy in the same way as any other parent.

While Irish schools make a considerable effort to be welcoming to refugee children, the way schools operate may exclude children who differ from the norm. Until recently there was little recognition of difference in educational provision in Ireland, a situation that is only slowly beginning to change. The vast majority of Irish primary schools are Catholic. While schools respect the right of parents to remove their children from religious instruction, the ethos of schools is such that religion permeates. Often children who are not participating in religious ceremonies or services get sidelined, at times of preparation for communion or confirmation, for example. There is often a lack of awareness of other religions and children's religious practice may then be a source of fun for other children. Several children (Muslims) had had the experience of being asked by classmates how they prayed. They later saw these children imitating them in the yard and had felt slighted.

It is frequently assumed that all children have equal access to certain "knowledge". This "knowledge" may be a way of behaving or literally a point of information. A Bosnian girl in sixth class cited the example of a weekly homework worksheet given to the class that often included general knowledge questions on which they were tested at the end of the week. The children had to find out the answers to the questions themselves. One of the questions one week was, "Charlie Haughy's wife is the daughter of which famous politician?" As she commented, "How can I know this? My mum, my auntie, nobody knows".

As a result, refugee children often find themselves very isolated in dealing with the education system. While their parents encourage them to do well in school and ensure that they are well provided for materially, their lack of knowledge of the Irish education system and lack of English limits their ability to advise and guide their children. The transition to secondary school can be a particularly difficult time as the responsibility for choosing a school, subjects and making the necessary applications often falls to the child. When parents or children do not fully understand the literature received they may miss deadlines for applications or end up making a poor subject choice.

HOUSING

The difficulties of many refugee children have been compounded by the prevailing housing crisis. Most refugees live in private rented accommodation, a trend that is likely to continue due to the current shortage of local authority housing. The most recently available annual report of the Refugee Agency (1999) shows that 6 per cent of Bosnians had purchased their own homes, 5 per cent were in local authority housing and 87 per cent in private rented accommodation. This poses problems as many families have to move after a couple of years and it is not always possible to be rehoused in the same area. Children are often uprooted and suffer further loss as they are forced to start in a new school and begin the difficult task of making new friends. The older the child, the more difficult the move. It is particularly hard for a child entering a class at the upper end of primary school where friendships and groups are generally well established.

A further effect of the current housing difficulties is that refugees are forced to live in certain areas where rents are suitably low. This raises the possibility of ghettoisation. The existence of a community of refugees provides an important support network and also facilitates the provision of services. Where there is a cluster of refugee children in a particular school, for example, it is easier to organise support for them. A negative effect is that refugee children then tend to socialise solely within their own community and are less likely to integrate with their Irish peers. This has been apparent from the contrasting experiences of Bosnian children living in different areas. A recent report by the Canal Communities Partnership (Boyle, 1999) highlighted similar difficulties among asylum seekers:

> Even when the children are at school if we're living in a hostel, it can be outside the area and we go and come from the hostel and collect the child and have no contact with the local community. In the school holidays the children stay at home, there's no activities. If the children meet after school we can't afford to let them go to sports etc. The children then don't even meet other children outside of school; they come back to the hostels which are full of other refugee children (Nigerian asylum seeker, cited in Boyle, 1999, p. 31).

CONCLUSION

This chapter has considered some of the issues affecting refugee children living in Ireland. In time most adapt well. Nonetheless, these children are a potentially vulnerable group who require an alternative support network when their families are in difficulty. In order to ensure their well-being, it is important that appropriate support structures be developed. Taking education as an example, such provision would ensure that refugee children have access to the mainstream school curriculum on a par with their Irish peers and in accordance with their academic potential rather than merely achieving a basic level of English competence.

To date, provision for refugee children in Ireland has been largely ad hoc. The lack of adequate supports has been such that it might be argued that many refugee children have thrived in spite of, rather than because of, the system. Their presence in schools challenges assumptions of homogeneity and introduces a potentially enriching diversity. While children are actively involved in creating their social worlds, "the structure of those worlds is already predefined by broader racial, gender and class relations" (Bourdieu and Wacquant, 1992, p. 144). As the school is a meeting ground for the cultures of home and school, the potential for conflict is not just a home/school divide but also a pupil/pupil cultural divide according to how pupils from different backgrounds have learnt to perceive the other. The resulting challenge for Irish education is twofold: to provide for the particular needs of refugee children and to prepare all children for life in a changing society.

In working and meeting with refugee children living in Ireland, more than anything, one would have to be impressed by how well they adjust and integrate with their Irish peers. Their success in rebuilding their lives, often against considerable odds, is a tribute to the resilience of children in the face of adversity.

References

Ahearn, F., and Athey,J. (eds.) (1991), *Refugee Children: Theory, Research and Services*, Baltimore, MD: John Hopkins University Press.

Bourdieu, P., and Wacquant, L. (1992), *An Invitation to Reflexive Sociology*, Chicago: University of Chicago Press.

Boyle, A. (1999), *Towards an Equality Strategy in the Canal Communities*, Dublin: Canal Communities Equality Strategy Publications.

Department of Justice, Equality and Law Reform (1999), *Integration A Two Way Process: Report of the Interdepartmental Working Group on the Integration of Refugees in Ireland*, Dublin: Department of Justice, Equality and Law Reform.

Drudy, S., and Lynch, K. (1993), *Schools and Society in Ireland*, Dublin: Gill and Macmillan.

The Future (1998), "My Homeland" by the Children in the Bosnian School, Bosnian Community Development Project, Dublin, April, 1998.

Faughnan, P. (1999), "Refugees and Asylum Seekers in Ireland: Social Policy Dimensions", Social Science Research Centre, University College Dublin.

Gibbons, P. (1996), "Learning to Learn in a Second Language", Primary English Teaching Association, Australia.

Gregory, E. (1993), "Sweet and Sour: Learning to Read in a British and Chinese School" in *English in Education*, Vol. 27, 3, Autumn 1993, NAT.

INTO (1998), *The Challenge of Diversity: Education Support for Ethnic Minority Children*, Dublin: Irish National Teachers Organisation.

Kos, A., and Derviškadić–Jovanić (1998), "What can we do to support children who have been through war?" in *Forced Migration Review*, December 1998, 3, RSP, Queen Elizabeth House, Oxford.

Little, D., and Lazenby Simpson, B. (1996), "Meeting the Language Needs of Refugees", Centre for Language and Communication Studies, University of Dublin, Trinity College.

Lodge, C. (1995), "Working with Refugees in Schools", *Pastoral Care in Education*, Vol. 13, No. 2, NAPCE.

MacGréil, M. (1996), "Prejudice in Ireland Revisited", Survey and Research Unit, St. Patrick's College, Maynooth.

McGovern, F. (1990), "Vietnamese Refugees in Ireland, 1979-1989: A Case Study in Education and Resettlement", unpublished M.Ed. Thesis, Trinity College, Dublin.

O'Regan, C., (1998), "Report of a Survey of the Vietnamese and Bosnian Refugee Communities in Ireland", Refugee Resettlement Research Project, Refugee Agency, Dublin.

Povrzanović, M., (1997), "Children, War and Nation, Croatia 1991-4" in *Childhood*, Vol. 4, No.1, February 1997.

Refugee Agency (1999), Annual Report 1998, Refugee Agency, Dublin.

Richman, N. (1993), "Annotation: Children in Situations of Political Violence" *Journal of Child Psychology and Psychiatry*, Vol. 34, 8.

Tomlinson, S. (1984), "Home, School and Community" in Craft, M., (ed.) *Education and Cultural Pluralism*, Falmer Press, Sussex.

Vrečer, N. (1996), "The Lost Way of Life: The Experience of Refugee Children in Celje from 1992-1994" in Jambresic Kirin, R. and Povrzanović, M. (eds.), *War, Exile, Everyday Life: Cultural Perspectives*, Zagreb: Institute of Ethnology and Folklore Research.

Westermeyer, J. (1991), "Psychiatric Services for Refugee Children: An Overview" in Ahearn, F., and Athey, J., (eds.) *Refugee Children, Theory, Research and Services*, Baltimore, MD: John Hopkins University Press.

Notes

[1] The Geneva Convention relating to the status of refugees in 1951 provided an international definition of the term refugee. In article 1(a)(2) a refugee is defined as one who:

> owing to a well founded fear of being persecuted for reasons of race, religion, nationality, membership of a particular social group or political opinion, is outside the country of his nationality and is unable, or owing to such fear is unwilling to avail himself of the protection of that country.

"Programme refugees" are people whose status as refugees is established prior to their arrival in Ireland. These refugees enter the country as a result of a Government Decision. They are entitled to social welfare benefits on a par with similarly placed Irish citizens. They also have the right to work and to state funded education and training. The main groups of programme refugees coming to Ireland have been the Hungarians (1957), Chileans (1970s) Vietnamese (since 1979), Bosnians (from 1992) and most recently Kosovars (1999). The Refugee Agency is the Government body which oversees the resettlement of programme refugees.

"Asylum seekers" are people who come to Ireland seeking to be recognised as refugees in accordance with the terms of the 1951 Conventon. They must then go through a process at the end of which they may or may not be granted refugee status. In some cases while they may not fully meet the definition of a convention refugee, they may be given leave to remain on humanitarian grounds. Such a decision is at the discretion of the Minister for Justice.

While their applications are being processed, asylum seekers are entitled to social welfare benefits on a par with Irish citizens but they do not have the right to work. The process may take several years. The children of asylum seekers may attend school but the area of educational provision for adults is more ad hoc. The Vocational Education Committees (V.E.C.) around the country provides some classes for adults.

[2] Numerically small and a relatively recent phenomenon, refugee children in Ireland have to date been a low priority for researchers and policy makers. McGovern's seminal work on the resettlement of the Vietnamese highlighted the difficulties experienced by Vietnamese children in Irish schools (McGovern, 1990). A 1996 report "Meeting the Language needs of Refugees" (Little and Lazenby Simpson, 1996) looked at some of the issues affecting refugee children in that context. In 1998, the INTO published its report on educational support for ethnic minority children, "The Challenge of Diversity", which discussed the educational needs of refugee children and examined current provision. Both reports drew on the experiences of teachers of the Primary Refugee Support Service. An inter-departmental research project that focused on the resettlement of the Bosnian and Vietnamese refugee communities in Ireland was carried out in 1997. Its findings add little to our knowledge of refugee children. As noted by its author, the report's conclusion that the children were adapting well socially and academically must be treated with caution in light of the small sample size (11 Vietnamese and 20 Bosnians) and wide age range (5-18 years) of those surveyed (O'Regan, 1998).

Chapter 13

"Tá Gaeilge agam . . . ach níl ag mo chara" — Irish-speaking Children

Máire Nic Ghiolla Phádraig

Irish-speaking children form a curious minority in the population. They belong to a linguistic tradition of over 2,000 years on the island (Ó Murchú, 1985, p. 9) which is honoured in the Constitution (Bunreacht na hÉireann, 1937, Airteagal 8) as the National Language and has been given varying degrees of political party support since the foundation of the State. On the other hand, while a large proportion of the Irish population have at least a smattering of Irish (41 per cent), mainly learnt as a school subject, the percentage of adults aged 20 years and older who use it daily is just under 3 per cent. (Census 1996, Vol. 9, pp.12, 26, 68). The areas in which Irish is in daily use as a community language are referred to as the Gaeltacht. All of them are rural areas, mainly located on stretches of the West coast periphery. They form a tiny, scattered proportion (2.4 per cent) of the population of the State. Even in the Gaeltacht, the proportion of the adult population using Irish daily is only 36.6 per cent (ranging from about 6 per cent to 92 per cent depending on the district). (Ibid, pp. 27, 69). In order to encourage the survival of the Gaeltacht, certain grants and subsidies additional to those available in other parts of the State have been provided to boost the socio-economic structure.

In practice, all Irish-speakers are, or soon become, fluent in English, "the second official language", and find this necessary to be able to avail of most services, including those provided by the State.[1] While Irish speakers show some degree of clustering in certain regions and educational and occupational groups, with the exception of organisations specifically established to provide services to Irish speakers, there is no sector in which communication is predominantly organised through Irish (Ó Riagáin, 1997, pp. 166-167).

Since 1926, Irish has been a compulsory school subject at primary and second-level, but only a small proportion of students emerge with fluency in Irish from the school system. Because of this, since the 1970s, the Gaelscoileanna movement has been responsible for setting up a network of Irish-medium primary (national) schools, which are found mainly in urban areas throughout the State. The supply of second-level schooling through Irish has been much more limited in contrast. Irish-speaking families have been prominent in the establishment of Gaelscoileanna. However, in every case, their children form a minority within the Gaelscoil (Ó Riagáin, 1997, p. 265). In official Gaeltacht areas, the schools also teach through Irish regardless of parental preference or actual community language.

The other main institution through which Irish-speaking children have contact with Irish is the television service, Teilifís na Gaeilge (TnaG) now renamed TG4, which began broadcasting in October 1996. Its stated policy has been to focus on children and young people's programmes. Prior to the establishment of TnaG there was very scant provision of programmes in Irish on the other two State-commercial channels, RTE1 and Network 2, and programmes in Irish for children were particularly scarce.

It has been noted that Irish speakers, because of their dispersal throughout the population and their knowledge and use of the majority language, English, maintain their usage of Irish mainly through networks (CLAR, 1975, p. 231; Ó Riagáin, 1997, pp. 166-167). However, adult networks do not always provide adequate opportunities for child networks. The realisation of this was a major impetus to the foundation of an organisation of Irish-speaking families, Comhluadar, in 1993. This organisation provides a variety of social activities for children and their parents and acts as a support group for parents who are encountering difficulties in bringing up their children with Irish. The membership in 1997, when this study was initiated, was 180 families, mainly in the Greater Dublin and Cork city areas, but it has since grown to over 300 families and achieved a greater geographical spread.

The data[2] in this chapter are drawn from two sources: (1) a postal survey of the 180 Comhluadar families carried out in 1997. Completed questionnaires were received from 65 per cent of the parents, and there was no apparent bias in the non-response rate. (2) Two focus group discussions with Comhluadar children (9-15 years) were held in 1999. For comparative purposes, a small focus group of three Gaeltacht teenagers (13-15 years) was also convened. These give some indication of the experience of being a child of the Irish-speaking minority and provide some additional data to the work of Maguire with Belfast children who were brought up as Irish speakers in the Shaw's Road community (Maguire, 1991).

The 1996 census data on the Irish language includes questions both on ability to speak Irish and frequency of use of Irish for all aged over 3 years. The 3-4 years category provides us with the best approximation of the percentage of children for whom Irish is a home rather than a school language. Forty-six in 1,000 of all children aged 3-4 years in the State are enumerated as speaking Irish on a daily basis; just under a fifth of these live in official Gaeltacht areas, but even there they form a minority accounting for only one-third of their age cohort. The percentage of the population recorded as speaking Irish on a daily basis varies widely within the Gaeltacht, so it is likely that while some of these children live in Gaeltacht areas where most or all children are raised as Irish speakers, most live in areas where this is a minority situation.

Globally speaking, bilingualism is more prevalent than monolingualism (Grosjean, 1982, Ch. 1). However, in Ireland and other parts of the English-speaking world, it is much less common. Monolinguals sometimes regard bilingual children as either prodigies or handicapped! Medical, paramedical and educational specialists are also frequently unaware of the "normalcy" of bilingualism and sometimes counsel parents against it, particularly if there are language, behavioural or medical problems (Nic Ghiolla Phádraig, 1999, p. 21). Further-more, there has been a shifting consensus in the literature on childhood bilingualism regarding the optimum means of en-suring acquisition of both languages. The dominant view was "one language, one parent", i.e. that each parent would use one language only to the child to ensure a "balanced" input and to keep the languages separate (e.g. Saunders, 1988). The main case studies on which such a recommendation was based were those carried out by (male) linguists on their own chil-dren. However, the experience of parents where one of the languages was a minority language with little or no community usage indicated that equal input of the two languages by each parent would not produce equal output (see *Bilingual Family Newsletter*, various, and Skutnabb-Kangas, 1981, pp. 20-21). The emerging consensus is that the minority language must be strengthened at every opportunity if the child is to acquire an adequate fluency in that language (Skutnabb-Kangas, 1981, p. 21). The "pull" of the majority language is very strong and often results in bilingual children refusing to use the minority lan-guage, at least for a time (*Bilingual Family Newsletter*, various). In Ireland, the minority position of Irish and the near universal fluency in English means that such pressures to conform to use of English are very strong.

For most Gaeltacht Irish-speaking children, Irish was the first language of their parents and ancestors in an unbroken chain. But Comhluadar children, who are brought up as Irish speakers in the Gaeltacht, are mainly the children of "revival-ists" who learnt Irish as their second language to varying de-grees of fluency. One or both parents were from the Gaeltacht, in the case of 23 per cent of the children, but a similar proportion were born to parents neither of whom had ever heard a word of Irish in their family of origin. About half of the children had one parent for whom Irish had been used, to a greater or lesser de-gree, by their family of origin. The majority of Comhluadar had largely English-speaking extended family relationships (Nic Ghiolla Phádraig, 1999, p. 4). Just over one-third of the parents had both been Irish speakers prior to meeting their partners. For 46 per cent of couples, one partner was an Irish speaker. In 15 per cent of families neither partner had used Irish regularly prior to meeting each other. There was a shift towards increased use of Irish between the couples subsequent to the birth of children (Ibid, p. 6).

Of 107 intact couples the following profile of language use with their children emerged:

Mainly English spoken by both parents	17%
English by one parent, Irish by the other	30%
"Bilingual" (mixture by both parents)	6%
Mainly Irish by both parents	48%

About half of eldest children were described by their parents as having acquired Irish as their first language and about one-fifth acquired Irish and English simultaneously. Those whose first language was English were still more fluent in that language at the time of the study, whereas those whose first language was Irish were mainly described as now equally fluent in English and Irish (Ibid, p.9).

A significant factor in the prominence of English as the first or most fluent language was the great difficulty parents experienced in accessing day care where even a smattering of Irish was used. A number of mothers and some fathers had made a decision to stay at home and look after their children themselves, mainly in the interest of ensuring they acquired Irish.

Parents' evaluations of changes over time in the use of Irish by their children varied in relation to the child's first language. Children whose first language was Irish were often reported as shifting to English as a result of attendance at a Naíonra (Irish medium playgroup) or Gaelscoil or acquiring English-speaking playmates. A form of diglossia often emerges at this stage with children identifying English as the norm when playing (in imitation of the majority of children), although others switch entirely to English at this stage. Children whose first language was English were reported as having increased their use of Irish following attendance at a Naíonra or Gaelscoil (Ibid, p. 14). The latter would be the normal pattern for children from English-speaking homes who attend Naíonraí and/or Gaelscoileanna (Hickey, 1997, p. 59; Ó Riagáin and Ó Gliasáin, 1979, p. 84).

Focus Group Participants

The two focus groups were recruited by a mailshot to Comhluadar members asking for volunteers aged 9-15 years. They were offered the inducement of a book token or disc token for participation. While this might be regarded as unethical (Hill, 1998, pp. 16-17) it had the desired effect of recruiting children and teenagers with negative or indifferent attitudes towards Irish as well as enthusiasts. While the two groups cannot be described as representative of children brought up as Irish speakers, or even of Comhluadar members, they do offer a range of opinions on the topics discussed.

Group A comprised eight participants, three of whom were teenaged and attending second level schools. All had attended a Gaelscoil and of the three second level pupils, one was now at an English-medium school and the others at Irish-medium schools. The three teenagers, one boy (Cian)[3] and two girls (Clíona and Síofra) were the main contributors. Síofra was particularly negative in her views towards the language, which ironically (and significantly) she spoke with closer proximity to native speaker ability than any other participant.

All but one of the eight Group B participants were still attending a primary school, a Gaelscoil. Their views ranged from very positive to indifferent regarding the Irish language.

The small Gaeltacht focus group consisted of three teenagers, one boy (Breandán) and two girls (Bríd and Úna) who were attending second level schools in a town which was largely English speaking although in an official Gaeltacht area. They lived and had attended primary school in a "strong" Gaeltacht area in which Irish dominated in daily usage.

The participants were requested to fill in brief questionnaires which offered some points of comparison of experience and views with those in the parents' questionnaire. Amalgamating the findings from Groups A and B we find:

Of the 16 participants, eight reported themselves as speaking Irish and seven as speaking Irish and English as their first language(s) with only one reporting English. None of those whose first/sole language had been Irish seemed to have difficulty in "picking up" English, although some recalled not having sufficient English, when they were younger, to understand everything being said by other children. This had not been a hurtful experience for any of those who reported it.

The majority (nine) reported themselves as equally fluent in both languages, with three claiming English and four claiming Irish as their most fluent language.

Eight claimed that more Irish than English was spoken in their homes, five claimed equal usage, three claimed that English was used more than Irish. Despite their claims that Irish dominated at home, only two reported speaking Irish to siblings, nine used both Irish and English and five used English only.

There was greater usage of Irish with other children who attended Gaelscoil than with other children in the family. This corresponds with the parents' perceptions also. Nine children reported speaking Irish to other Gaelscoil children and six to using both Irish and English. None reported using English only. They were not questioned about out of school usage of Irish with classmates, which is likely to be considerably lower than school usage. Parents are usually responded to in the language in which they address their children, although the more indifferent/negative were more likely to respond in English. When asked about their opinion about the Irish language, seven selected "proud" (Bród), four selected "Respect/Regard" (Meas) and four selected "No interest"/I don't care (Neamhshuim/is cuma liom). Comparing these responses to the evaluations of parents regarding the population of Comhluadar children the distribution is reasonably similar:

	Child 1	Child 2[4]
Proud	41.1%	24.7%
Respect	45.8%	41.4%
No interest/shame/hatred	13%	25.2%
Total, net of children too young to have opinion	(107)	(87)

Five sets of siblings participated in the focus groups, two in each group with one divided between the two groups. These accounted for 11 of the 16 children. Ten families in all were represented in the groups. Where siblings participated, there was some intra-family variation in overall individual usage of Irish, but, with one exception, all siblings positioned themselves similarly as either favourable or unfavourable in their opinion of Irish and made similar responses to a pictogram of children playing in Irish identifying themselves as central or marginal to this group.

GAELSCOILEANNA

For children from an Irish-speaking background, the main sources of regular contact with Irish, apart from their parents, are the schools and more recently TnaG. The movement to establish Irish-medium education has gathered strength over the last 20 years, Naíonraí (preschools) Gaelscoileanna (Irish-medium national schools) and, to a limited extent, second level schooling having been provided in most major urban centres. Almost all of the parents in the study sent their children to Gaelscoileanna (the exceptions being, mainly, those living abroad). This entailed a special effort on the part of almost half of these families (e.g. relocating beside a Gaelscoil, helping to establish one in their area or commuting considerable distances each day). The majority of parents believed themselves well-served by the Gaelscoil, although a minority argued that these schools focus on children from non-Irish speaking backgrounds. Some claimed that their children's command of Irish had disimproved as a result of their attendance at Gaelscoil. A recent study has asserted that the children in Gaelscoileanna often develop an argot for use amongst themselves which largely reflects English syntactic structures, although using a mixed Irish and English vocabulary (Ó Catháin, 1998). Maguire also refers to "interlanguage" as prevalent among the young people of the Shaw's Road community (1991, pp. 181-187). This researcher does not have the competence to examine this aspect, but noted that several of the children in both focus groups exhibited this form of speech which differed from the role models provided by their parents or, probably, their teachers.

All but one of the children indicated overall satisfaction with their Gaelscoil (with the usual disclaimers regarding "obair bhaile" (homework)). Síofra in Group A was the exception to this. She found the school rule requiring use of Irish on top of her home use of Irish as "brú, brú, brú" (pressure). She was afraid to use English in case she got a black mark, although the rule to speak Irish was largely ignored in the playground. As a result, she had had only one friend and felt isolated. Her progression to an English-medium second level school had brought relief from this pressure, and new friends.

Clíona responded with a different kind of experience. Her Gaelscoil had been successful in inculcating Irish as the school language, even in the schoolyard. However, the transition to an Irish-medium second level school brought problems. During her first month there, she and one other friend spoke only Irish, however no one would speak to them and they felt obliged to switch to English ("bhí orainn athrú go Béarla").

The children in Group B were positive about their Gaelscoil, even those who were least favourable in their opinions about Irish. A number mentioned their friends as the best-liked aspect of school. While initial problems in understanding some of the English words used in their schools were mentioned by two of the children, it was not a cause of embarrassment to them in their memory of early schooldays.

Boys in both Galltacht discussion groups were more dismissive of peer pressure to speak English than were girls. Ciarán (10):

> I mo rang labhrann a lán daoine Béarla sa chlós ach labhraim Gaeilge ar ais leo agus ní deireann siad aon rud is ní deireann mise aon rud. . . . Gach éinne i mo rang is maith leo Gaeilge.

> (Lots of people in my class speak English in the school yard, but I just speak Irish back to them and they don't say anything [about it] and I don't say anything [about it] . . . everyone in my class likes Irish)

By comparison, Cian who was 13 years and in 1st year adopted a retreatist strategy:

> Níor chuir sé as dom go mór mar bhí daltaí eile ag labhairt Gaeilge agus d'fhan mé leo. Níor bhac mé leis na daoine eile.

> (It didn't trouble me greatly because there were other pupils who did speak Irish and I stayed with them. I didn't have anything to do with the other people.)

Diarmuid (10), who described himself as indifferent to Irish, took a pragmatic view:

> Labhrann beagnach gach duine Béarla sa chlós, ach nuair a thagann na múinteoirí timpeall bíonn siad ag labhairt Gaeilge.

> (Almost everyone speaks English in the school yard, but when the teachers come around they [pupils] speak Irish.)

The difference in responses by gender to pressure to speak English in the schoolyard are worth considering. Among Gaeltacht girls, this experience had occasioned some distress and led to switching to English, even by committed Irish speakers, whereas the boys were dismissive. In view of the relatively greater importance of conversation in girls' peer relationships, as compared with boys' (see Thorne, 1993, Ch. 6), girls would appear to be more vulnerable to pressures to switch to the dominant language. The importance of females in initiating language shift in communities has been documented in a variety of circumstances (Milroy and Milroy, 1992, Coates, 1993, Ch. 8). The participants in the present study rejected an interpretation of these pressures as bullying as such, although it could probably be rated on a continuum of bullying. Again, the experience of bullying by girls is more often verbal than in the case of boys (see O'Moore, 1989, pp. 5-6; Smith and Sharp, 1994, pp. 6, 16). Use of Irish may possibly draw a more negative peer reaction among girls than boys, but that could only be resolved by further research. In contrast, the pre-teenaged did not appear to perceive any real negative pressures from school peers about their use of Irish.

The Gaeltacht teenagers had attended an Irish-medium national school in their locality where, they reported, everyone spoke Irish. The transfer to second level schools brought a more linguistically mixed situation. Although these schools taught through Irish and Irish was the medium of communication with pupils, they drew on a wide catchment area which, while part of the official Gaeltacht, was largely English-speaking. Although the national schools in these areas would have followed an Irish-medium curriculum, the home language of most of the pupils would be English and the degree of fluency in Irish attained by them was weaker than that of the Gaeltacht participants in the study. They reported that such pupils experienced difficulty in following what was going on in second level school initially, but that they had made the effort and had mastered the language. Some pupils attended who had not been through Irish-medium national schools and found it very difficult to cope. They had not objected to the linguistic norm of the school. The language of the schoolyard was reported to be Irish. This posed problems for those whose home language was English.

> Ni thuigfeadh na daoine le Béarla cad a bheadh á rá againn agus bheadh sé deacair acu fáil amach cad a bheadh á rá againn.

> (The English speakers would not understand what we would be saying and it would be hard for them to find out what we'd be saying.)

Whereas in the girls' school it was claimed that everyone mixed together and English speakers got in on the use of Irish, in the boys' school the ethos appeared to be different, and friendship groups largely corresponded to linguistic background.

TEACHER'S PET?

A number of the children reported that their teachers had greater expectations of them than of their classmates because they had been brought up with Irish. They were sometimes used as a resource by teachers and fellow pupils when stuck for a word or phrase in Irish. This seemed a source of satisfaction to them. Only Síofra viewed this negatively:

> Anois, má fhaighim Grád A sa Ghaeilge, deireann daoine cén fáth?

> (Now, when I get an A grade in Irish, people ask why?)

PEER RELATIONSHIPS AND IRISH

The tensions around use of Irish or English and the linguistic management skills required in the schoolyard have already been outlined. The Gaeltacht children were usually members of the only Irish-speaking family in their neighbourhood. English was the exclusive language used by all but two when playing with neighbours' children.

Where neighbouring children attended the same Gaelscoil, Irish had a minor role in their after-school play activity. It appeared to have been used mainly to communicate without other children understanding what was being said, or to baffle and tease them.

Early experiences of "going out to play" prior to school age confronted some of those for whom Irish was the first language with difficulties in understanding some of what was being said. But they soon "picked up" English.

With the exception of the Gaelscoil and whatever extra-curricular activities were organised there, Comhluadar children had little contextual/structural support for the use of Irish with peers. Children from one family who participated in the focus group were members of a youth club organised through Irish. About half of the participants were regular attenders at events organised by Comhluadar. When asked for suggestions as to what should be organised through Irish for young people, youth clubs, musical and sporting activities were proposed.

For the Gaeltacht group, there was a vibrant Irish-speaking social life outside school based on sporting clubs. They were very athletic and had no interest in any other form of activity. Had non-sporting young people been included their perception of support for Irish in the local community might have been much weaker.

GAELTACHT/IRISH COLLEGE

Over half of the families in the survey took a holiday in the Gaeltacht at least once a year, but one in six families had never managed to holiday in the Gaeltacht. About two-thirds of those who spent time in the Gaeltacht believed it had been helpful to the children to hear Irish spoken in a "natural" community setting.

References to Gaeltacht areas as holiday venues were very favourable. For the younger children there was a magical fusion of the sand, sea, open spaces, the tramping over hill and bog and exploring shorelines with engagement with an Irish-speaking community. Ciarán (10):

> Is maith liom Ciarraí. Níl a lán daoine ann. Téann muid go dtí an trá agus is féidir linn siúl timpeall agus gach rud.
>
> (I like Kerry. There aren't many people there. We go to the strand and we can walk around and everything.)

A number of children reported that while there they played with Gaeltacht children, but it seems that not all spoke Irish. As well as family holidays in the Gaeltacht, some of the children expected to spend a couple of weeks there with their classmates and teacher from the Gaelscoil.

The Gaeltacht teenagers had spent one or more periods at Gaeltacht summer colleges, with varied results. Typically, Síofra and Clíona in Group A reported diametrically different experiences. For Clíona, her college in Connemara reinforced all of her enthusiasm for the Irish language:

> Chuaigh mé go dtí an Ghaeltacht anuraidh agus tá mé ag dul go dtí an Ghaeltacht arís an Samhradh seo. Thaitn sé go mór liom, bhí sé go híontach. Bhí mé i gColáiste X. Bhí sé go hanmhaith agus thaitn sé go mór liom. . . . Tá mo dheirfiúir

ag dul agus tá go leor cairde eile agam ó chontaetha eile
gur bhuail mé leo an bhliain seo chaite.

(I went to the Gaeltacht last year and I'm going again this
summer. I really enjoyed it, it was wonderful. I was in X
College and I really enjoyed it. My sister is going and lots of
friends from other counties that I met last year.)

For Síofra, however, the Gaeltacht college which she attended
reinforced the sham she perceived and the negative experiences she had had regarding the Irish language:

Bhí sé díreach mar an gcéanna leis an scoil. Bhí ort Gaeilge a
labhairt ach ní raibh an chuid is mó de na daoine á hiarraidh.
Bhí sé an-deacair Gaeilge ar bith a aimsiú leis an méid sin
Béarla thart — fiú labhair fear a'tí agus bean a'tí Béarla.

(It was just like school. You had to speak Irish, but most
didn't want to. It was very difficult to discover any Irish,
there was so much English around — even the man and
woman of the house spoke English.)

In contrast, Clíona reported that she had heard no English at all
for the full three weeks and she appeared to have integrated
very well:

Bhí mé ar an duine is óige san teach ina raibh mé ag fanacht
agus uaireanta d'imir mé le páistí muintir an tí agus bhí
Gaeilge álainn acu agus d'fhoghlaim mé go leor uathu.

(I was the youngest [student] in the house where I stayed
and sometimes I played with the children of the house and
they had lovely Irish and I learnt a lot from them.)

On the whole, the views expressed were very positive about
the experience of staying in the Gaeltacht. Additionally, a number of children referred to the Gaeltacht as a sign of the
strength and future endurance of the Irish language.

It was decided to explore the views of the Gaeltacht teenagers regarding the annual influx of visitors and summer college
students. Were these a source of irritation? They articulated a
tolerant, welcoming view, although most of their contact was at

a distance. They believed that where there were teenagers in a host family the scholars mixed with them. Apart from this, there appeared to be no structures (e.g. sporting or social occasions) in which the teenagers from the Gaeltacht could mix with those attending the Coláiste. However, the door appeared to be open

> Uaireanta imíonn cupla daoine ón gceantar go dtís na céilí.

> (Sometimes a couple of people from the area go to the céilí.)

There was also some appreciation of the effort involved for students at the Irish college:

> Tagann siad go dtí an cheantair chun Gaoluinn a fhoghlaim agus bíonn sé deacair orthu Gaoluinn a labhairt. Ach tar éis cupla seachtain faigheann siad taithí agus bíonn sé níos fusa Gaoluinn a labhairt le chéile.

> (They come to the area to learn Irish and it's hard for them to speak Irish. But after a couple of weeks they get practice and it's easier for them to speak Irish to each other.)

Only one of the teenagers had ever visited another Gaeltacht area. She had found it easy to understand the dialect there, but preferred her own area.

THE IMPACT OF TEILIFÍS NA GAEILGE

More than three in four parents believed that TV had an impact on the use of language by their families. About one-quarter believed that TV had increased their use of English, while almost half claimed that the introduction of TnaG had reinforced their use of Irish. Almost one-fifth of the parents specifically referred to the interactive children's programme, Hiúdaí, with its cheeky Troll cartoon character, as having given a whole new set of phrases which were gleefully quoted by their children.

When asked about TnaG, Hiúdaí was the exclusive choice of the younger children, all of whom had been part of the studio audience on one or more occasions, and a number who regularly phoned to take part in competitions. Hiúdaí was judged as less enjoyable after the first year or so ("bhí sé níos fearr anuraidh") but was still their favourite programme. The older children (13+) were less impressed by the children's programmes, viewing them as aimed only at pre-schoolers. Their favourite programmes were drawn from the adult soap and a comedy series — Ros na Rún and C U Burn (these were also mentioned by the younger children).

Níl go leor rudaí do dhaoine dár aois

(Not enough for our age group)

was a frequent comment by the teenagers and none mentioned the music programmes purportedly aimed at them. The Gaeltacht teenagers were sports fans and were warm in their praise of the sports programmes on TnaG and also of Ros na Rún (soap). The use of English subtitles on many programmes was also seen as a distraction and led to yet another spirited exchange between Clíona and Síofra (Group A) as to whether these might assist people to learn Irish. It was interesting to note that even those hostile or indifferent to Irish still took an interest in what was on offer on TnaG and had their own favourite programmes.

REFLECTIONS ON THE EXPERIENCE OF BEING BROUGHT UP WITH IRISH AS THE HOME LANGUAGE

While it is a cliché to claim that parents impose their own culture on their children, for many there is no great choice in the matter and it is done unreflexively. This is less likely where parents are bilingual, particularly where the language is a minority language and, more acutely, when this language has been acquired as a second language at school rather than at home (as would be true of 70 per cent of the individual parents and 46 per cent of couples) and not shared with members of the extended family. These parents were more likely to reflect on and discuss which language(s) to use and what the likely consequences would be. Over half of the parents had engaged in "linguistic family planning". Only just over one-quarter of parents assessed the family use of language to be precisely as planned. About two-thirds found that more English was now being spoken than they had bargained for and about one in 20 were now more Irish-speaking than planned. A major obstacle to the use of Irish by their children was lack of day care facilities through Irish. A majority of couples each worked full time and so the linguistic environment became bilingual much earlier than anticipated, with the introduction of minders and crèches. While many parents attempted to find Irish-medium care for their children, very few were successful.

While parents pointed out many difficulties and lack of support from the State and the community for parents who raise their children as Irish speakers, the vast majority were happy that their children had benefited from the experience and would not change their decision, given a chance to start their family over again. The few who would make changes said they would use more Irish (Nic Ghiolla Phádraig, 1999, p. 21). They referred to a variety of advantages accruing to the use of Irish, ranging from deeper understanding of Irish culture, cognitive flexibility, to greater facility in learning other languages. Only a minority referred to advantages at school and examinations. Sixty per cent of parents had attempted to explain their own views on the importance of Irish to their children. The children/teenagers in the study were mainly positive[5] about their upbringing as Irish speakers. Some viewed themselves as having something extra compared with other children

> Tá Gaeilge agam agus ag mo chlann ach níl ag mo chara.
>
> (I have Irish and so have my family, but my friend doesn't.)

Even the more negative/ambivalent participants found it an advantage to speak Irish when abroad, in order to communicate privately:

> Bheith in ann rudaí a rá i nganfhios agus tú thar lear.
>
> (Being able to say things unbeknownst when you're abroad.)

Some articulated nationalistic views. Cian, 13:

> Is teanga álainn í an Ghaeilge agus is teanga na tíre í.

(Irish is a lovely language and the language of the country.)

Clíona, 13, had similar views:

> Teanga álainn í . . . taispeánann sé go bhfuil muid difriúil
> agus neamhspleách mar go bhfuil ár dteanga féin againn.
>
> (It's a lovely language . . . it shows we are different and in-
> dependent because we have our own language.)

Only one took an instrumental view. Tiarnán (10):

> Is breá liom an Ghaeilge agus gheobhaidh tú marcanna níos
> airde sa Ghaeilge san Ardteist.
>
> (I love Irish and you'll get higher marks in Irish in the Leav-
> ing Cert.)

EXPECTATIONS REGARDING OWN AND GENERAL USE OF IRISH IN THE FUTURE

The final topic raised for discussion concerned the issue of whether they saw themselves as continuing to use Irish as adults. Linked to this was the broader question as to whether the number of Irish speakers was expected to increase or to decline.

The groups varied in their responses to these questions. Group B were younger overall and were positive on both aspects. Róisín (10):

> Ceapaim nuair a bhéas páistí agamsa go labhróidh mé
> Gaeilge leo agus iad a chur go dtí Gaelscoil freisin.
>
> (I think that when I have children I'll speak Irish to them and
> also send them to a Gaelscoil.)

Ten year old Ciarán had planned for every contingency!

> B'fhéidir má fhaigheann tú pósta, níl a lán daoine a phósfadh
> tú go mbeadh Gaeilge acu ach muna bhfuil, Gaeilge a
> fhoghlaim dóibh. Mar, muna bhfuil Gaeilge acu beidh tú ag
> caint Béarla leo ach má dhéanann tú Gaeilge a fhoghlaim
> dóibh beidh tú ag caint as Gaeilge.

(Perhaps if you get married, there's not a lot of people you would marry that would have Irish, but if not to learn them Irish. Because, if they don't have Irish you will be talking English to them, but if you learn them Irish you'll be talking in Irish.)

Other members of Group B also envisaged use of Irish when adults and two hoped to get jobs where they might use Irish.

Opinions diverged in Group A. Síofra (13):

Ní féidir liom dearmad a dhéanamh ar an Ghaeilge, ach tar éis an rud a thárla ar an mBunscoil agus sa Ghaeltacht, níl mé ag iarraidh Gaeilge. Tá a fhios agam gur rud uafásach é sin a rá. Tá mé ag iarraidh a bheith i mo mhúinteoir agus beidh orm Gaeilge a theagasc do na páistí mar mhúinteoir Bunscoile ach dáiríre níl mé ag iarraidh . . .

(I cant forget Irish, but after what happened at primary school and in the Gaeltacht I don't want Irish. I know it's a terrible thing to say. I want to be a teacher and I'll have to teach Irish to the children as a primary teacher, but I really don't want to . . .)

The other teenage participants in Group B wished to use Irish in their adult lives but saw difficulties and obstacles to its use in their teens. Cian (13):

Déarfainn go mbeidh [Gaeilge á labhairt aige] ach nuair a bhíonn daoine óg bíonn go leor Gaeilge ach nuair a fhásann siad suas timpeall 12, 13, 14 — timpeall an aois sin bíonn na cairde go léir ag labhairt Béarla níos mó agus ag titim den Ghaeilge.

(I'd say I'll continue [to speak Irish] but when people are young there's plenty of Irish, but when they grow up — around 12, 13, 14 — around that age the friends are all speaking more English and falling away from Irish.)

Clíona (13) agreed but also hoped to continue using Irish.

It was interesting that they perceived difficulties in using Irish in their teens. The Advisory Planning Committee (1986, p. 26) pointed to several studies which charted the movement of

people in and out of Irish-speaking networks over their life-
times. This was precisely the hazard that these young people
foresaw, with its attendant possibility of not having opportunities to mix with Irish speakers in the future. Maguire also noted
the increased pressures to use English with peers as they enter
their teens and leave primary school (1991, p. 166). Ó Riagáin
(1997, p. 274) estimated that only about one-quarter of those
who grew up in Irish-speaking homes use Irish with the same
intensity in their current homes.

The Gaeltacht teenagers all saw themselves as continuing to
use Irish. Úna (13):

> Labhróidh mé Gaoluinn nuair a fhásaim suas mar bíonn
> daoine ag dul ar chúrsaí ag iarraidh Gaoluinn a labhairt
> agus tá an t-ádh orainn.

> (I'll speak Irish when I grow up because people go on
> courses trying to learn to speak Irish and we are lucky.)

They hoped to live in the Gaeltacht when adults, although without plans as to what they might do when finished second-level
education. Their social life revolved around sporting activities,
which were conducted through Irish.

When asked for their views as to whether the Gaeltacht was
growing stronger or weaker, Bríd, 13, made an accurate assessment:

> Is doigh liom go bhfuil sé ag fáil saghas níos laige . . . Níl an
> ceantar seo [ag éirí níos laige] ach tá cupla áit agus is cuma
> le daoine cén teanga a labhrann siad.

> (I think its getting sort of weaker. . . . not this area but there
> are a couple of places and people don't care what language
> they speak.)

Breandán, 15, was more optimistic:

> Ceapaim go bhfuil sé ag dul i bhfeabhas toisc go bhfuil níos
> mó Gaoluinne á labhairt agus daoine eile ag teacht isteach.

> (I think its improving because more Irish is being spoken
> and people moving into [the area].)

This was linked to his belief that TnaG had sparked off an interest in people coming to learn Irish in the Gaeltacht.

CONCLUSION

The way in which the children deviated from parental and school norms by using English in interaction with their siblings and in the schoolyard indicates that socialisation never results in a perfect reproduction of the adult model (Berger and Berger, 1976, pp. 64-5; Wrong, 1961). It provides further evidence of the limitations of power (Foucault, 1980; Devine, 2001). Furthermore, as the case of Síofra illustrates, some degree of deviation by the children may be important if the overall norm is to survive (Merton, 1968, Ch. VII). Síofra's rejection of the hypocrisy she identified in the non-enforcement of the rule to speak Irish at school and in the Gaeltacht Coláiste Samhraidh, led her to reject the Irish language itself. Síofra also spoke a very pure "adult" model of Irish, while other participants exhibited some degree of argot/interlanguage. While parents often view this as slippage, it may alternatively be viewed as Irish on the child's terms and provide immunity from outright rejection.

Overall, the children were optimistic about the future of Irish as a spoken language, although the teenagers were aware of difficulties and weaknesses in the situation. The Gaeltacht children referred to the establishment of TnaG, the growth of the Gaelscoil movement and for some also the Gaeltacht as indicators that Irish is growing in strength and popularity. A number volunteered that they would bring up their own children as Irish-speakers.

The Gaeltacht teenagers were also quite optimistic. They claimed that their own Gaeltacht area was strong. They did not refer to the Gaelscoil movement, but like their Gaeltacht peers, they interpreted the establishment of TnaG as a very positive sign. They also claimed that more people were coming to the Gaeltacht to learn Irish as a result of TnaG.

The limitations of all of these phenomena — the erosion of the Gaeltacht, the minority status of Gaelscoileanna, the competition for TV viewers, etc. — did not impinge on these young people's evaluations of an expanding role for the Irish language. It would take longitudinal research to establish whether such "reality checks" provoke a "crisis of confidence" in late adolescence/early adulthood. At present, however, the majority have a very positive "definition of the situation" which constructs their minority language status as a positive and valued element of their experience of childhood.

References

Advisory Planning Committee (1986), *The Irish Language in a Changing Society: Shaping the Future*, Dublin: Bord na Gaeilge.

Berger, P.L. and Berger, B (1976, revised ed.) *Sociology: a Biographical Approach*, Harmondsworth: Penguin.

Bilingual Family Newsletter, published quarterly by Multilingual Matters, Clevedon.

Bunreacht na hÉireann, 1937.

Census 1996

CLAR: Committee on Language Attitudes Research (1975), *Report*, Dublin: Government Publications.

Coates, Jennifer (1993, 2nd ed.), *Women, Men and Language*, London: Longman.

Devine, D. (2001), "Locating the Child's Voice in Irish Primary Education", in Cleary, A., Nic Ghiolla Phádraig, M. and Quin, S., *Understanding Children (Vol. 1): State Education and Economy*, Dublin: Oak Tree Press.

Foucault, M. (1980), *Michel Foucault: Power Knowledge,* Hertfordshire: Harvester Wheatsheaf.

Grosjean, Francois (1982), *Life with Two Languages: An Introduction to Bilingualism,* Cambridge MA: Harvard University Press.

Hickey, Tina (1997) *Early Immersion Education in Ireland: Na Naíonraí,* Dublin: Institiúid Teangeolaíochta Eireann.

Hill, Malcolm (1998), "Ethical Issues in Qualitative Methodology with Children" in Hogan, Diane and Gilligan, Robbie (eds.) *Researching Children's Experiences: Qualitative Approaches,* Dublin: The Children's Research Centre, TCD.

Maguire, Gabrielle (1991), *Our Own Language: an Irish Initiative,* Clevedon: Multilingual Matters.

Merton, Robert K. (1968, 3rd ed.), *Social Theory and Social Structure,* New York/London: The Free Press; Collier Macmillan.

Milroy, L. and J. (1992), "Social Network and Social Class: Toward an integrated sociolinguistic model", *Language in Society,* Vol. 21, pp. 1-26.

Nic Ghiolla Phádraig, Máire (1999), *Comhluadar agus a Bhaill — Tuairisc ar Shuirbhéireacht ar Theaghlaigh Galltachta ag a bhfuil an Ghaeilge mar Theanga Bhaile,* Ionad Taighde na hEolaíochta Comhdhaonnaí, An Coláiste Ollscoile, Baile Átha Cliath.

Ó Catháin, Brian (1998), unpublished study; personal communication.

Ó Cinnéide, Mícheál agus Ní Chonghaile, Sorcha (1996), *An Ghaeilge san Earnáil Phoiblí i gCeantar na Gaillimhe,* An tIonad Taighde sna hEolaíochtaí Sóisialta, Coláiste na hOllscoile, Gaillimh.

O'Moore, A.M. (1989), "Bullying in Britain and Ireland: An Overview" in Roland, E. and Munthe, E. (eds.) *Bullying: An International Perspective,* London: David Fulton Publishers.

Ó Murchú, Máirtín (1985), *The Irish Language,* Dublin: Department of Foreign Affairs and Bord na Gaeilge.

Ó Riagáin, Pádraig agus Ó Gliasáin, Mícheál (1979), *All-Irish Primary Schools in the Dublin Area,* Dublin: Institiúid Teangeolaíochta Éireann, Publication No. 16B.

Ó Riagáin, Pádraig (1997), *Language Policy and Social Reproduction: Ireland 1893-1993,* Oxford: Oxford University Press.

Saunders, George (1988), *Bilingual Children from Birth to Teens,* Clevedon: Multilingual Matters.

Skutnabb-Kangas, Tove (1981). *Bilingualism or Not: The Education of Minorities,* Clevedon: Multilingual Matters.

Smith, Peter K. and Sharp, Sonia (1994), "The problem of school bullying" in Smith and Sharp (eds) *School Bullying: Insights and Perspectives,* London: Routledge.

Thorne, Barrie (1993), *Gender Play: Girls and Boys in School,* Buckingham: Open University Press.

Wrong, D.H. (1961), "The oversocialized conception of man in modern society", *American Sociological Review,* Vol. 26, April, pp. 183-193.

Notes

[1] This is true even in Gaeltacht areas, see O Cinnéide, Mícheál agus Sorcha Ní Chonghaile (1996) *An Ghaeilge san Earnáil Phoiblí i gCeantar na Gaillimhe*, An tIonad Taighde sna hEolaíochtaí Sóisialta, Coláiste na hOllscoile, Gaillimh.

[2] The fieldwork and analysis were funded by a research grant from the Social Science Research Committee of the Royal Irish Academy, whose assistance is gratefully acknowledged. Research assistance for the survey was provided by Iarfhlaith Watson — mo bhuíochas leis.

[3] All names are fictitious.

[4] Eldest children have also been reported as more committed to the language than subsequent children by Maguire (1991, p. 68).

[5] None said that they rejected Irish to annoy or defy parents as some of Maguire's respondents did (1991, p. 167). This may have been because the author is herself a Comhluadar parent.